AN ALBUM OF AMERICAN BATTLE ART

1755-1918

AN ALBUM OF AMERICAN BATTLE ART

1755-1918

Reprint of a 1947 Library of Congress Publication
With Text By
Donald H. Mugridge and Helen F. Conover

DA CAPO PRESS • NEW YORK • 1972

Library of Congress Cataloging in Publication Data

United States. Library of Congress
    An album of American battle art, 1755-1918.

    Reprint of the 1947 ed.
    1. Engravings—Washington, D. C.—Catalogs.
2. Battles—United States—Pictorial works.
1. Mugridge, Donald Henry. II. Conover, Helen Field.
III. Title.
NE955.U5   1972   769′.4′9973   72-6278
ISBN 0-306-70523-0

This Da Capo Press edition of *An Album of American Battle Art, 1755-1918,* is an unabridged and slightly altered republication of the first edition published in Washington, D.C., in 1947 by the Library of Congress.

The quotations (pages 179-180, 205) from *John Brown's Body* by Stephen Vincent Benét (Holt, Rinehart and Winston, Inc.) are copyright 1927, 1928 by Stephen Vincent Benét; copyright renewed 1955, 1956 by Rosemary Carr Benét. They are reprinted by permission of Brandt & Brandt.

Published by Da Capo Press, Inc.
A Subsidiary of Plenum Publishing Corporation
227 West 17th Street, New York, New York 10011

Manufactured in the United States of America

Publisher's Note/1972 Edition

All illustrations in this edition of *An Album of American Battle Art, 1755-1918,* have been reproduced from new photographic prints. The publishers are grateful to the following institutions for providing these prints:

Eleutherian Mills Historical Library, Wilmington, Del. (Plate 45)
Franklin D. Roosevelt Library, Hyde Park, N.Y. (Plate 32)
Library of Congress (see page 319 for complete list)
Maryland Historical Society, Baltimore, Md. (Plate 31)
National Archives (Plates 138–140, 144, 145, 149)
Naval History Division, U.S. Navy Department, Washington, D. C. (Plate 23)
New York Public Library, Phelps Stokes and Bancroft Collections (Plates 1, 11–15)
Peabody Museum, Salem, Mass. (Plate 33)
Peale Museum, Baltimore, Md., Hambleton Collection (Plate 46)
U.S. Naval Academy Museum, Annapolis, Md. (Plate 24)
U.S. National Museum, Smithsonian Institution (Plates 141, 142, 146, 148, 150)
Yale University Art Gallery, New Haven, Conn. (Plate 27)

The negative for Plate 138 in the first edition could not be located. A different photograph from the same event—the Philippine insurrection—has been provided by the National Archives and is reproduced in this edition. All other illustrations reproduced in this volume correspond with those in the first edition.

The publishers are grateful to Brandt & Brandt for permitting use of the quotations from Stephen Vincent Benét's *John Brown's Body* which appear on pages 179–180 and 205.

Finally, the publishers wish to emphasize that the Library of Congress has not participated in the preparation or publication of this edition of *An Album of American Battle Art, 1755–1918,* other than to provide the same generous help that is available to any interested citizen or organization. The responsibility for this edition is entirely that of the publisher.

Contents

List of Plates

I. THE FRENCH AND INDIAN WAR AND ITS AFTERMATH, 1755–1765

II. THE AMERICAN REVOLUTION, 1770–1783

VIII

VII. THE CIVIL WAR, 1861–1865

XIII

Acknowledgments

THIS ALBUM took its origin in an Exhibition of American Battle Art which was held at the Library of Congress from July 4 to November 1, 1944, and which was intended to be complementary to the Exhibition of American Battle Painting held at the National Gallery of Art from July 4 to September 4, and later at the Museum of Modern Art, New York, from October 2 to November 18, 1944. Both exhibitions owed their primary inspiration to Pvt. Lincoln Kirstein of the Army of the United States, whose mastery of the subject and infectious enthusiasm for it set things in motion and in considerable degree directed their course. Private Kirstein's enthusiasm was communicated practically intact to the then Librarian of Congress, Archibald MacLeish, to whose glowing personal interest and participation the Battle Art Exhibition owed much of its unusual success.

To secure a well-rounded exhibition, with adequate coverage of all our major wars from the French and Indian War to the World War of 1914–18, the Library of Congress drew upon the resources of a number of other institutions and individuals, both within and outside the United States Government. These institutions and individuals have been generous, not only in lending their materials to the Library of Congress for the hundred days of the exhibition, but in permitting their reproduction in this book. The Library of Congress takes the present opportunity to express its deep obligation to the late President of the United States, Franklin Delano Roosevelt, for permission to reproduce Plate 32; to the New York Public Library and to the Chief of its Reference Department, Paul North Rice, for permission to reproduce Plates 1, 11–14, 15, and 18; to the Maryland Historical Society, Baltimore, and to its Director, James W. Foster, for permission to reproduce Plate 31; to the Municipal Museum of the City of Baltimore and to its Director, Richard Carl Medford, for permission to reproduce Plate 46; to the Peabody Museum of Salem, Mass., and to its Curator of Natural History, Ernest S. Dodge, for permission to reproduce Plate 33; and to the Yale University Art Gallery and its Director, Theodore Sizer, for permission to reproduce Plate 27. Mr. Irving S. Olds, of New York City, was kind enough to send us a photograph of one item from his distinguished collection of naval prints, which unfortunately it did not prove feasible to include in this volume. The following branches of the United States Government have placed us in their debt by substantial contributions: the U. S. Naval Academy Museum, Annapolis, and its Curator, Capt. H. A. Baldridge, for Plates 23 and 24; the U. S. National Museum, Smithsonian Institution, and its secretary, Alexander Wetmore, for Plates 141, 142, 146–148, and 150; and the National Archives and the Acting Chief of its Division of Photographic Archives and Research, Josephine Cobb, for Plates 112, 138–140, 144, 145, and 149.

The Library of Congress makes further grateful acknowledgment for permission to make certain extended quotations in the text of our annotations: to Messrs. Brandt and Brandt, agents for the estate of Stephen Vincent Benét, for permission to quote from *John Brown's*

Body (published by Farrar and Rinehart; copyright, 1927, 1928 by Stephen Vincent Benét); and to Mr. André Smith, for permission to quote from his *In France with the American Expeditionary Forces* (New York, 1919).

The *Album of American Battle Art* now published by the Library of Congress is the work of many hands. David C. Mearns, Director of the Reference Department, has planned and advised at all stages, and has made all the essential decisions. Robert C. Smith, former Assistant Chief of the Prints and Photographs Division, organized the Exhibition of Battle Art, participated in planning the Album, and made the first selection of materials for inclusion. Hirst Milhollen, Curator of Photographs, has been indispensable at all stages of both Exhibition and Album, from his unique knowledge of both the prints and the photographs collections. Hugh Clark, of the Photoduplication Laboratory, has made uniformly excellent photographs of the materials to be reproduced. Margaret D. Garrett, of the National Gallery of Art, has turned over her files of notes on battle art and artists, which have proved of much service in the preparation of the annotations. Kenneth Stubbs, late of the United States Navy and now of the Corcoran Gallery, has been kind enough to view many of the plates with the eye of a practicing artist.

As to the text, the labor of research and writing has been shared by Helen F. Conover, of the Division of General Reference and Bibliography, and the undesigned. It is safe to say that without Miss Conover's able assistance this Album would not have appeared at all. In addition I have supplied editorial supervision in the task of selecting and securing the pictures, as well as in the preparation of the text.

DONALD H. MUGRIDGE,
Fellow in American History.

Introduction

AN ALBUM of American Battle Art is, as its name sufficiently implies, a picture book. In it the Library of Congress offers to the American public 150 plates, all scenes from or directly related to the wars in which this Nation has been engaged from the close of the Colonial Period through the First World War. The graphic side of the Second World War, so recently concluded, is a vast and uncharted subject which we have thought best not to approach in this Album; and before 1755, the outbreak of the French and Indian War, there is so little graphic material, as well as so little national feeling on the part of the American participants in colonial warfare, that we have been well content to begin with that date, the year of the first American historical print.

Since this is a picture book, we have endeavored to secure the best and clearest form of reproduction possible without making the volume too expensive for the average pocketbook. The bane of print and map reproduction has always been the difficulty of reproducing a large view, meant for framing or consultation on a table, on the page of a book not too large to go on the shelf. Figures and details only too easily become microscopic or blurred, and the whole crowded plate stuns rather than enlightens the reader. We have therefore omitted some oversize items otherwise deserving of inclusion, spread some pieces over two or even three plates (Plates 2–4, 19–20, 87–88), and in two instances enlarged the central and most vital portion of a large and crowded subject (Plates 38 and 47). Another defect of reproduction is that we are compelled to give in black-and-white plates the originals of which glow with charming, brilliant, or riotous color. We have therefore attempted to emphasize line and design in our selections, but must admit that in a number of instances (notably Plates 7, 68, 105, 110, and 127), the reader is deprived of a great deal; we can only recommend that, when opportunity offers, he stop in at the Library of Congress and inspect the originals. In the case of Plate 133, however, he is spared a great deal of pain.

We have intended this Album to reach the American public—the average citizen and the general reader, if such there still be. We have all endured the agony and shared the glory of the war of 1941–45. After eagerly scanning the most recent bulletins of disaster, disappointment or victory we have all turned to the pictures from the fighting fronts in order to see the terrible face of war as it appears to the eyes of those who wage it. We have all gone to newsreels and documentary films and so visually experienced the war as no other war has ever been experienced by noncombatants. The Library has supposed that very many of us will take a genuine interest in the graphic record of the earlier wars of the American Nation. To be sure, for the first century or so there were no photographs, but anyone who goes through this Album with understanding will probably discover what artists have always known, that the photograph has its limitations. We could not do without it, of course, but it should supplement rather than supplant the other forms of illustration. We hope that most of our readers will find in these old pictures of America's wars a deep charm as well as a source of pride. We have photographs too, of course—13 of them from 1863 onward.

Since this Album is intended to reach as wide a public as possible, we have not been able to take anything for granted. We have therefore provided each plate or group of related plates with an annotation which, we hope, will serve the purposes of various kinds of readers. Our only object is to explain the picture from every relevant point of view. In each case we begin with a technical description of the item reproduced—legend, classification, dimensions, location, etc.—which anyone who is not interested is invited to skip. We have then tried to explain the nature and the significance of the historical event or situation which the plate portrays, getting as close to its individuality as possible. Then we turn to the illustration itself, discussing the artists or craftsmen who brought it into being, the nature of the processes which they employed, and, in many cases, the characteristics of the illustration, both as art and as representation of historical fact. On the latter point it may be said that, just as we do not have more than a few pieces of "fine art," so our "art criticism" is not at all pretentious and is limited to fairly elementary and obvious considerations. We fear that many of our historical annotations will seem banal to historical specialists, while our graphic annotations will be tedious to those versed in illustration. We can only suggest that historians should read our graphics, and print-collectors read our history, while those equally versed in both fields may look at the plates.

The annotations, of course, do not as a rule represent research in primary source material, which would be quite beside the point in most cases, and for which in any event there has not been time. We have relied in considerable part upon standard works of reference—without Stauffer on engravers, Peters on lithographers, and the Dictionaries of American Biography and American History we should have been at sea—and we have brazenly helped ourselves to other peoples' epigrammatic summaries. What is the sense in flatly rewording a point which has been expressed as neatly as possible elsewhere? We have, however, tried to be both intelligent and accurate in our compilation. We have taken some pains to be readable, and shall be disappointed if we have failed.

The process of selecting material for this Album requires some commentary. As stated in the acknowledgments, the Album is the result of, and is based upon, an Exhibition of American Battle Art held at the Library of Congress from July 4 to November 4, 1944. The exhibition was based upon the existing collections of the Library, and was supplemented by borrowed materials only at points in which our own collections were inadequate. The Album is therefore a particular selection of materials; possibly 15 of our plates are pieces which would have to appear in any comprehensive book illustrating American battle art, but for the rest there are manifold alternatives possible. Of our 150 plates 123 are from the collections of the Library, the great majority from those of the Prints and Photographs Division; 15 come from other branches of the United States Government; while 12 are reproduced through the courtesy of non-Federal institutions or of individuals. Of the 150, about 110 were included in the Battle Art Exhibition;

much first-class material could not be turned up in the haste of organizing a large exhibition. This will explain, we trust, why the Album is fuller for those wars in which the Library's collections are the strongest—particularly the Mexican War and Civil War.

With paintings we have nothing to do. The Library's exhibition was the complement of the Exhibition of Battle Painting organized by the National Gallery of Art, of which a well-illustrated catalogue has been issued; and oil paintings are not library materials. Many of our engravings and lithographs, however, were made from paintings. We do have three plates of watercolor sketches, included among a total of 33 drawings in various media: pencil, wash, pencil-and-wash, pen-and-ink, charcoal, and crayon. Of our 30 copper-plate engravings, 25 are in the older and most usual form of line engravings, three in the later development of stipple, and two in the most difficult craft of mezzotint. There are five etchings—a process not well adapted to historical illustration—and six instances of a later refinement of etching which proved to be much more so adapted, aquatint. Most numerous are the lithographs, the popular print of nineteenth-century America, of which we have 53—some printed in black- or gray-and-white; some so printed and colored by hand, some tinted, some printed in light colors, and some printed in the heavy, oily colors of chromolithography. Our six wood engravings, with one exception, are not very distinguished specimens of graphic art. There are, as we said, 13 photographs, five of which are by U. S. Government photographers, and the rest the product of private enterprise. Finally, there are four plates of maps, three of them hand-drawn and the other partially so. One of the engravings and one lithograph are properly sheet music. This prosaic inventory at least shows the variety of means by which America's battles have been illustrated. For the benefit of the uninitiated, we have attempted to say something concerning the graphic processes in our annotations—the expert will skip these passages as a matter of course. These processes all have their times and their seasons—copper-plate engraving, for instance, once the backbone of illustration, is now a dead art.

Our plates are grouped in 10 sections, each representing a war or a group of wars—excepting our Volunteer Companies, who were characteristic of the 30 years of peace, broken only by Indian wars, from 1815–47. Until 1861 our wars were all wars of expansion, in one sense or another—the colonial frontier expanding against French and Indian compression; American nationality expanding against the shackles of British imperial control; American commerce expanding against French and Barbary depredations; War Hawks expanding into Canada—or trying to; Gringoes expanding over the Mexican Southwest. In 1861 came the question whether all this expansion would not break into fragments—a question happily though bloodily resolved in the negative. In 1898 we were expanding again—across the Pacific, as it happened, although we started out with the most disinterested purposes. Since 1898 our two wars have been strictly defensive. We hope that this Album will give many people a clearer sense of the appearance, the individuality, and the significance of each of these American wars, without the occurrence of any one of which we should have been a different people from what we are. This plain recognition of the importance of warfare in a nation's history does not mean that war is preferable to peace, or that we are a nation of warmongers, which the record shows that we are emphatically not.

In conclusion, a few remarks on some books that are related to our Album. There seems to be nothing exactly like it, which is certainly not the result of trying to be unduly original. *American Battle Painting, 1776–1918* (Washington and New York, 1944) is a catalogue of the exhibition at the National Gallery, with 41 halftone plates and two frontispieces in color. There is an excellent brief introduction by Lincoln Kirstein, but no annotations. *The United States Navy, 1776 to 1815, Depicted in an Exhibition of Prints* (New York, Grolier Club, 1942), is a splendid, well-nigh complete catalogue, with notes on actions and artists, but only a handful of the dozens of prints listed are reproduced, and not too satisfactorily. I. N. Phelps Stokes and D. C. Haskell, *American Historical Prints, Early Views of American Cities, from the Phelps Stokes and Other Collections in the New York Public Library* (New York, 1932) is a magnificent catalogue from the most important repository, with many reproductions; annotation is slim. Mr. Phelps Stokes' *Iconography of Manhattan Island, 1498–1909* (6 vols., New York, 1915–28) is the most important single contribution, on a geographically limited theme, to the graphic side of American History; it is superbly produced and cost a small fortune. Ralph Nevill, *British Military Prints* (London, 1909) approximates a British counterpart to our Album; but he was more interested in uniform than we are, and put his sketchy commentary in an introduction. Albert Eugene Gallatin, *Art and the Great War* (New York, 1919) covers the whole war, but is generous to the American contribution; there are 100 illustrations, including some of the official A. E. F. drawings, which we also sample. Carl W. Drepperd, *Early American Prints* (New York, 1930) is a manual for the new-fledged print-collector, and does not go very deep; but it does pay particular attention to historical views. Robert Taft, *Photography and the American Scene: A Social History, 1839–89* (New York, 1938) is an altogether admirable survey of the new medium from every conceivable point of view; there are good chapters on the Civil War and the Frontier. Harry T. Peters' several books on American lithography are all one could wish; they are noticed under Plates 70 and 71. Two books pursue our method of plate-and-annotation; they are the Metropolitan Museum's *Life in America: A Special Loan Exhibition of Paintings held during the World's Fair* (New York, 1939), which is a sheer delight; and Allan Nevins and Frank Weitenkampf, *A Century of Political Cartoons: Caricature in the United States from 1800 to 1900* (New York, 1944). If we had been able to match the quality of Mr. Nevins' notes in the latter, we should have had cause for pride. A relative of the last-named book is William Murrell, *A History of American Graphic Humor, 1747–1938* (2 vols., New York, 1933–38). The *Album of American History,* edited by J. T. Adams and R. V. Coleman, an attempt to document our national past from strictly contemporary graphic materials, is now approaching completion.

DONALD H. MUGRIDGE.

XX

I

The French and Indian War and Its Aftermath 1755-1765

FRANCE and Britain were intermittently at war, in Europe and America, from 1689 until 1783—the Second Hundred Years' War, Sir John Seeley called it. During the first three intercolonial wars, down to 1748, the pattern was one of depressing sameness, and was set in the first year or two of the struggle. The French were the masters of Indian diplomacy, and the Indians were the masters of the wilderness. The French and their savage allies could come undiscovered across the forest trails and strike at the exposed settlements on the English frontier; Pemaquid in 1689 and Schenectady in 1690 were the victims of surprise, fire, pillage, and massacre. Against this constant menace, the only retaliation possible on the part of the disunited, unmilitary, and specieless English colonies was to organize costly and difficult expeditions by sea. In 1690, Sir William Phips took Port Royal in Acadia, but failed utterly before Quebec. And so it went until the French and Indian War of 1755, when the full weight of British imperial power was thrown into counterattack in America. But Britain, like her American provinces, was unmilitary, and the first years of the offensive ended in futility or worse. Then in 1757 arose a warmaker of genius, the elder William Pitt. "The success of the Seven Years' War was almost entirely due to Pitt's torrential energy, to his farseeing preparations, to his wise choice of commanders on land and sea, and still wiser trust in them when they

were chosen, and above all to his strategic insight into the crucial objects of his world-wide campaigns" (Basil Williams). With such men as Boscawen and Saunders, Amherst and, above all, Wolfe at the head of the British fleets and the British-and-provincial armies, French Canada was utterly overwhelmed in three seasons of campaigning.

PLATE No. 1. *A Prospective Plan of the Battle fought near Lake George on the 8ᵗʰ of September 1755, between 2000 English with 250 Mohawks under the Command of General Johnson and 2500 French and Indians under the Command of General Dieskau in which the English were Victorious, captivating the French General with a number of his Men, killing 700 and putting the rest to flight. ☆ S. Blodget del. Thoˢ Johnston Sculp. ☆ [Dedication to William Shirley, Captain-General and Governor of Massachusetts Bay Colony.]*
Line engraving, colored by hand. 13¾ x 17½ inches.

ORIGINAL IN THE PHELPS STOKES COLLECTION, NEW YORK PUBLIC LIBRARY, NEW YORK.

In the first months of 1755 the British Government sent out to America Gen. Edward Braddock—"a barrack-square general without the slightest conception of American conditions of warfare"—and two regiments of regulars to wage the undeclared colonial war.

After Braddock had arrived and set up his headquarters at Alexandria, a council of colonial governors was called, which, convened on April 14, "marks the nearest approach which was ever made to the realization in practice of a British plan of concerted action for the American colonies." In large part at the instance of the energetic Governor of Massachusetts, William Shirley, a large-scale plan for the year was worked out: Braddock was to move against Fort Duquesne, the present Pittsburgh; Shirley himself was to go to Oswego on Lake Ontario and thence against Niagara; and Colonel Monckton was to attack Fort Beauséjour on the isthmus of the Acadian peninsula. The fourth enterprise was aimed against Crown Point on Lake Champlain, on the direct route into the heart of Canada, and was entrusted to Sir William Johnson, the extraordinary Irishman who had established himself in the Mohawk Valley 17 years earlier and had acquired such a reputation among the Indians "that they revered him like one of their natural chiefs." He had no military experience, but his general abilities were imposing.

This ambitious attempt on the part of the American provinces to invade and conquer Canada with a minimum of British help came to naught. Braddock was ambushed and slaughtered together with his redcoats in the western wilderness; Shirley reached Oswego but could get no further; and while Monckton took Beauséjour he remained so insecure that it was thought necessary to evict the whole French population of Acadia. Twenty-eight hundred men were raised in New England and joined with 800 from New York to make a respectable force with Sir William Johnson and the Indians who followed him. The Hudson made their advance easy as far as the Great Carrying Place, where they now constructed Fort Edward; and they pushed on 14 miles across the wilderness to the shores of the Lake which the French called St. Sacrement but which Johnson renamed Lake George after his sovereign. Here he fortified his camp.

The French Government had countered Braddock's expedition by sending out to Canada 3,000 regulars under a new commander in chief, Baron Dieskau; and the latter had prepared an expedition along the Lake Champlain route which reached the debatable ground soon after Johnson had established himself on Lake George. Coming by the eastern branch of the Lake, Dieskau overshot Johnson's camp, but turned north to attack it as soon as he realized the true situation. Learning of the approach of a French force from the southward, Johnson unwisely divided his force and sent out a detachment, under Col. Ephraim Williams and Lieutenant Colonel Whiting, to oppose their advance. This body, advancing in column, walked into Dieskau's ambush and were terribly punished in the "bloody morning scout." Williams and the old Mohawk chief Hendrik were shot down, but Whiting managed to keep his rear guard in sufficient order to cover the retreat of the rest to the camp. Dieskau now pressed on to complete his victory by overwhelming the camp, but found himself met by the most determined resistance. When his regulars formed to assault *en masse,* they were broken up by the fire of the provincial artillery. Johnson was wounded in the leg, and withdrew to his tent, but his lieutenant, Phineas Lyman of Connecticut, took sturdy charge of the defense. Finally, after a last French effort failed, the New Englanders came over their entrenchments and drove their assailants off the field. Dieskau himself, several times wounded and unable to escape, fell into their hands. It was a famous victory, but it remained without strategic result, for Johnson, apparently much shaken by his wound, made no further attempt to advance during the season.

"On the adjacent hill stood one Blodget, who seems to have been a sutler, watching, as well as bushes, trees, and smoke would let him, the progress of the fight, of which he soon after made and published a curious bird's-eye view." (Parkman). This view, we have it on no less an authority than I. N. Phelps Stokes, was "the first historical print engraved in America," and we are pleased to reproduce the copy in the Phelps Stokes collection as our first plate. SAMUEL BLODGET (1724–1807) was a Yankee-of-all-trades who in the course of a long and active career kept a trader's shop in Boston, sat on the judge's bench, and projected a canal, as well as plying the sutler's trade and designing the unusual combination of map-and-view with which we are concerned. With praiseworthy journalistic promptitude he had his solitary venture into art on the market before the end of the year; the Boston *Gazette* carried an advertisement of the *Prospective Plan* as "this day published" in its issue of December 22, 1755. With the view Blodget was able to offer a five-page quarto pamphlet, *An Explanation thereof: Containing a Full, tho' short, History of that important Affair*. To engrave his plan, Blodget enlisted the services of a local "japanner, painter, and engraver," THOMAS JOHNSTON (1708–67), a man of considerable experience in engraving maps and heraldic bookplates, who had, six years before, engraved the first view of Yale College.

Since Blodget was born in Woburn, Mass., and Johnston in Boston, and the subject-matter was purely American, this, our first view, was an all-American production, in which we may justly take some pride. Blodget's design was re-engraved at London in the following year by the well-known Thomas Jeffreys, who likewise incorporated it in his *Topography of North America* (1768); his is certainly a more polished production, but has neither the wilderness atmosphere nor the fascination of its Boston prototype. The Blodget-Johnston view really consists of four elements: at the left a small view of the "bloody morning scout," with the head of the New England column broken and completely surrounded by the ambushing French; beside it, a larger view of the assault on Johnson's camp, with the white-coated French regulars receiving the fire of three provincial field pieces; along the top, a map of Hudson's River, from New York City on the left to the Great Carrying Place on the right; and finally, in the upper left-hand corner, inset plans of Fort William Henry (constructed after the battle at the site of Johnson's camp) and of Fort Edward, which is still termed "Lyman's Fort" in the map of the river.

PLATE NOS. 2, 3, 4. *Plan du Cap Breton dit Louisbourg Avec ces environs Pries par Lamiralle Bockoune [i. e., Boscawen] Le 26 juillet 1758.*

Figurative map, in water color and ink. 20 x 80 inches.

Londoners as well as Bostonians did well to gloat over their respective editions of Blodget's view, since it would be nearly three years before they were vouchsafed another glimmering of victory, and in the meanwhile they were presented with an almost uninterrupted series of

3

disasters, in Europe as well as in America. The British nation was not yet organized for war, and the one man who could set its feet on the road to victory did not achieve a secure tenure of office until June 29, 1757. William Pitt had attempted to form a ministry of his own in the preceding year, but under the system of organized corruption which then constituted British politics, he had not sufficient "interest" behind him, and was dismissed after less than five months. But in 1757 Pitt entered into a coalition ministry with the Duke of Newcastle, "on the sensible understanding that Newcastle should continue to exercise the patronage he loved, while Pitt should be solely responsible for the conduct of the war he understood" (Basil Williams). It was, as we who have lived through the grim months after Pearl Harbor can understand, some time before Pitt's reinvigorating influence could make itself felt upon the battlefield; but in the course of 1758 a number of important projects were set on foot, including an expedition against the island fortress of Louisbourg.

By the Treaty of Utrecht, which brought the War of the Spanish Succession to a close in 1713, France ceded Acadia, as the French called Nova Scotia, to Great Britain. This left the River of Canada and its valley devoid of outer fortification, and, in order to supply the lack, the French Government set about constructing a mighty fortress at the northeastern corner of the Ile Royale, better known as Cape Breton Island, a northeastward extension of the Acadian peninsula which had not been included in the cession of 1713. Settlers were brought to Louisbourg, as the royal fortress was to be called, from the relinquished French settlements on Newfoundland, directly after the conclusion of peace. The work of fortification was early begun, continued for years, and was never really finished, in the sense of all the paper plans being carried out in masonry. But from about 1720 Louisbourg was in being, "the one real fortress ever heard of in America." In 1745–48 occurred one of the most famous episodes of our colonial history: a New England expedition, planned by Governor William Shirley and conducted by Sir William Pepperell, and assisted only by the British squadron already on the North American station, took Louisbourg by themselves, only to have it returned to France by the British Government at the inconclusive Peace of Aix-la-Chapelle. By 1755 the fortifications had been repaired and extended, and the job, become more difficult, had to be done over.

Early in 1758, before the winter was over, Pitt had his expedition ready to start. There were 39 warships under Admiral Edward Boscawen and 12,000 men under General Jeffrey Amherst, seasoned veterans both, although it was Amherst's first large command. They collaborated so well as to win the commendation of Amherst's junior brigadier, James Wolfe, a man not easily pleased, as is often the case with geniuses: "The Admiral and the General have carried on public service with great harmony, industry and union. Mr. Boscawen has given all, and even more than, we could ask of him." By June 1 they were before Louisbourg, where the governor, the Chevalier de Drucour, was able to dispose of some 4,500 men, now completely isolated within their massive fortifications. Amherst's conduct of the siege proceeded much too slowly and methodically to suit Wolfe, but the garrison was nevertheless ready to surrender by July 26, 1758, and the fortress became permanent British property on the following morning.

4

There is little information available concerning the fascinating figurative map which we reproduce on three separate plates, save that the Library of Congress purchased it from a Parisian dealer in 1903. That it was made by a Frenchman is obvious, and it is probably safe to assume that he had been at the siege and that it was made either for the information of the home government or for publication as a print. It is not drawn accurately to scale, and it is far more elaborately pictorial than any of the other French maps of the siege which J. S. McLennan reproduced in his *Louisbourg from its Foundation to its Fall* (London, 1918). It would yet seem to deserve description as a map rather than a view. In the first, or left-hand, plate may be seen Boscawen's ships anchored in Gabarus Bay, which is southwest, not due west, of Louisbourg. On the right of the first plate and the left of the second is depicted the landing effected by the British on June 8 under Brigadier Wolfe; the first attempt to land on the beach at Freshwater Cove came under a murderous fire from the shore, and Wolfe gave the order to turn back; but three boats on the right of the line made a craggy section of the shore out of reach of the French barrage, and Wolfe, perceiving and seizing the opportunity, redirected his whole force to land there, thus turning the flank of the main French defense in this area. This was the most crucial single action of the whole siege. In the second or central panel is shown the general English advance upon the fortress, although there is little or no indication of the elaborate siege-works which Amherst constructed directly in its front: the map is probably intended to represent the events of June 8 rather than those of July 26, the date it bears. In the third, or right-hand section, we see the

fortress itself, the French fleet in the bay, and above it, the Grand Battery on the northern shore of the harbor, which formidable construction the French commander abandoned on the night of June 8th–9th.

PLATE No. 5. *A View of the Taking of Quebeck by the English Forces Commanded by Genl Wolfe Sep: 13th 1759. ☆ For the London Mag: 1760. From The London Magazine, or Gentleman's Monthly Intelligencer, Vol. XXIX (1760), June issue, opposite p. 280.*

Line engraving. 6¾ x 9⅞ inches.

The fall of Louisbourg left the St. Lawrence highway into the heart of Canada open to the British navy. It was now 1759, and the results of Pitt's genius for organization and his eye for ability were becoming apparent. Twenty-two thousand British regulars were concentrated in America, and enough provincial troops had been raised to bring the total forces available for the campaigns of 1759 well over 50,000. As a result it was, in Horace Walpole's phrase, an *annus mirabilis,* when the church bells were worn threadbare with ringing for victories. The greatest effort was to be a joint naval and military expedition against Quebec, a fleet of 49 ships mounting nearly 2,000 guns in addition to 76 transports and 152 small craft, and an army of 9,000 men. The fleet Pitt entrusted to Admiral Charles Saunders, "one of the uncrowned Kings of the sea," who "had everything in his life to make him great, except the one supreme opportunity of commanding a fleet in action" (William Wood). For the army Pitt selected the young brigadier who had distinguished himself at Louisbourg the year before, James Wolfe. His passed-over seniors objected that the young-

5

ster, obnoxious for his professional zeal, was mad. The old King, George II, anticipated Abraham Lincoln on Grant: "Mad, is he? Then I wish he would bite some of my other Generals!" But such abilities might have cancelled each other out if jealousy had ensued; instead Saunders and Wolfe "for over two months gave one of the happiest examples of perfect unison in amphibious operations by army and fleet."

The great expedition rendezvoused at Louisbourg, set out from there on June 1, 1759, and, after a masterly navigation of the treacherous St. Lawrence, arrived at the Isle of Orleans before Quebec, and set up their base there, on June 26. Montcalm, the French commander in chief, had withdrawn from the frontier to take personal charge of the defense of the capital, and had arranged the heterogeneous forces at his disposal in a position which seemed well-nigh impregnable. The bulk of his army was posted to the east of Quebec, between the St. Charles and the Montmorenci Rivers; for the defense of the river bank above the capital, Montcalm had to trust to the high cliffs which stretched westward from the rock of Quebec, along which sentries were placed to watch for a possible British concentration. For over two months, from June 26 to September 10, Wolfe vainly sought for a weak spot in the French defense, and made sundry tentative dispositions for attack, all of which were seen to be futile almost as soon as made. It was a nerve-racking time, and Wolfe was seriously ill for a time in the course of August. But on the latter date, September 10, Wolfe's sharp eye perceived, in the course of a reconnaissance above Quebec, a concealed but practicable path up the cliff at Anse-au-Foulon (the Fuller's Cove), now known as Wolfe's Cove. It was on this occasion, and not on the night of the assault,

that Wolfe, after reciting passages of Gray's *Elegy in a Country Churchyard,* made the famous remark to his officers: "Gentlemen, I would rather be the author of that poem than take Quebec." Three days were required for preparation, but by the night of the 12th–13th, Wolfe was ready to strike. Diversionary threats and cannonades were made at various points of the extended line, completely mystifying Montcalm, while a forlorn hope of 24 men followed by three light infantry companies swarmed up the path and overpowered its defenders. By daylight Wolfe had an army of 4,800 men drawn up on the crest of the heights and advancing on the Plains of Abraham just outside Quebec.

We reproduce an anonymous engraving of the action which the *London Magazine,* a competitor of the *Gentleman's Magazine* for the subscriptions of genteel readers in eighteenth-century England, presented to the public in its issue of June 1760. No great matter as art, it is a jolly piece of graphic journalism, employing a device of great antiquity which was well-nigh obsolete by the mid-eighteenth century. The successive stages of the action are all presented simultaneously: the barges filled with redcoats are rowing up the river; the advanced guard are scaling the cliffs and meeting the fire of the defenders in darkness; the armies are drawn up at the top, in daylight, and the French are already beginning to break! The plate is one of the many line engravings to be found in this book: line engraving on copper, by means of a *burin* or *graver*—a steel bar with a lozenge-shaped cutting end—was developed in the course of the fifteenth century, finding its greatest master, Dürer, at its close, and remained the primary and all-round form of illustration until the early years of the nineteenth.

6

With Wolfe's army drawn up on the Plans of Abraham, Montcalm's right flank was turned, his sources of supply cut off, and his whole defensive arrangement imperiled. He had no choice but to attack with the least possible delay and this, like the good soldier he was, he promptly did, leading his army across the bridge over the St. Charles and through the narrow streets of Quebec. The English array awaited the charge of the French until they were within forty paces, and then let loose a murderous volley of musketry before which the French columns wilted. Seeing the enemy in confusion, Wolfe gave the order for counterattack, and himself led the charge on the right of his line, at the head of the Louisbourg grenadiers. Here, although the main bodies of the enemy were broken, there were sharpshooters in the bushes and cornfields. A shot shattered the English leader's wrist, and he wrapped his handkerchief about it; a second struck him in the groin, and failed to stop his advance; a third struck him full in the breast, and he staggered and sank to a sitting position. A little group of four officers and men carried him toward the rear, until he begged them to lay him on the ground. Here he sank into a lethargy, until some one on a knoll in front cried out, "They run, they run!" Wolfe roused up to ask, "Who run?" When told that it was the French who were everywhere in flight, he gave one final order, turned on his side, and murmured, "Now, God be praised, I will die in peace." In a few moments he was gone.

With the death of Lt. Col. James Wolfe—for such he remained on the army list although he had the temporary rank of a general in America—at the age of 32, the British nation lost its finest military intellect between Marlborough and Wellington. This tall, thin-chested, *retroussé*-nosed youth, who was commissioned an ensign soon after his fifteenth birthday, approached the duties of his calling in a professional spirit altogether different from that of the average British officer of that age. The model state of things which Wolfe brought about wherever he was in command soon marked him out for early preferment; he was a battalion adjutant at 16, a brigade-major at 20, and a lieutenant colonel at 24. He was a diligent student of military science, and was deep in Polybius, Montecucculi, and Vauban while most of his colleagues, whom he thought "an effeminate race of coxcombs," were dedicated to "Soup, and Venaison and Turtle." He took little credit to himself, and wrote to his mother, "I reckon it as a very great misfortune to this country that I, your son, who have, I know, but a very moderate capacity and a certain degree of diligence a little above the ordinary run, should be thought, as I generally am, one of the best officers of my rank in the service." Wolfe enjoyed far from robust health, was prostrated after the capture of Louisbourg and in the middle of the Quebec campaign, and it has been suggested that he was marked for an early death from tuberculosis. In any event, it was fortunate for the United States of America that James Wolfe, rather than Howe, Burgoyne, or Clinton, was not on hand to lead the British army in 1776.

The engraving which is here reproduced is the joint production of two first-rate artists, the American painter BENJAMIN WEST (1738–1820), and the English engraver WILLIAM WOOLLETT (1735–85). West has not received overmuch praise in recent years, because the whole trend of painting has been in a different direction from those effects which he wished to produce; but of his ability to produce those effects there can be no serious question. His *Death of Wolfe,* painted in 1771, aroused great enthusiasm and attracted greater crowds than any picture hitherto exhibited in England. King George III failed to purchase the original, which was bought by Lord Grosvenor and now hangs in the National Gallery of Ottawa; but he soon repented of the omission and commissioned a replica, for which he paid 350 pounds. Two other full-sized replicas were painted by West, for the Monckton family and for the Prince of Waldeck. In 1772 West was appointed Historical Painter to the King, a fact of which the engraving reminds us, as it does of the royal patronage of Woollett. The latter, an inn-keeper's son who made his first engraving on one of his father's pewter plates, was largely self-taught, and is said to have "carried landscape engraving to a perfection unknown before his time, and still unsurpassed." His engraving of *The Death of Wolfe* was three years in the making, since subscriptions were set on foot on January 1, 1773, and publication followed on the same day in 1776. In it he has practically recreated the original in a different medium, securing with an uncanny skill the utmost contrast of various textures within the picture. Woollett, we are told, had the amiable idiosyncrasy of firing a cannon from the roof of his house whenever he finished an important plate; this one surely deserved a salvo! West, it need hardly be remarked, has thrown historical fact out of the window in order to create a magnificent symbol of Conquest and Death; the principal officers of Wolfe's army were busy pursuing the foe, and had no time to form an awe-struck group about their dying leader. The Indian is a pure invention, but he serves to remind us that Benjamin West was one of the earliest, and one of the best, painters of the American Indian.

PLATE NO. 7. *Mort De Montcalm. [Biographical sketch of Montcalm: 2 columns of 16 lines each.] ☆ Desfontaines del. 1789 Moret Sculp. ☆ À Paris, chez Blin, Imprimeur en Taille-Douce, Place Maubert, n.º 17, vis-à-vis la rue des 3-Portes. A. P. D. R.*

Aquatint, printed in color. 9⅛ x 6½ inches.

The vanquished, too, had their paladin. Louis-Joseph de Saint-Veran, Marquis de Montcalm-Gozon was in 1756 a seasoned soldier of 44 years who had begun his soldiering at 15 and his campaigning at 17. A Christian gentleman and a lover of letters, he had proved himself a commander of outstanding ability as well as a man of great courage and fortitude. Such qualities were needed for the defense of Canada in 1756, and the Minister of War, D'Argenson, was free to make use of them, as Parkman says, because none of the Court favorites wanted a command in the backwoods. When Montcalm arrived at Quebec on May 13, 1756 he found himself confronted with a task intrinsically impossible, and

8

tackled it manfully. "Louis XV and Pompadour sent 100,000 men to fight the battles of Austria, and could spare but 1,200 to reinforce New France" (Parkman). There were but 5,300 regulars in the whole of that imperial domain, eked out by a fluctuating militia unfit for pitched battles and an uncertain number of notoriously erratic Indian allies.

In addition to this fatal lack of resources, Montcalm was handicapped by a vacillating and jealous Governor-General, Vaudreuil, under whose orders he was placed, and by a systematically peculating Intendant. Nevertheless with such means Montcalm kept the English at bay through three years of strenuous campaigning. In 1756, while Lord Loudoun dawdled, he pounced on the outpost of Oswego and took it with its garrison of 1,400 and its hundred light cannon; in 1757, when Loudoun's main effort went into a bungled expedition against Louisbourg, he besieged Fort William Henry at the southern end of Lake George and compelled the capitulation of its garrison of 2,200 while the British commander, Daniel Webb, looked on from Fort Edward, impotent to give assistance; and in 1758, he butchered General Abercrombie's men to the number of 2,000 as they made their vain onslaught against his stockade at Ticonderoga. All might yet have been well if Pitt had not concentrated overwhelming numbers under first-class leadership against the isolated province. But in 1759 Wolfe found his way to the Plains of Abraham, and Montcalm, like every one of his senior officers, was struck down as he tried to rally his beaten and fleeing army beneath the walls of Quebec. Two soldiers supported him on his horse as he returned to the city for the last time through the St. Louis Gate, and as he came within, one of a group of women

recognized him, saw the blood streaming from his wound, and cried out, *"O mon Dieu! Mon Dieu! le marquis est tué!"* *"Ce n'est rien,"* Montcalm answered her, *"ce n'est rien; ne vous affligez pas pour moi, mes bonnes amies."* He was taken to the house of the surgeon Arnoux and, when told that he had but a few hours to live, replied, "So much the better. I am happy that I shall not live to see the surrender of Quebec." At five o'clock the next morning he died.

The print here reproduced is an *aquatint,* the first of our six plates in this medium (see also Nos. 36, 37, 45, 46, 47). Aquatint is an extension of the etching process, technically rather complex, whereby tones of various intensities can be produced instead of only lines. A granular substance, such as powdered resin, is applied to the copper plate before it is exposed to the acid, and such protection as the granules afford results in the effect of tone. Aquatint was developed in the latter part of the eighteenth century, from about 1762, and a few decades later an ingenious Frenchman, François Janinet, discovered a method of using multiple plates to produce aquatints in color. Among his followers were Louis-Philibert Debucourt, one of whose later pieces is our Plate 47, and, of less eminence, JEAN-BAPTISTE MORET or MORRET, who was active at Paris during the three decades 1789–1820. In the present print he has reproduced the work of a painter named Desfontaines: there were several French artists of this name at the time, all rather undistinguished; it was perhaps MICHEL-CLAUDE-PHILIPPE DESFONTAINES, who had died in 1785. It is impossible to say whether the inferior drawing of the print is to be ascribed to painter or aquatinter; but its fresh and charming colors, which unfor-

9

tunately cannot be reproduced here, are certainly to be credited to Morret.

The scene presented by the print is obviously inspired by *The Death of Wolfe,* and was not the only *Mort de Montcalm* to be begotten in France by West's painting. It is even less historical, since Montcalm died in a house at five in the morning, and not before his pavilion on the battlefield in the full colors of daylight. The *rococo* grace of the attitudinizing figures presents, at any rate, an interesting contrast to West's far greater work.

PLATE No. 8. *The Indians giving a Talk to Colonel Bouquet in a Conference at a Council Fire, near his Camp on the Banks of Muskingum in North America, in Oct.ʳ 1764. ☆ B. West inv.ᵗ Grignion sculp. From William Smith, An Historical Account of the Expedition against the Ohio Indians, in the Year MDCCLXIV. Under the Command of Henry Bouquet, Esq:, London, T. Jefferies, 1766, opp. p. 14.*
Line engraving. 8 x 6 inches.

PLATE No. 9. *The Indians delivering up the English Captives to Colonel Bouquet, near his Camp at the Forks of Muskingum in North America in Nov.ʳ 1764. ☆ B. West inv.ᵗ Canot sculp. ☆ From William Smith, An Historical Account of the Expedition against the Ohio Indians, in the Year MDCCLXIV. Under the Command of Henry Bouquet, Esq:, London, T. Jefferies, 1766, opp. p. 28.*
Line engraving. 8 x 6 inches.

The Seven Years' War drew to its end, and England, France, and Spain in 1763 concluded a general peace. To the American colonies, where world-wide conflict had brought the added cruel danger of uncivilized foes, the peace

was hailed as a "most happy event." But "just at the time when we concluded the Indians to be entirely awed, and almost subjected by our power, they suddenly fell upon the frontiers of our most valuable settlements, and upon our outlying forts, with such unanimity in the design, and with such savage fury in the attack, as we had not experienced, even in the hottest times of any former war."

William Smith has recently been reëstablished as author of the *Historical Account of the Expedition against the Ohio Indians.* This "haughty, self-opinionated, half-learned Character," as his contemporary Ezra Stiles branded him, was Provost of the College, Academy and Charity School of Philadelphia, and a power in the province. In 1755 he had published *A Brief State of the Province of Pennsylvania,* urging more active cooperation in the French and Indian War, and in 1756 an answer to the strictures against his first work, *A Brief View of the Conduct of Pennsylvania in 1755.* His account of Bouquet's expedition, published anonymously, won high favor abroad, and appeared in several London and Dublin editions as well as in Philadelphia.

In the war of 1763–64, to which the greatest of the Eastern Indian leaders, Pontiac, gave his name, the confederacy he had welded struck simultaneously from Fort Pitt, the present Pittsburgh, to Mackinac at the northernmost straits of the Great Lakes. Three only of the outlying forts stood, Niagara, Detroit, and Fort Pitt. Pontiac himself directed the siege of Detroit which was finally relieved in 1764 by Col. John Bradstreet and his army. In the summer of 1763 the expedition from Pennsylvania was sent, under Col. Henry Bouquet, to relieve Fort Pitt, "a long and tedious land march of near 200 miles beyond the settlements; and through those dangerous passes where the fate of Braddock and others still rises on the imagination."

Colonel Bouquet marched from Carlisle, in central Pennsylvania, with 500 redcoated regulars. Twenty-five miles east of Fort Pitt, at Bushy Run, the Indians attacked (August 5–6, 1763). The first day there was no decision and the English passed the night watchful under arms. In the morning Bouquet placed companies in ambush and feigned retreat, "the savages gave entirely into the snare," and were utterly routed on the second charge.

The Indians retreated beyond the Ohio, and for the winter there was quiet. But "the ensuing spring of 1764 presented these savage enemies afresh on our frontiers ravaging and murdering with their usual barbarity." Bradstreet was despatched to the lakes, but the peace he made at Detroit was not observed. On May 30th, 1765, the Pennsylvania Assembly finally passed a bill calling for a thousand militiamen. Bouquet assembled them at Carlisle, but desertions were such that he had to call for Virginia volunteers to meet him at Fort Pitt. He started on the 2d of October with about 1,500 men. Preliminary Indian embassies had already come with peace overtures. The army marched with a fine show of force, and the need of meeting the enemy in combat passed. On October 17th Bouquet met the leaders, in a "bower" erected for the conference near the British encampment at the Muskingum River (Plate 8). The English colonel was well attended; "most of the regular troops, Virginia volunteers and light horse" stationed themselves about. Through this formidable array came the Indians, Kiyashuta, chief of the Senecas, with 15 warriors, Custaloga and Beaver, chiefs of the Wolf and Turkey tribes

of the Delawares, with 20 warriors, and Kiessinautchtha, a chief of the Shawanese, with six warriors. "Being seated, they began, in a short time, to smoak their pipe or calumet, agreeable to their custom. This ceremony being over, their speakers laid down their pipes, and opened their pouches, wherein were their strings and belts of wampum."

The Indians sought to avert wrath, offering "excuses for their late treachery and misconduct, throwing the blame on the rashness of their young men and the nations living to the westward of them, suing for peace in the most abject manner." They delivered up 18 white prisoners, and swore that all captives would be returned. Bouquet accepted their terms, but marched on into the heart of the Indian country, to the forks of the Muskingum. Day by day the leaders of the tribes came in, bringing their white captives, but Bouquet "refused to shake hands or have the least talk" with the chiefs until, on November 12, 206 prisoners had been returned, 81 men and 125 women and children from Pennsylvania and Virginia. Then the Colonel met the chiefs and told them "that though he had brought a Tomahawk in his hand, yet as they had now submitted he would not let it fall on their heads, but let it drop to the ground, no more to be seen." Everything was settled, and the army marched back to Fort Pitt. The remaining hostages, too far away to be collected before the winter, were delivered there the next spring.

"And here," writes Smith, "I am to enter on a scene . . . which language indeed can only weakly describe; and, to which the Poet or Painter might have repaired to enrich their highest colourings of the variety of human passions . . . the arrival of the prisoners in the camp; where were to be seen fathers and mothers recognizing and clasping their once-lost babes; husbands hanging on the necks of their newly-recognized wives; sisters and brothers unexpectedly meeting together after long separation, scarce able to speak the same language . . . In all these interviews, joy and rapture inexpressible was seen, while feelings of a very different nature were painted in the looks of others; flying from place to place in eager enquiries after relatives not found . . ., stiffened into living monuments of horror and woe, on learning their unhappy fate."

There were many instances of tenderness on the part of the Indians toward their late hostages, and the children protested bitterly the separation from their adopted parents. "But it must not be denied that there were even some grown persons who shewed an unwillingness to return . . . some . . . clung to their savage acquaintance at parting, and continued many days in bitter lamentations, even refusing sustenance. For the honour of humanity, we would suppose those persons to have been of the lowest rank . . . For, easy and unconstrained as the savage life is, certainly it could not be put in comparison with the blessings of improved life and the light of religion, by any persons who have had the happiness of enjoying, and the capacity of discerning, them."

Benjamin West's drawings, from which the engravings were made for the book, may have been a debt of gratitude to William Smith, for it was the Philadelphia Provost who had first called attention to the genius of the young painter in the *American Magazine and Monthly Chronicle,* which Smith published from 1757. West had gone to Italy in 1760, and in 1763 had established his studio in London. It was there that he made the drawings which decorate the first London edition of the *Historical Account.* The two engravers who executed West's designs bear French names, and one of them, PIERRE CHARLES CANOT (1710–77) was of French birth, but had lived in England since his thirtieth year. He enjoyed a considerable reputation in his adopted country for his landscapes and sea pieces. Some of the latter were after paintings by Richard Paton, who did the canvas of Paul Jones' sea fight which was engraved in our Plate 23. The other, CHARLES GRIGNON (1716–1810; the name in the plate is anglicized as GRIGNION) was born in London of French parents. He likewise is credited with some masterly work, and was one of the committee which set up the Royal Academy in 1755. Canot was elected as Associate-Engraver of this body in 1770.

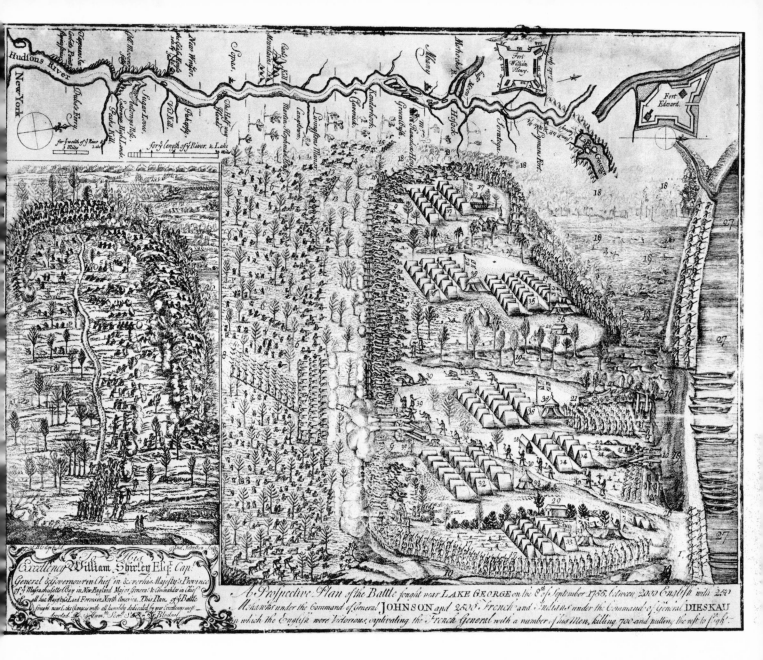

PLATE No. I. *A Prospective Plan of the Battle Fought near Lake George, September 8, 1755. Engraving by Thomas Johnston, 1755.*

13

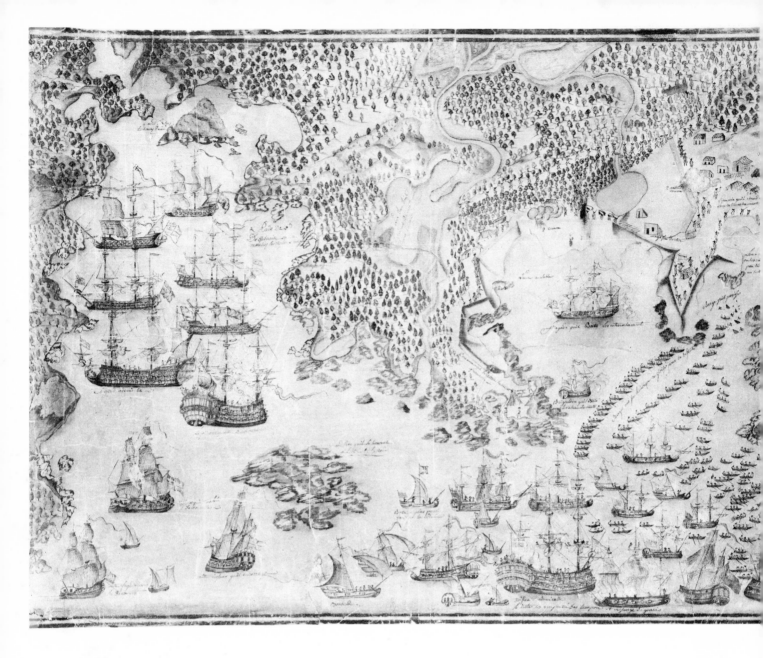

PLATE No. 2. *Plan du Cap Breton dit Louisbourg avec ses environs, July 26, 1758. Manuscript figurative map, Part I.*

14

PLATE No. 3. *Plan du Cap Breton dit Louisbourg avec ses environs, July 26, 1758. Manuscript figurative map, Part II.*

15

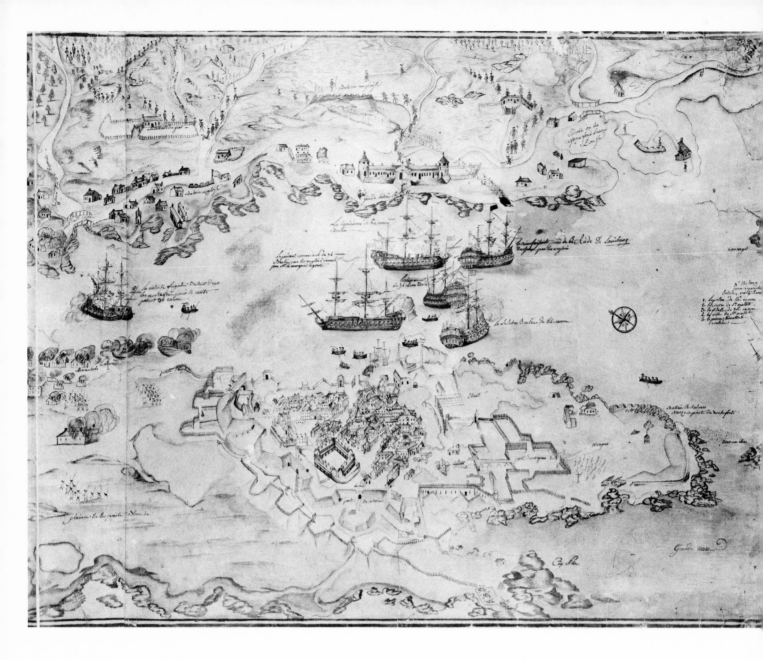

PLATE NO. 4. *Plan du Cap Breton dit Louisbourg avec ses environs, July 26, 1758. Manuscript figurative map, Part III.*

16

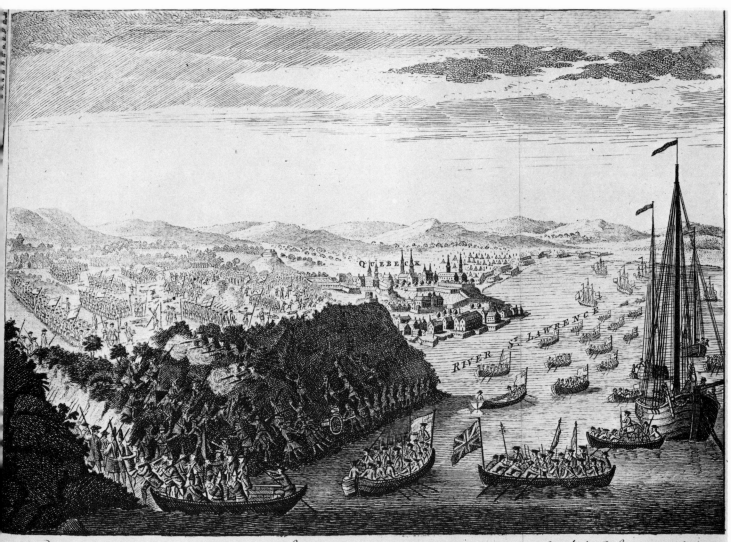

View of the Taking of QUEBECK by the English Forces Commanded by Gen.ᵗ Wolfe Sep: 13.ᵗʰ 1759.

PLATE No. 5. *A View of the Taking of Quebeck, September 13, 1759. Engraving from the London Magazine, 1760.*

To the King's most excellent Majesty this plate THE DEATH OF GENERAL WOLFE, &c.

PLATE No. 6. *The Death of General Wolfe, September 13, 1759. Engraving by William Woollett, after Benjamin West, 1776.*

18

Desfontaines del.   1789   Moret Sculp.

MORT DE MONTCALM.

Louis-Joseph de Saint Véran, Marquis de Montcalm, naquit en 1712, et porta les armes de bonne heure. Il fut fait Colonel du Régiment d'Auxerrois en 1743, se signala dans plusieurs commandemens particuliers, reçut trois blessures en 1746 à la bataille donnée sous Plaisance, et deux coups de feu à l'affaire de l'Assiette. En 1756 il obtint le grade de Maréchal de Camp et le titre de Commandant en Chef des troupes Françoises dans l'Amérique septentrionale; il arrêta, par ces bonnes dispositions, l'armée du Général Anglois Loudon au Lac Saint-Sacrement. Les Campagnes de 1757 et 1758 ne lui firent pas moins d'honneur; il repoussa avec un très-petit nombre de troupes les Armées ennemies, et prit des forteresses munies de garnisons considérables. Le froid, et la faim se réunirent aux efforts des Anglois pour accabler ses soldats depuis l'automne de 1757 jusqu'au printems de 1758. Montcalm soutint ces revers avec constance, partagea les peines et les fatigues de ses troupes, s'oublia pour les secourir et les soulager, leur inspira la patience par son exemple, et se maintint ainsi contre les Anglois. Le Général Abercombry ayant remplacé le Lord Loudon, n'eut pas plus d'avantages que son prédécesseur. Montcalm remporta sur lui une victoire complette le 8 Juillet 1758. C'est par ces moyens que le Général François soutint pendant quatre années la destinée de la Colonie du Canada. Les Anglois accrurent leurs forces pour tenter de faire des progrès dans cette partie du Continent de l'Amérique. Montcalm étudia longtems les efforts d'une armée beaucoup supérieure à la sienne, et ceux d'une flotte formidable; mais enfin, engagé malgré lui dans un combat qui se tivra près de Quebec, il reçut au premier rang et au premier choc une blessure dont il mourut le lendemain 14 7bre 1759. On l'enterra dans un trou creusé par la chute d'une bombe, sépulture digne d'un héros guerrier.

A Paris, chez Blin, Imprimeur en Taille-Douce, Place Maubert, N.º17, vis-à-vis la rue des 3-Portes.

A.P.D.R.

PLATE No. 7. *Mort de Montcalm, September 14, 1759. Aquatint by Jean-Baptiste Morret, 1789.*

19

The Indians giving a Talk to Colonel Bouquet in a Conference at a Council Fire, near his Camp on the Banks of Muskingum in North America, in Octr. 1764.

B. West invt.　　　　　　　　　　　　　　　Grignion sculp.

PLATE NO. 8. *The Indians Giving a Talk to Colonel Bouquet, October 1764. Engraving by Charles Grignon, after West, 1766.*

B. West inv.^t   Canot sculp.

The Indians delivering up the English Captives to Colonel Bouquet, near his Camp at the Forks of Muskingum in North America in Novr 1764.

PLATE No. 9. *The Indians Delivering up the English Captives to Colonel Bouquet, November 1764. Engraving by Pierre C. Canot, after West, 1766.*

21

II

The American Revolution
1770-1783

THE elimination of France from the North American continent placed the relation between Great Britain and her thirteen colonies on an entirely different footing. The home government turned to the tightening of administration and the increase of revenue; the provinces, freed of the horror from the northwest, began to look more seriously into their constitutional rights and grievances. What was the imperial authority of King, and of Parliament; and what was the status of the colonial legislatures? Did not Englishmen in America have all the rights and liberties of Englishmen at home? For 12 years there was friction, now becoming more acute, and now subsiding for a time. Massachusetts and Virginia led with equal firmness the movement for autonomy, but, as things went, the crisis occurred in Massachusetts. The city of Boston was to be drastically punished for its rash flouting of imperial sovereignty, and was occupied by a sizeable garrison of redcoats. This state of affairs naturally intensified the resistance movement, which received the sympathy and active assistance of Whigs throughout the other 12 colonies. In 1775 fighting broke out, and in 1776 the Continental Congress declared the United States of America a free and independent nation.

Could Britain reconquer her revolted provinces? At first sight the military disparity in her favor was enormous; population, wealth, sea power, military skill, all were heavily weighted on the side of the homeland. Nevertheless, the task of subduing America required a major effort, and this could not be forthcoming, because Britain was not of one mind. King George III, who was seeking to restore the dwindling power of the monarchy, was distrusted; there was much active sympathy with the colonial Whigs; and enlistments for service in America were hard to obtain. British armies could go where they would on the seaboard—New York was taken in 1776 and Philadelphia in 1777—but inland, problems of transportation and supply mounted up. Burgoyne, seeking to open the Hudson, was immobilized, surrounded and overwhelmed at Saratoga in 1777. France now saw her way clear to enter the war, in 1778. The earlier experiences of the alliance were disappointing, but it was de Grasse's fleet and Rochambeau's army which enabled Washington to descend upon Cornwallis and pen him up in Yorktown, where he surrendered on October 17, 1781. All three major parties to the conflict were now approaching exhaustion, and peace was soon made. By the Treaty of Paris, September 3, 1783, America, with her western frontier at the Mississippi, was independent; England lost the best part of her empire but salvaged Canada and the West Indies; while the decaying monarchy of France had at least inflicted a serious humiliation on an ancient rival.

The early days of resistance and revolution saw a noteworthy efflorescence of the historical print in America, and we lead off with six crude but vigorous and expressive native productions. In the strain and poverty of the war, this could not continue, and our remaining fourteen plates are either of foreign or much later domestic origin.

PLATE No. 10. *The Bloody Massacre perpetrated in King-Street Boston on March 5*[th] *1770, by a party of the 29*[th] *Reg*[t]*. [Three columns of verse of six lines each.] The unhappy Sufferers were Mess*[s]*. Sam*[l]*. Gray, Sam*[l]*. Maverick, Jam*[s]*. Caldwell, Crispus Attucks & Pat*[k]*. Carr Killed. Six wounded; two of them (Christ*[r]*. Monk & John Clark) Mortally. Engrav'd Printed & Sold by Paul Revere Boston.*

Line engraving, colored by hand. 11¼ x 9½ inches.

The *Boston Gazette and Country Journal,* published each Monday by Edes and Gill, was not equipped in March 1770 to issue extras. They went to print as usual with No. 779, March 12, a full week after the greatest news event of Boston's 140 years. It was already history. Most "freeholders and other inhabitants of the town" had spent the week in Town Meetings. Committees had been formed, a military watch set, and Sam Adams had brought about the withdrawal of the troops from their city quarters to Castle Island. The black mourning borders of the *Gazette's* inside news pages surrounded the columns of a story that had lost, and for years to come was to lose, none of its horror in the telling. In the first column of the right hand page is a cut—four coffins arow. Each has in its center a skull and crossbones, with initials above: SG, for Samuel Gray; SM, for Samuel Maverick; JC, for James Caldwell; and CA, for the

Negro, Crispus Attucks. The fifth coffin, ordered with the four others, had to be held till next week; the Irishman Patrick Carr had not yet died. The coffins were engraved for Edes and Gill by Paul Revere.

In popular memory the Boston silversmith patriot's character of Man on Horseback has outweighed his other attributes, not least of which was the use of his engraving tools for propaganda. His pen-and-ink diagram of King Street on the night of March 5, with four bodies lying where they had fallen, was used at the subsequent trial of Captain Preston and the eight soldiers of the 29th Regiment. And no less than the speeches and papers of Samuel Adams, John Hancock or Joseph Warren, than the editorials of the *Gazette,* or the fiery blasts from Boston pulpits, Revere's famous print, which by March 26 was "To be Sold by Edes & Gill (Price Eight Pence Lawful Money)", was an instrument for inflaming and uniting Massachusetts public opinion, and setting it on its way toward the Declaration of 1776.

The Revere "Representation of the late horrid Massacre in King St." is probably the most famous of American engravings. Existing copies are hand-colored, with emphasis on scarlet uniforms and Yankee blood (which, said the *Gazette,* was "running like Water thro' King-St.") While Revere's diagram, used at the trial, is considered accurate, the scene in the print is arranged completely in accord with Whig propaganda—a straight line of brutal soldiers, waved on by the sword of their evil captain, firing point-blank into the group of citizens innocent of clubs, reinforced snowballs, or other weapons. More close to the real facts, as they seem to historians of the "brawl" of Monday, March 5, is the report sent by Lt. Col. Maurice Carr, commander of the 29th Regiment, to General Gage:

"About half after Nine that Night a Number of Towns people Armd with Clubs & Other Weapons, came and Attacked the Sentry Posted at the Custom House upon Which the fire Bells Rang. (Which is a Call for the Mob.) Which Made Cap[t] Preston Who was Cap[t] of the Day run to the Main Guard to see what was the Matter, and found the Mobb Attacking the Sentry at the Custom house very Violently, upon Which He got the Guard under Arms & went with a party of men to Relieve the Sentry. Which party of Men were allso Attacked Near the S[d] Sentry Some of them nocked down, others got wounded and Cap[t] Preston allso struck several times, during this Scuffle some of this Party fired on the Mobb, without any orders from Him and Killd three Men on the Spot and wounded others, this Obliged the Mobb in some Measure to Desperse, and then they Brought the Sentry off His Guard. Upon Which the Governour and Counsel Met, and Demanded Capt[n] Preston and several of the Men to be delivered up to Goal for the same, two or three people have Sworn that they Heard Cap[t] Preston order the Men to fire, and some of Sworn that they Heard Him say they Should not fire, and one Gentleman that was by will Swear that He heard a Porter that was Standing on the Custom house Steps Cry out fire Several times."

The original copperplate for this most celebrated of Revere's engravings is still in existence, preserved in the office of the State Treasurer of Massachusetts. Miss Esther Forbes in her fascinating recent study, *Paul Revere and the World He Lived In* (Houghton Mifflin, 1942), quotes a letter of March 27, 1770, from Henry Pelham, a young rival Boston engraver, to Revere, accus-ing the older craftsman of stealing his drawing for the engraving. As Miss Forbes points out, such practises were not unknown to the most scrupulous of eighteenth-century engravers. The authoritative study of the many copperplates executed in the patriot cause by Paul Revere is that of William Loring Andrews, *Paul Revere and His Engraving* (New York, 1901).

PLATE NO. 11. *The Battle of Lexington, April 19th 1775. Plate I. [6 References at bottom.] A. Doolittle. Sculpt.*

Line engraving, colored by hand. First of a set of four prints. 11¾ x 17⅝ inches.

PLATE NO. 12. *Plate II. A View of the Town of Concord [6 References at bottom.] A Doolittle Sculp[t]*

Line engraving, colored by hand. Second of a set of four prints. 11⅝ x 17½ inches.

PLATE NO. 13. *Plate III. The Engagement at the North Bridge in Concord [2 References at bottom.] A Doolittle Sculp[t]*

Line engraving, colored by hand. Third of a set of four prints. 11¾ x 17¼ inches.

PLATE NO. 14. *Plate IV. A View of the South Part of Lexington [9 References at bottom.] A. Doolittle Sculp[t]*

Line engraving, colored by hand. Fourth of a set of four prints. 11¾ x 17½ inches.

ORIGINALS OF PLATES 11–14 IN THE BANCROFT COLLECTION, NEW YORK PUBLIC LIBRARY, NEW YORK.

In a book intended for American readers it is surely unnecessary to rehearse the events of April 19, 1775—how Gen. Thomas Gage decided to send a detachment out to Concord to destroy the military stores which the provincials had been collecting there, and to secure, if possible, the persons of Samuel Adams and John Hancock; how James Warren sent William Dawes and Paul Revere riding through the night to warn and rouse the countryside; how Lt. Col. Francis Smith and Major Pitcairn with a miscellaneous force made their way to Lexington and fired upon a body of militia which they found drawn up on the common, killing eight and wounding ten; how they pressed on to Concord and were engaged in destroying such stores as could be discovered when a strong force of minute-men appeared on the farther side of the North Bridge and before long forced their way across it; how Smith's command was nearly used up on its retreat through Lexington, and was saved only by the appearance of Earl Percy with his entire brigade; and how this whole British force reached Charlestown neck and the protection of its warships only in the nick of time, just at sunset, narrowly avoiding being cut off by the powerful body of minute-men coming south from Marblehead and Salem. The stirring action of this famous day and year brought the American Revolution out of the realm of potentiality and into the world of fact.

Perhaps the most interesting among the numerous first-hand and primary records of that day is the series of four engravings here presented, the joint work of the painter Ralph Earle (1751–1801) and the engraver Amos Doolittle (1754–1832). This, as we are well aware, is not the first historical print, but it is the first set or series of related historical prints, to be produced in America. As art, the prints cannot pretend to much sophistication, and commentators have been having their fun with them

ever since. Says the Rev. William A. Beardsley, "We are told that Doolittle was entirely self-taught as an engraver. That is charitable, since there is no use in incriminating anyone else." Harold Murdock likewise gets in some neat digs, which anyone interested may look up in *The Nineteenth of April, 1775* (Boston, 1923), pages 51 and 87. Both men improved later: Earle went to England, studied under Benjamin West, and painted some very creditable canvases before he drank himself to death. Doolittle never became very precise or in the least inspired, but in spite of Mr. Murdock, he certainly produced more finished work than these maiden efforts. As a contemporary graphic record of the great day, they are unique, and deserve our gratitude rather than our criticism. Incidentally, the general design of the landscape is rather surely handled, and there is a fresh open-air effect to the several scenes.

It has been questioned whether Earle actually participated in these engravings, the first statement to that effect not having appeared till 1831. But Doolittle was still alive in 1831 if Earle was not; and the original advertisement says that the plates are neatly engraven from original paintings taken on the spot. Earle was already painting portraits, of a sort, and there is no reason to believe that Doolittle ever meddled with paint. The tradition recorded by John W. Barber is that Doolittle and Earle went up to Cambridge with the New Haven Cadets under Capt. Benedict Arnold soon after the news of Lexington reached Connecticut, and remained three weeks at the front; that Earle visited and sketched the scenes of the late battles, and that Doolittle posed for him when human figures were to be added, so that when Earle "wished to represent one of the Provincials as loading his gun, crouching behind a stone wall when firing on the enemy, he would require Mr. D. to put himself in such a position." There is no evidence that Earle was like Doolittle a member of the company, but he may have gone along as a volunteer or a hanger-on.

They of course saw the sites and not the action, but there is no doubt that they took eye-witness evidence of what had gone on, and the prints themselves are weighty evidence for the events of that day. In the first, for example, it is clear that the Lexington minutemen are dispersing without offering any concerted resistance, and are being shot down as they disperse, a fact which was for long lost sight of, but has been reëstablished by Mr. Murdock. In the second, the portly Smith stands by as Pitcairn looks for provincials through his telescope, while in the background redcoats are throwing supplies into Concord Millpond, long since drained. In the third, the shot heard round the world has just been fired, as the Bedford and Acton companies prepare to force their way over the North Bridge. The fourth print contains some demonstrable inaccuracies: Earl Percy had already reformed his brigade from column into line before Smith's detachment found shelter with him, and since Smith had received a ball in the leg, he could hardly have conferred with Percy on horseback.

Amos Doolittle returned to New Haven and had his four engravings completed before the end of the year. The *Connecticut Journal* for December 13, 1775, advertised the set as "this day published, and to be sold at the store of Mr. James Lockwood, near the College, in New Haven." "The plain ones" were to be had at six shillings for the set, and the colored (by hand, necessarily) for eight shillings. A New Haven

man could not have made a better investment for his great-grandchildren. Only four complete sets are known, and the price, if one were to come on the market, can only be conjectured.

PLATE No. 15. *An Exact View of The Late Battle at Charlestown June 17ʰ 1775. In which an advanced party of about 700 Provincials stood an Attack made by 11 Regiments & a Train of Artillery & after an Engagement of two hours Retreated to their Main body at Cambridge Leaving Eleven Hundred of the enemy Killed and Wounded upon the field ☆ B: Romans in AEre incidit ☆ [At top: References 1–9]*
Line engraving. 11¼ x 16¼ inches.
ORIGINAL IN THE PHELPS STOKES COLLECTION, NEW YORK PUBLIC LIBRARY, NEW YORK.

PLATE No. 16. *The Battle of Bunker's Hill. ☆ Painted by J. Trumbull Esq. Engraved by I. G. Müller. London, Published Feb: 1798, by A. C. de Poggi, Nº 91. New Bond Street.*

Line engraving. 22¾ x 31¼ inches.

For two months after Lexington and Concord the British lay besieged in Boston by a large provincial force in which the original volunteer minutemen were gradually replaced by regularly enlisted regiments under a commander in chief, Artemas Ward. Organization and discipline remained of the loosest kind, however, until after General Washington had taken over the chief command on behalf of the Continental Congress on July 10, 1775. It was this vagueness of structure that makes it so difficult to understand what really happened at Bunker Hill. In May, a joint committee of the Massachusetts council of war and the committee of safety had recommended the fortification of Bunker Hill, on the Charlestown peninsula which thrusts its nose out between the Mystic and Charles Rivers against the nose of Boston peninsula. But they had evidently contemplated the simultaneous fortification of the nearest hills on the landward side of Charlestown Neck, the narrow causeway, flooded at highest water, which connected the peninsula with the mainland. On June 16 a council of civilians and military officers at Cambridge decided to fortify Bunker Hill at once, without making any provision for the landward hills. As soon as night had fallen Col. William Prescott took three regiments—perhaps 3,500 men; the provincial army did not go in for statistics—and passed over Charlestown Neck; Israel Putnam and other general officers went along, but did not exercise any definite command. Colonel Prescott marched past Bunker Hill to Breed's Hill, farther down the peninsula and 35 feet lower; and there, during the summer night, his men constructed an entire earth-and-wood redoubt, the perfection of which aroused the astonishment of the British officers after they had captured it.

As soon as the American advance was perceived the next morning, June 17, General Gage in Boston called a council of war, at which Clinton and others urged the use of the British ships to land troops near Charlestown Neck, in the Americans' rear. Gage, however, insisted on an immediate frontal assault, and commissioned Gen. William Howe to cross over to Charlestown and carry it out. As one of our most trenchant military critics, Charles Francis Adams, has put it: "So far as the American, or what we call the patriot cause was concerned, the operation ought to have resulted in irretrievable disaster, for on no correct military principle could it be defended; and yet, owing to the superior capac-

ity for blundering of the British commanders, the movement was in its actual results a brilliant success; and, indeed, could hardly have been made more so had the Americans controlled for that occasion the movements of both sides, and so issued orders to their opponents." Three times Howe's redcoats charged up the slopes of Breed's Hill. Twice they recoiled from the deadly fire of New England musketry which Prescott wisely restrained until they were 40, and the second time, 20 yards from redoubt or breastwork; the third time, the Americans' ammunition was exhausted, and without bayonets the redoubt could not be held. Prescott's force retreated in fair order over the Neck, Putnam exerting himself in the rear guard, but suffered most of their casualties as they went. The British had secured Charlestown peninsula, but at a terrible cost: 1,054 out of about 3,500 men engaged, and one in ten of them officers.

We reproduce two versions of Bunker Hill (the battle, as is well known, took its name from the wrong hill): one an engraving published at Philadelphia during the same year, and evidently before Doolittle had completed his labored work on the Lexington plates, by BERNARD ROMANS (c. 1720–c. 1784); the other an engraving made in Germany after a painting by JOHN TRUMBULL (1756–1843). Both men were active participants in our Revolution: on the day of the battle Adjutant Trumbull was on Roxbury hill on the other side of Boston, and could get a distant view of the smoke of firearms along the ridge of Breed's hill and the whole of Charlestown enveloped in flames. Romans, on May 12, 1775, had captured Fort George near Ticonderoga single-handed—its garrison consisted of two men—and would shortly begin constructing, for the New York committee of safety, the earliest fortifications about West Point. For this versatile Dutchman was both "civil engineer, naturalist, cartographer, author, and captain of artillery"—the *Dictionary of American Biography* does not even mention his prowess as an engraver. In this same year of 1775 he published at New York his best-known book, *A Concise Natural History of East and West Florida.* Five years later he was taken prisoner while on his way to join the southern army in South Carolina, and was carried off to Jamaica. In 1784, he took ship to return to the United States, but never reached it, and presumably either died or was murdered at sea. His *Exact View* is panoramic and shows, from right to left, the guns from Copp's Hill in Boston, as well as the British warship *Somerset,* firing on Charlestown, which is sending up flames and a billow of smoke; the British assaulting Breed's hill in line—column would have been more correct—while one group which has suffered heavily has turned back, leaving its dead behind it, and is being rallied by its officers, swords drawn; the Americans behind a very solid-looking breastwork—there is no sign of the redoubt; and finally, a monstrous General Putnam on a huge white charger, brandishing his sword for the encouragement of his riflemen. But where are we, the spectators, and who is the "Broken Officer" who waves his sword beneath the giant tree in the left margin? The drawing may be termed loose but lively.

In 1777 Col. John Trumbull decided that his merit was insufficiently appreciated by the Continental Congress, and returned to art; three years later he went *via* Paris to London to study under Benjamin West, only to be arrested on "suspicion of treason," perhaps as a reprisal for the hanging of Major André, with departure from Britain made the condition of his release. The war over, Trumbull made a beeline for London and West's studio. In the course of 1785 there came to him the inspiration to undertake historical subjects from the history of his own country in the grandiose manner of West, and during that year and the following spring he completed, under West's supervision, "the death of General Warren at the battle of Bunker's hill, and of General Montgomery in the attack of Quebec"—manifestly both lineal descendants of the master's *Death of Wolfe.* In 1786–89 came a new series, with one more death, that of General Mercer at Princeton, but also *The Declaration of Independence, The Surrender of the Hessians,* and *The Surrender of Lord Cornwallis at Yorktown.* Unfortunately, if comprehensibly, there was little market for such productions in England, and Trumbull had to turn to other means of livelihood. Meanwhile, he arranged with West's publisher, the Italian Antonio C. de Poggi, to have the series engraved, and suitable craftsmen were sought for on the continent, where Trumbull traveled in 1785–86. Ultimately, de Poggi found an engraver for *Bunker Hill* in JOHANN GOTTHARD VON MÜLLER (1747–1830) of Stuttgart, professor of engraving in the *Akademie* of that city, who had studied in Paris in his youth and was now an acknowledged master. He took his time over Trumbull's painting; the painter paid him a visit in 1794 to see how he was getting on, and another in 1797 to pick up the finished plate as well as his canvas. Neither painter nor engraver came quite up to the mark set in *The Death of Wolfe,* but it is nevertheless an impressive work, most carefully and elaborately engraved; one of von Müller's two *Hauptblätter.*

Joseph Warren, whose death it commemorates, was one of the mainstays and hopes of the patriot cause. President of the Provincial Congress and member of the committee of safety, and also major general of Massachusetts troops, he came to Breed's Hill as a volunteer, after having vainly opposed the advance in the councils of the day before. There he was killed, just after the Americans were compelled to abandon the redoubt.

PLATE NO. 17. *Représentation du feu terrible à nouvelle Yorck, que les Américains ont allumé pendant la nuit du 19. Septembre 1776. par lequel ont été brulés tous les Bâtimens du coté de Vest, a droite de Borse, dans la rue de Broock jusqu'au collége du Roi, et plus de 1,600. maisons avec l'Eglise de la Sᵗᵉ Trinité la Chapelle Luthérienne, et l'école des pauvres.* ☆ *A Paris chez Basset Rue S. Jacques au coin de la rue des Mathurins.*

Line engraving, colored by hand. 10½ x 15¼ inches.

The command of the Howe brothers in the early years of the Revolutionary War has formed one of the enigmas of American history. In their own time and frequently since they have been accused of sympathy if not downright collusion with the rebels, and few critics fail to brand their conduct of the campaign as incompetent. Dilatory they unquestionably were in the evacuation of Boston and the transfer of operations to New York. General Washington had full time, after the defeat of Long Island (August 27, 1776) to withdraw his men in orderly fashion and evacuate New York, which was clearly untenable in view of the disparity between his small army and the 30,000 British and Hessian regulars

under Sir William, not to mention the fleet under Admiral Lord Howe in New York harbor. On September 2, Washington wrote to the Continental Congress asking for an immediate decision as to whether the city should be destroyed or be left as winter quarters for the enemy. "They would derive great convenience from it on the one hand; and much property would be destroyed on the other." Congress replied with a resolution that in case General Washington "should find it necessary to quit New York" special care must be taken "that no damage be done to the said city by his troops on their leaving it; the Congress having no doubt of their being able to recover the same." On September 15 Washington retreated to Harlem Heights and left the city to the British.

On September 22, 1776, a brief report went to Congress from the commander in chief:

"On Friday night (Sept. 20–21), about Eleven or Twelve O'Clock, a fire broke out in the City of New York, near the New or St. Paul's Church, as it is said, which continued to burn pretty rapidly till after Sunrise the next morning. I have not been Informed how the Accident happened, nor received any certain Account of the damage. Report says many Houses between the Broadway and the River were consumed."

On the same day Washington wrote to Governor Trumbull of Connecticut:

"By what means it happened we do not know; but the Gentleman who brought the Letter from Genl. Howe last night, and who was one of his Aide De Camps, informed Col. Reed, that several of our Countrymen had been punished with various deaths on Account of it; some by hanging, others by burning, &c., alledging that they were apprehended when Committing the fact."

The English and Loyalist view was unanimous—the fire had been started by "a Number of Villains" concealed in town to burn it after the evacuation. Howe so reported to Lord George Germaine, and Governor Tryon contributed his opinion that Washington had been "privy to this villainous act" because he had had the bells of the city sent off ostensibly to be cast into cannon, really to prevent the ringing of the alarm. The magnificent *Iconography of Manhattan Island* by I. N. Phelps Stokes quotes many columns (v. 5, p. 1020–24) of detailed accounts from contemporary journals, letters, newspapers and documents. Most of them agree that "many of the villains were apprehended, with Matches in their Hands to set Fire to the Houses," and that combustibles had been found in concealment. On the other hand, many Americans were convinced that it was a wanton act of barbarism on the part of the British. Admittedly "the Destruction was very great; between a third and a fourth of the City is burnt. All that is West of the New Exchange, along Broad Street to the North River, as high as the City Hall, and from thence along the Broad Way and North River to King's College, is in ruins. St. Paul's Church and the College were saved with the utmost Difficulty. Trinity Church, the Lutheran Church, the Parsonage, and Charity School, are destroyed" (Loyalist letter). And thus perished in flame and smoke all the physical remains of old New Amsterdam, the quaint little Dutch town which never dreamed of its megalopolitan destiny.

The engraver and publisher of this plate was ANDRÉ BASSET, a Parisian craftsman of the second half of the century, who turned out a large number of caricatures, portraits, and costume plates. In spite of the popularity of the American cause in France, he confidently swallowed the story of American responsibility for the fire without any reservations. The goings-on in the street are drawn with great animation in the figures, which are individually activated instead of being made to a pattern.

PLATE No. 18. *The Landing of the British Forces in the Jerseys on the 20th of November 1776 under the command of the Rt Honl Lieut Genl Earl Cornwallis.*
Watercolor, probably by Thomas Davies. 12½ x 17½ inches.
ORIGINAL IN THE EMMET COLLECTION, NEW YORK PUBLIC LIBRARY, NEW YORK.

Washington's attempt to hold the area about New York against a better-trained and better-equipped force enjoying the advantages of sea power ended, as it had begun, in disaster. The Continental Congress had unfortunately meddled so far as to resolve, on October 11, 1776, that Fort Washington, on the northern tip of Manhattan Island, should not be abandoned, and the commander in chief was unable, before it was too late, to make up his mind to withdraw the garrison across the Hudson. Howe, by well-calculated maneuvers, succeeded in isolating the fort and then, on the morning of November 16, concentrating superior forces against it. Its defensibility proved to be far below expectation, and on the same afternoon Colonel Magaw surrendered, nearly 3,000 men, 146 pieces of artillery, and a great quantity of ammunition falling into British hands. It was the hardest blow so far to the American cause, and Washington's eyes filled with tears as, from Fort Lee on the other side of the Hudson, he watched the British flag unfurled over the fort which bore his name.

For once Sir William Howe was not in the least dilatory, and the second day after the capitulation he had General Cornwallis on his way across the Hudson from Yonkers, with 12 regiments or about 5,000 men. It was the intention of Howe and Cornwallis to surprise Fort Lee by an approach from its rear. Washington, learning of the advance, did not tarry but abandoned the fort and its stores and began his long retreat across the Jerseys.

One of the officers with the British army made the vigorous watercolor of Cornwallis' crossing and his ascent of the Palisades which is here reproduced. Either he has misdated it (November 20 for 18) or it represents a later crossing of troops rather than the vanguard which sought to surprise Fort Lee. This watercolor formed a part of the collection made by Francis Rawdon, in 1776 a captain with Howe's army, but later adjutant general to the British forces in America, the victor of Hobkirk's Hill over Nathaniel Greene (April 1781), Governor General of Bengal (1812–22), and first Marquis of Hastings. It has apparently been understood by some that this drawing was Rawdon's own work, but the drawings in his collection were by several hands, none of them, apparently, his own. His grandson's unthriftiness caused the collection to be put up for sale, and about 1870 a number of the sketches passed into the ownership of Dr. Thomas Addis Emmet, "one of the most generous and liberal of the few Americans who in-

dulge in the costly but delightful and useful pastime of gathering up for preservation such precious grain of the fine gold of our history, which might otherwise be forever lost" (*Harper's Monthly*, 1873). The drawing is unsigned, but is almost certainly the work of THOMAS DAVIES, Captain in the Royal Regiment of Artillery, who made a signed water color of the attack on Fort Washington a few days earlier, which is in the Phelps Stokes Collection (reproduced as Plate 24 in the Stokes catalogue, *American Historical Prints*), and which displays a similar drawing technique and an almost identical script in the title. Some of Davies' drawings had been engraved in the *Scenographia Americana* series, 1768. As an artillery officer he would take particular notice of the guns in the larger boats, those being unloaded, and those already on their way up the steep path to the top of the Palisades.

PLATES No. 19, 20. *View of Mud Island before it's Reduction 16ᵗʰ Novʳ. 1777 under the Direction of John Montrésor Esqʳ. Chief Engineer in America, taken from the Dyke in the Front of the Six Gun Battery on Carpenter's Island.*

Topographical drawing, in watercolor and ink, by Pierre Nicole. 11¼ x 29¾ inches.

In the spring of 1777 Sir William Howe, after taking the advice of the rebel prisoner and ex-officer of the British army, Gen. Charles Lee, changed his plans and determined to attack the American capital, Philadelphia, from the south, by sea. In the course of July and August Howe took his army around by the Capes of Virginia to the head of Chesapeake Bay, and, proceeding overland, administered a brisk defeat to Washington at the Battle of the Brandywine, September 11, 1777. Howe was an able tactician but a muddle-headed strategist; instead of exploiting his advantage by a ruthless pursuit of Washington's beaten army, he chose the city for his objective, and neatly maneuvered his way into Philadelphia without further fighting. But his achievement remained incomplete and insecure as long as the navigation of the Delaware was not open to British ships; and it remained closed by "three rows of chevaux de frize, composed of immense beams of timber bolted and fastened together, and stuck with iron pikes fastened in every direction" (Stedman). The chevaux de frize was buttressed by two fortifications: Fort Mercer, at Red Bank on the Jersey shore, and Fort Mifflin, on Mud Island near the Pennsylvania side of the River. This stoppage of navigation made Howe's supply problem difficult; he was obliged to detach 3,000 men to bring his supplies overland from the Chesapeake, and it was while he was thus weakened that Washington undertook his surprise counterattack at Germantown, a counterattack which failed only through miserable luck amid the fog of war. It was high time to reduce the American forts on the Delaware, and on October 22, Howe sent Count Donop and a strong force of Hessians to assault Fort Mercer. Donop was killed and his Hessians cut to pieces; and it was evident that more systematic measures would have to be undertaken.

At this point we encounter one of history's more ironical situations. In 1771 John Montrésor, barrackmaster for the ordnance in North America, had constructed the fort on Mud Island for the protection of Philadelphia against His Majesty's enemies. In 1777, John Montrésor, chief engineer in America, prepared for Sir William Howe a plan for reducing the fort on Mud Island, now called Fort Mifflin by those

rebels who held it so tenaciously against His Majesty's authority. Thirty-nine pieces of ordnance were to be concentrated against the fort, in batteries, floating batteries, and a warship, with an assault to follow after the artillery fire should take sufficient effect. On November 10, 1777, Montrésor wrote in his journal, "We opened our Batteries against Mud Island Fort." The bombardment continued for five days, and on the sixth, five warships came right up to the chevaux de frise to join in. The assault was never necessary. The engineer who had built the fort battered it to pieces, killing or wounding 250 of the 300 Americans who garrisoned it; and on the night of the 15th–16th, the survivors set what structures remained intact on fire and slipped away to Fort Mercer. This in its turn was abandoned on November 20, and Sir William could look forward to a comfortable and well-fed winter in Philadelphia.

Like Lord Rawdon, Captain Montrésor collected "Views of North America," as his endorsement reads on this gemlike drawing of the doomed fort. But, although he was doubtless capable of producing one himself, this does not seem to have been his own work. The Library of Congress has another item from Montrésor's collection, a map entitled, "A Survey of the City of Philadelphia and its Environs shewing the several Works constructed by His Majesty's Troops . . . since their possession of that City 26th September 1777." This map was surveyed and drawn by P. Nicole; and the inset view of Fort Mifflin, reduced but identical with ours in all but trifling detail, is inscribed "P. Nicole Fecit." Capt. PIERRE NICOLE was a Draughtsman in the Corps of Engineers under Montrésor in the campaign of 1777. Twenty-two years later Montrésor was still trying to get

33

his accounts passed by the British Treasury; and we find the following in one of his petitions: "There was in the Department of your Memorialist, as Draftsman and Captain of the Guides, a man named Capt. Pierre Nicole, a Swiss, very intelligent, well acquainted with the Country and with the people," who engaged in intelligence work and served as "the confidential person acting between the British army and the Loyalists." But Captain Nicole had died in 1784 and so could no longer testify on behalf of his old commander's claims on the public purse.

PLATE No. 21. *McColloch's Leap. In the year 1777 Major McColloch hotly pursued by the Indians, saved his life by boldly leaping down a precipice about 150 feet high into the Wheeling Creek, Va ☆ On Stone by G. W. Fasel. Print by Nagel & Weingärtner. ☆ New York, Published by Emil Seitz, 233 Broadway. ☆ [Copyright notice, 1851]*

Lithograph, colored by hand. 11⅜ x 15¼ inches.

Where the great highway of Route 40, the "National Old Trails Road," passes over Wheeling Creek in West Virginia, on its way from Atlantic City via Baltimore, Frederick, Columbus, Indianapolis and points west to San Francisco, there is set up a historical marker. *McCulloch's Leap,* it reads, *1777.*

Wheeling was a new settlement in 1777. Its Indian name was Weeling, "the place of the skull," and when in 1769 Ebenezer Zane came there to build his cabin he found a row of poles on which stood the heads of murdered palefaces. But frontiersmen were not easily frightened, and in eight years "Zanesburg" had a num-

ber of inhabitants. A fort had been built there during Lord Dunmore's War in 1774, named Fort Fincastle after the Earl's viscountcy, but in 1776 the western Virginians changed its name to Fort Henry. Patrick Henry's ringing words, "Give me liberty or give me death" made a slogan which the border liked.

The militia who defended settlers on the Ohio frontier against the savage allies of Britain were daring Indian fighters. Samuel McCulloch—this is the spelling found in histories—had come as a venturous lad of twenty to the Wheeling Creeks country on the border between Virginia and Ohio in 1770. In 1776, when militia were called to garrison the border forts south of Fort Pitt, McCulloch was made a major and given command of a blockhouse on Short Creek.

Early in 1777 raiding parties, mainly Indians, but directed by the British Col. Henry Hamilton in Detroit, were sent out against the frontier. In August friendly Indians brought to Zanesburg the rumor that a party was drawing near Fort Henry and that its leader was the notorious renegade Simon Girty. Scouts on August 31st reported smoke to the south. Next morning a small group from the fort was surrounded by Indians, only one or two escaping. Then the savages, nearly 400 strong, broke from cover and besieged the fort. Throughout the day a heroic defense went on within the stockade; its garrison, outnumbered ten to one, repelled every howling assault, while the women and children loaded and passed the guns. Someone, maybe from the fort, maybe a nearby settler, got clear and carried the news to Short Creek and the other settlements.

Maj. Samuel McCulloch assembled 40 or 50 men, his blockhouse command and ablebodied settlers, and came early on September 2 to relieve the besieged fort. The rescuers made a bold dash through the Indian host, and as the gates of the stockade were opened a crack, surged inside—all but McCulloch. The major, directing the charge, was cut off from the body of his men. The gates were closed, and the Indians all about him. He turned his horse and galloped up steep Wheeling Hill, only to run into another Indian band on the summit. The savages were behind and before, all escape cut off—except to a bird or a fearless horseman. McCulloch plunged his steed straight down the precipitous bank to the creek 150 feet below, across and to safety. The Wheeling historians do not claim the clear leap into open space that G. W. Fasel depicted, but after making allowances for helping underbrush still declare the exploit one of the most daring in western annals.

The siege was raised next day by the Indians and the ravaged settlement started rebuilding. A petition to the Virginia House of Delegates for "just and reasonable" relief was rejected. In 1779 the settlers chose McCulloch to represent their new Ohio County in the legislature. But an Indian fighter of his caliber could not be kept safe in halls of debate. He was called in August 1779 to go with Brodhead's campaign on the upper Allegheny. Then he was given command of Van Metre's fort on Short Creek. In 1782, the worst though almost the last of the years of Indian strife on that border, crops could be planted only under the protection of scouts on constant patrol. Toward the close of July, Major McCulloch, riding on scout duty, was shot by a party of Indians near the fort. "His name had been a terror to savage foes for years, and it was thought the Indians had marked him for destruction. In addition to scalping

him, it is said his slayers cut out his heart and ate it to impart to themselves his courage."

This and the following plate are part of a series of six lithographs, "Heroic Deeds of Former Times," all scenes of Indian warfare, which the New York importer and publisher of prints, Emil Seitz, brought out in 1851. Though drawn long after the events they depict, and not without some comic aspects, they make unusually vigorous and satisfying representations of frontier warfare. All six were handsomely drawn on stone by G. W. FASEL, otherwise known for his views in a *Central Park Album* of 1862. They exist in both uncolored and colored state. The printing was carried out by the well-known New York firm of NAGEL AND WEINGÄRTNER, who are credited with "a considerable mass of very important and interesting work" during their partnership of 1849–57, including views of New York City and portraits. It may well have been this Louis Nagel who drew on stone our Plate 56. This is the first *lithograph* which we reproduce; lithography was neither invented nor introduced into America until long after the American Revolution, and we shall have more to say of it in those periods of which it was a characteristic mode of illustration.

PLATE No. 22. *Heroic Deeds of Former Times.* ☆ *5.* ☆ *Benjamin Logan saving Harrison from being scalped who was one of a party of three men guarding the women while milking the cowes, outside the station, when they were suddenly attacked by Indians and fired upon, two were killed instantly and Harrison disabled, when Logan seeing his friend writhing in agony, sprang forward at the risk of his own life, and*

Benjamin Logan was of Scotch-Irish ancestry, born in Augusta County, Va., about 1743. At the age of 14 he took his dead father's place as head of his family. In 1764 he went as a sergeant with Bouquet's expedition. In 1775 he removed to the new land of Kentucky, in whose frontier annals his name stands beside those of Boone and Harrod. His great size, strength, and courage were renowned throughout the border.

After Dunmore's War (1774) against the trans-Ohio Shawnee Indians there began a movement of southwestern Virginians to the rich new lands to the West. Richard Henderson of North Carolina had acquired from the Cherokee Indians a huge tract of land, Transylvania, between the Kentucky and Cumberland Rivers. James Harrod had begun his fort in June 1774, before Dunmore marched, and Harrodsburg was the chief base of operations for the pioneers. In 1775 Daniel Boone blazed a trail across Cumberland Gap and built his stout stockade at Boonesborough. That same year Logan crossed the mountains and established his station, which he called St. Asaph's, and to which in the next year he brought his wife and family.

Harrod's Fort, Boone's Fort, Logan's Fort, three small blockhouses, each a cleared space enclosed by a strong fence in the great wilderness, behind every tree of which might lurk a hostile Indian. "Never perhaps," wrote the chronicler Alexander Scott Withers, "lived three men better qualified by nature and habit, to resist that hostility, and preserve the settlers from captivity and death, than James Harrod, Daniel Boone, and Benjamin Logan. . . . They were placed at the head of the little colonies planted around them; not by ambition, but by the universal voice of the people; from a deep and thorough conviction, that they only were adequate to the exigencies of their situation."

On March 5, 1777, under orders and commissions from Virginia, a militia was assembled and organized, with George Rogers Clark at Harrodsburg as its major, and Harrod, Daniel Boone, and Benjamin Logan captains at their own stations. In the same month the Shawnees came back from their winter villages across the Ohio. They assaulted the three forts, and from each one they were repelled with unexcelled heroism. At Logan's Station the garrison consisted of thirteen men. The Indians, 50 or 60 painted warriors, hid near the stockade in a swamp. The famous episode, here illustrated by G. W. Fasel, took place the morning of the attack, Friday, May 30. According to Withers (1831):

"Early in the morning the women went out to milk, guarded by most of the garrison; and before they were aware of impending danger, the concealed Indians opened a general fire, which killed three of the men, and drove the others, hastily within the fort. A most affecting spectacle was then presented to view, well calculated to excite the sympathies of human nature, and arouse to action a man possessed of the generous sensibility and noble daring, which animated the bosom of Logan.

One of the men who had fallen on the first fire of the Indians and had been supposed by his comrades to be dead, was in truth though badly wounded, yet still alive; and was observed feebly struggling to crawl towards the fort . . . The magnanimous and intrepid Logan resolved on making an effort to save him. He endeavored to raise volunteers, to accompany him without the fort, and bring in their poor wounded companion . . . [One Martin reached the gate, but there] the spirit of Martin forsook him, and he recoiled from the hazardous adventure. Logan was then alone. He beheld the feeble, but wary exertions of his unfortunate comrade, entirely subside; and he could not hesitate. He rushed quickly through the gate, caught the unhappy victim in his arms, and bore him triumphantly into the fort, amid a shower of bullets aimed at him; and some of which buried themselves in the pallisades close by his head. A most noble and disinterested achievement, and worthy of all commendation."

The assault was beaten off, and Logan managed to leave the fort and go for ammunition and relief. St. Asaph's still stood, and so did Harrodsburg and Boonesborough. In the retaliatory expeditions against the Indians in 1778, 1780, and 1782, Logan was a leader. In 1781 he was named chief militia officer of the district, now Lincoln County. He was sent for three terms to the Virginia General Assembly, as the most trusted of Kentucky leaders. In 1788 he led the Kentucky troops in his last Indian fight, the expedition against the Indians of the Northwest. Washington appointed him a member of the Board of War in the West in 1790, and Governor Shelby of Kentucky made him a brigadier general of state militia. In 1792 he was a member of the Kentucky Constitutional Convention. He died in 1802.

Most of our readers will, we trust, be pleased with the scene as Fasel imagined it three-quarters of a century later, even if his stockade is much too low. It does not, to be sure, put its strongest emphasis on the deed of Logan; that and most of the rest of the picture has a curious placidity typified by the cud-chewing cattle in the middle distance; but in the lower right-hand corner there is going on, sketched in bolder and accented lines, the savage frenzy of the most effective piece of scalping in American illustration.

PLATE NO. 23. *[At top, mirror-wise:] Combat Memorable entre le Pearson et Paul Jones.* ☆ *Collection des Prospects.* ☆ *[Right-hand column:] Combat memorable entre le Pearson et Paul Jones doné le 22 7bre 1779, le Capitaine Pearson comendant le Serapis et Paul Jones commandant le Bon home Richart, et son Escadre. [Left-hand column: Same in Dutch.]* ☆ *Richard Paton peignot Lugdun Gravé par Balth. Frederic Leizelt.* ☆ *Se vend à Augsbourg au Negoce comune de l'Academie Imperiale d'Empire des Arts liberaux avec Privilege de Sa Majesté Imperiale et avec Defense ni d'en faire ni de vendre les Copies.*

Line engraving, colored by hand, 12 x 16½ inches.

ORIGINAL IN THE NAVAL HISTORY DIVISION, U. S. NAVY DEPARTMENT, WASHINGTON, D. C.

On December 7, 1775, the Continental Congress handed a lieutenant's commission in the American navy to a 28-year-old Scottish ship master, a refugee who bore the recently acquired surname of Jones. At Tobago in the West Indies in 1773 John Paul, master of the *Betsy,* had killed a mutinous sailor. The noise of the affair sent him to Virginia, and America acquired the first and not the least of her naval heroes.

Four days before his lieutenantcy arrived, Jones had hoisted the new flag of the American colonies, thirteen stars on a blue ground, thirteen stripes, red and white, over the first ship procured for the American navy, the *Alfred.* He proved successful in taking prizes, and by the summer of 1777 Captain Jones was in command of the sloop *Ranger.* With her he was sent to France, and with her, in true Elizabethan corsair style, he raided the coasts of England and Scotland. In Paris in 1779, with the blessing of Benjamin Franklin, he was given a French ship, the wornout East Indiaman, *Duras,* 40 guns. He rechristened her *Bonhomme Richard* after the philosopher-diplomat whose *Maxims of Poor Richard* had taken Paris by storm. On August 14 Captain Jones put to sea from L'Orient, commander of a squadron—seven vessels, of mixed and discordant elements, flying the new flag but paid for by His Most Christian Majesty. The only force that held together the ships with their French captains and motley crews, recruited with the greatest difficulty in L'Orient and Nantes, was the indomitable personality of their leader.

Off Flamborough Head on the Yorkshire coast, September 23, 1779, Captain Jones lay in watch for the Baltic trade fleet. The coast from Scarborough down to Hull was in alarm, the Northumberland militia was called out, and the men of the coast villages mustered at the quays armed against the pirate. At 2 p. m., Jones sighted 41 merchant vessels, escorted by

His Majesty's ships *Serapis,* 44 guns, Capt. Richard Pearson, and *Countess of Scarborough,* 20 guns, Commander Thomas Piercy. Of Jones' fleet, three had disappeared, the *Pallas,* Captain Cottineau, was lending cooperation, the *Vengeance* was in the offing, and the most intransigent of the squadron, the *Alliance,* lay to in the distance, her half-mad commander, Captain Pierre Landais, not to be relied on for the coming fight.

At six the battle was joined in the gathering dusk, Jones intercepting the *Serapis* and *Countess of Scarborough* as they stood in for the coast. The *Pallas* engaged the smaller vessel, her 32 eight-pound guns silencing the *Countess of Scarborough's* 22 six-pounders, and compelling her surrender in an hour. But the *Bonhomme Richard* met the *Serapis* in single combat: the *Serapis* had two decks, 18-pound guns, and a crew of 400 British tars, the unquestioned lords of the sea. The *Bonhomme Richard* was essentially a 12-pounder, one-deck vessel, though on a lower deck gun ports had been cut to mount six old-fashioned 18-pounders. Her crew was 322—75 Americans, many of them young boys, Englishmen, Portuguese, Irishmen, Scotsmen, scum of the French ports, and 137 French marines; while a number of trustworthy minor officers had been detached to bring off the prizes already taken. The great victory was a personal achievement, due to the single factor of the unquenchable courage of the great captain.

The details of the battle are told in a hundred books. Suffice it to say that Jones manoeuvered the *Richard* close to the *Serapis,* that two of the large guns on his makeshift lower deck burst, that on both sides the dead were heaped high, that the *Richard,* hardly seaworthy to begin with, was soon leaking badly. Pearson called again and again for the surrender which was not forthcoming. The two ships locked and fought at arm's length. The perverse *Alliance* drew close, but her fire, by accident or design, was turned partly on the *Bonhomme Richard*. British prisoners earlier captured in prizes were released from the hold by the terrified master at arms, and only Jones' firm order which set them to save their lives at the pumps, kept them from stampeding the crew. Fires burned on both ships. Wrote Jones, "The scene was dreadful beyond the range of language." The marines and sailors in the *Richard's* tops cleared the decks of the *Serapis* again and again. One valiant topman, after three hours' combat, climbed out far on the mainmast above the enemy deck and flung hand grenades down the *Serapis'* hatchways, exploding an 18-pounder. At last Jones wore down Pearson's brave resistance, and as the mainmast of the *Serapis* threatened to fall, she called for quarter. Pearson with his own hand struck his flag, then sent his sword to Capt. John Paul Jones. British historians have minimized the triumph, saying that it permitted the valuable Baltic fleet to escape. But it firmly established the American naval tradition.

RICHARD PATON (1717–91) was an English painter specializing in marines and sea fights. A poor boy who had been picked up in the streets of London by an Admiral of the Royal Navy and sent to sea, he was eventually seen to have talent, and was more or less subsidized by an appointment in the Excise. He was thereby enabled to paint all the great sea battles of his day, from about 1757 on. His paintings, greatly popular, were exhibited at the Royal Academy and promptly engraved by contemporary masters of that art. Paton made a fine

canvas of the *Bonhomme Richard's* battle; whether because, as an inscription in Lerpinière's engraving suggests, Captain Pearson's "Bravery & Conduct saved the Baltic Fleet under his Convoy tho' obliged to submit to a much superior force," or because it was such a famous fight to the finish, can only be conjectured. The authorized engraving was made by Daniel Lerpinière and James Fittler in a handsome, smoothly executed moonlit scene, a reproduction of which will be found in the Grolier Society's catalog, *The United States Navy, 1776 to 1815* (New York, 1942), opposite page 10. Paton's picture was also reproduced at least three times on the Continent, twice at Paris and once far away in south Germany, at Augsburg, a free city of the Holy Roman Empire. It is unlikely that any of these engravers actually saw Paton's canvas; the Frenchmen do not even mention his name, and it is probable that they simply reworked the Lerpinière-Fittler engraving. It is the version engraved at Augsburg by BALTHASAR FRIEDRICH LEIZELT that we reproduce; it has none of the suave finish of the English production, and the light of the moon has given way to ordinary daylight. Since it is the reverse, from left to right, of the English view, and since the style of engraving is considerably more crude, vigorous, and archaic—it reminds one of the Dutch plates of nearly a century earlier—it is not readily perceived to be the same scene. The mirror-wise inscription at the top, it is said, indicates that the print was designed for transfer onto glass, like so many contemporary engravings. Leizelt was active at Augsburg for a considerable period in the latter part of the Eighteenth Century, and was making plates of the great war at its close; although he did views of German cities, he also kept his eyes on the world outside, and engraved one of New York, as well as of Versailles and Ranelegh Gardens in London.

PLATE No. 24. *Capt. Paul Jones shooting a Sailor who had attempted to strike his Colours in an Engagement.*

Mezzotint, printed for R. Sayer and J. Bennett, London, 1780. 13¼ x 9¾ inches.

ORIGINAL IN THE U. S. NAVAL ACADEMY MUSEUM, ANNAPOLIS, MD.

After the first hour's close engagement, Pearson called for surrender, but Jones chose to grapple. When the *Alliance* had fired on her consort and drawn away to safety, fires broke out on the *Richard*. The officers begged Jones to surrender, but he answered, "No, I will sink, I will never strike." A shot carried away one of the four pumps, and the master gunner, believing the ship sinking and being told that Jones and his splendid first officer, Richard Dale, had both been killed, ran aft on the poop to haul down the colors. He would have succeeded, save that the flag had been shot away. Pearson from his deck shouted again his demand for surrender. It is Dale who reported the famous answer—the words whose spirit is alive today, as witness the *Franklin* and the *Laffey*—"I have not yet begun to fight." At the same moment Jones, standing on his quarter-deck, hurled his two pistols at the defeatist master gunner. One of them struck him down at the foot of the gangway ladder.

This is, we suppose, the reality behind the British mezzotint of the following year, unless the master gunner had become confused with the mutineer whose summary execution sent Jones to Virginia. The British public liked to make its flesh creep with tales of the terrible Jones, and this print, manifestly designed for nonaristocratic consumption, is a good specimen of such thrillers. As a mezzotint, of course, it is not to be thought of in comparison with the following plate.

PLATE No. 25. *General Marion in his Swamp Encampment Inviting a British Officer to Dinner. ☆ Painted by John B. White, Charleston, S. C. Engraved by John Sartain. ☆ Published by the Apollo Association for the Promotion of the Fine Arts in the U. S. Nº 1. 1840.*

Mezzotint. 16¾ x 20 inches.

On May 9, 1780, Maj. Gen. Benjamin Lincoln surrendered Charleston and his army of 7,000 Continentals to General Clinton, and the British commander sailed back to New York, leaving Cornwallis with 5,000 men to hold the supposedly conquered territory. It was "the most serious defeat of the Americans in the Revolution. For the South, it meant that all the American forces in South Carolina had been eliminated" (Thomas G. Frothingham). Cornwallis moved in leisurely fashion from the city to occupy the hinterland, and walked into a hornet's nest. The countryside, thorny tangle, piney woods, cypress swamps, rose to sting him in the form of warfare most inacceptable to disciplined redcoat armies, partisan raids. Here one moment, on swift horses, striking down British outposts, gone the next like a shadow into the pathless forest—the militiamen who made up the band of the "Swamp Fox" became the terror of the Carolinas.

Gen. Francis Marion, romantic partisan leader whose tactics were of the highest value in the recovery of the South, was the subject of a biography by the egregious Parson Mason L. Weems, based on an account by one of Marion's officers, Horry. An eloquent sentence describes the reactions of a British colonel who had been sent out with a heavy force to capture Marion and who met with a singular lack of success— 20 men dead on the ground and several wagons full of wounded. Hurrying back to headquarters he "encamped on the plantation of Mr. Trapier, to whom he told a dreadful story about Marion and his *damned rebels,* who would not, as he said, *sleep and fight like gentlemen,* but, like savages, were eternally firing and whooping around him by night; and by day, waylaying and popping at him from behind every tree he went by."

Marion's men were recruited from the countryside, and like other State militia, came and went as they fancied. At times he had no more than 30 followers. Their fortress was the good greenwood, their tent the cypress tree, familiar to American schoolboys in William Cullen Bryant's "Song of Marion's Men." The story of the dinner offered to a British officer is from Parson Weems, but it need not for that reason alone be rejected as apocryphal. The officer had been sent out under a flag to make some arrangements about exchange of prisoners, and had been conducted into Marion's swamp encampment. "When led into Marion's presence, and the bandage taken from his eyes, he beheld in our hero, a swarthy, smoke-dried little man, with scarce enough of threadbare homespun to cover his nakedness! and in place of tall ranks of gaily dressed soldiers, a handful of sunburnt yellow-legged militia-men; some roasting potatoes and some asleep, with their black firelocks and powderhorns lying by them on the logs!"

Business over, Marion requested the pleasure of his company to dinner. "At mention of the word *dinner,* the British officer looked around him; but to his great mortification, could see no sign of a pot, pan, Dutch-oven, or any other cooking utensil that could raise the spirits of a hungry man." The dinner was produced, "no other than a heap of sweet potatoes, that were very snugly roasting under the embers," and which a soldier wiped on his shirt and offered on a large piece of bark, set on the trunk of a fallen pine tree. At the officer's polite question, Marion launched into a magnificent discourse. "I am in love," quoth Marion, "and my sweetheart is *Liberty.* Be that heavenly nymph my companion, and these wilds and woods shall have charms beyond London and Paris in slavery." The officer returned to his post in the deepest dejection, telling his colonel that the worst had happened: "Why, sir, I have seen an American general and his officers, without pay, and almost without clothes, living on roots and drinking water; and all for *Liberty!* What chance have we against such men!" Even if we eliminate Weems' heavenly nymph and the final query, we still have left the perfectly credible idea of a beef-eating British officer amazed that a partisan force could support itself on roasted yams.

The episode just described is the subject of our plate, the joint work of two fine old American artists, the painter JOHN BLAKE WHITE (1782–1859), and the mezzotint engraver JOHN SARTAIN (1808–97). White, born in Marion's State in the year of the preliminary treaty of peace, was another of the succession of Americans who, like John Trumbull, went to London to study with Benjamin West. After his return to Charleston, White cannily provided himself with an income by practising law, while devoting his leisure to the historical canvases in which he excelled, and writing dramas on the side. In 1821 he assisted in the foundation of the South Carolina Academy of Fine Arts, a praiseworthy but short-lived enterprise, which failed to survive in a society that preferred horse racing. Among his other paintings of subjects from the history of his own State and section were *Mrs. Motte Presenting the Arrows* and *The Battle of New Orleans.*

John Sartain we have claimed as an American, which is perhaps inadmissible since he did not emigrate from London to Philadelphia until 1834, when he was 28; but he lived here for 63 years after that, and became so identified with American illustration that our claim is hardly unjust. Furthermore, after turning from line engraving to mezzotint, he had brought his second plate to America and marketed it at Philadelphia in 1830; and he saw so good a prospect here for his new skill that he brought his family over four years later. His judgment had been sound, for he had an abundance of work from the first. He acquired a number of magazines, handling the graphic side, and in the course of his long life he engraved about 1,500 plates. A noteworthy one, which might well have been reproduced in this Album, was his *Battle of Gettysburg* after Peter F. Rothermel.

Mezzotint, a process invented by a German soldier about 1642, might be described as ordinary copper-plate engraving in reverse. Instead of incising lines on a smooth plate, the mezzotinter begins by completely roughening his plate with a *rocker,* going over every fraction of its surface about 80 times, a process which takes a day or two for the average-sized plate. The design is then brought into being by the use of a *scraper,* which restores various degrees of smoothness, up to actual burnishing if white is desired in the print. Mezzotints consist entirely of minute dots, never of lines, and the better specimens have a velvety quality which is never seen elsewhere, save perhaps in portions of certain etchings and dryprints. The process was normally reserved for portraiture, but a master like Sartain had no hesitation in tackling more complex subjects, and for a while turned mezzotint into a rival of line engraving in the sphere of the large framing print. Neither, of course, could hold the field against the speed and cheapness of lithography.

PLATE No. 26. *This Representation of Peter Franciscos Gallant Action with Nine of Tarletons Cavalry in Sight of a Troop of Four Hundred Men Took place in Amelia County Virginia 1781 Is respectfully inscribed to Him by James Webster and James Warrell. ☆ [Centered bust of Washington] Design'd by Warrell Drawn by Barralett. Engraved by D. Edwin. ☆ Published Dec.ʳ 1 1814 by James Webster. Entered according to Act of Congress the 1ˢᵗ day of December 1814 by James Webster of the State of Pennsylvania.*

Stipple engraving. 21¼ x 25¾ inches.

Peter Francisco, soldier of the Revolution, is a nearly legendary figure in Virginia history, a model for all soldiers in the ranks, and indeed for all men of great stature. Because of the popularity of Warrell's print his gallant action in Amelia County is remembered as his greatest exploit, but according to his biographers it was only one among many herculean feats. He "possessed strong natural sense, and an amiable disposition. He was, withal, a companionable man . . . industrious and temperate, and always advocated the part of the weak and unprotected. On occasions of outbreaks at public gatherings, he was better in rushing in and preserving public peace, than all the conservative authorities on the ground."

This character estimate is given by the discursive Henry Howe in his *Historical Collections of Virginia*. With his account of Francisco most of the other authorities agree. A more detailed story, including family and local legends unvouched for elsewhere, is told by a descendant of the hero, Mrs. Nannie Francisco Porter (*The Romantic Record of Peter Francisco*, 1929). One point on which Howe and Mrs. Porter differ is Francisco's height; Howe says six feet, one inch, while Mrs. Porter gives him five inches more. Both agree on a weight of 260 pounds, and that he enlisted in the continental army in 1776, at the age of 16. The ordinary sword was not long enough for him, and he had a blade five feet long—his son said Washington himself ordered it made for him, and his granddaughter gave it to the Virginia Historical Society. At Stony Point he was the first soldier after Major Gibbon to enter the fortress. He fought at Brandywine under Lafayette, at Monmouth and other battles in the north, and then was transferred to the army under Greene in the south. At the battle of Camden, in default of horses, he picked up an 1,100-pound cannon and moved it across the field. Mrs. Porter tells that he was the friend and companion of Lafayette. In a petition Francisco wrote to the State of Virginia many years later, he declared "that he never felt satisfied, nor thought he did a good day's work, but by drawing British blood, and if that was not the case, could not have a good night's repose." Needless to state, he usually slept well.

Peter Francisco's origin was of a romantic obscurity. He turned up at City Point, Va., in 1765, a small boy (Mrs. Porter says five or six years old) speaking Spanish or Portuguese. Howe says he was Portuguese, and that he had been kidnapped and carried to Ireland, where he indented himself (at five years of age!) to a sea captain for seven years, in payment for his passage to America. Mrs. Porter hints at Spanish nobility and mentions his "suit of rich material, with collars and cuffs of fine lace, and . . . massive silver shoe buckles bearing the initials P. F. and a bit of marking too badly scratched to be deciphered." In the Amelia County episode the buckles figure, and Mrs. Porter has a cut of them, "Franciscos Shoe Buckles Said to be a Fine Picture." To return to 1765, Peter was taken into the household of Anthony Winston, Esq., of Buckingham County—"sold" says Howe; "adopted" says Mrs. Porter. He learned manly pursuits, but when he entered the army could not read or write.

For the Amelia County scene, let us depend on Howe:

While the British army were spreading havoc and desolation all around them, by their plunderings and burnings in Virginia, in 1781, Francisco had been reconnoitring, and while stopping at the house of a Mr. V . . ., then in Amelia . . . nine of Tarleton's cavalry came up, with three negroes, and told him he was their prisoner. Seeing he was overpowered by numbers, he made no resistance. Believing him to be very peaceable, they all went into the house, leaving him and the paymaster together. "Give up instantly all that you possess of value," said the latter, "or prepare to die." "I have nothing to give up," said Francisco, "so use your pleasure." "Deliver instantly," rejoined the soldier, "those massy silver buckles which you wear in your shoes." "They were a present from a valued friend," replied Francisco, "and it would grieve me to part with them. Give them into your hands I never will. You have the power; take them, if you think fit." The soldier put his sabre under his arm, and bent down to take them. Francisco, finding so favorable an opportunity to recover his liberty, stepped one pace in his rear, drew the sword with force from under his arm, and instantly gave him a blow across the skull. "Ben V . . . [Francisco observed] (the man of the house) very ungenerously brought out a musket, and gave it to one of the British soldiers, and told him to make use of that. He mounted the only horse they could get, and presented it at my breast. It missed fire. I rushed on the muzzle of the gun. *A short struggle ensued.* I disarmed and wounded him. Tarleton's troop of *four hundred men* were in sight. All was hurry and confusion, which I increased by repeatedly hallooing, as loud as I could, *Come on, my brave boys; now's your time; we will soon dispatch these few, and then attack the main body!* The wounded man flew to the troop; the others were panic struck, and fled."

In his letter of petition Francisco told the same tale more briefly, ending with, "This is the last favor I ever did the British." He got six out of the eight horses abandoned by the troopers, which may have been enough to set him up as a man of property, the keeper of a Tavern at New Store, Buckingham Co., after Yorktown. He married three times, into the first families of Virginia, and left many descendants. In his later years he was appointed sergeant at

arms to the House of Delegates at Richmond, in which service he died in 1831. His portrait hangs in the State Library. Tales abound of his strength and gentleness in times of peace. He used to carry lady visitors around his garden, one on the palm of each hand. A bully came from Kentucky to fight him, but Peter Francisco declined the trial of strength. Instead he dropped the Kentucky gentleman over the fence, then lifted his horse over after him. He may have borne a slight grudge against Kentucky. A Colonel Mayo, whom he had once rescued and presented with his horse, deeded him a thousand acres of land, which, he wrote in the aforementioned petition, couched in the third person, "he never got, as the title is disputed (this land lying on Richland creek, Kentucky) for services rendered his country and for saving his life."

This handsome piece of stipple engraving has four men concerned in its production. James Webster was the publisher, who was stirred up by the War of 1812 to issue patriotic prints; he commissioned Tiebout's fine stipple of the *Constitution-Guerrière* fight (Plate 25) and may have commissioned this. James Warrell is stated to have *designed* it, whereas John J. Barralet *drew* it, a distinction seldom seen. We may guess that Warrell interviewed Francisco and laid out the background, the figures to be included, and the action, whereas the task of turning these rough data into a coherent design was handed over to the professional draughtsman, Barralet. Barralet also designed our Plate 39, and more will be said of him there. The engraving of the Warrell-Barralet design was entrusted to DAVID EDWIN (1776–1841), who did an excellent job, as might have been expected from

44

"the most popular and prolific engraver of portraits in the United States." Edwin, the son of an English comic actor, ran away from the Dutch engraver to whom he had been apprenticed and arrived in Philadelphia at the age of 21. He found employment with a book publisher and the engraver Edward Savage, and struggled so manfully with the inferior tools and materials which were all that could be had in America that he was soon his own master and receiving as many commissions as he could execute.

Edwin did the best he could with the Warrell-Barralet design, which is better in detail than as a coherent composition. The stiffness of the three retreating figures beyond the horse may be noticed—they have struck such poses as one might expect in a ballet.

PLATE No. 27. [*Major John André. Sketch of himself drawn on the eve of his execution, 1780.*]
Pen-and-ink drawing. 12¼ x 14 inches.
ORIGINAL IN THE YALE UNIVERSITY ART GALLERY, NEW HAVEN, CONN.

PLATE No. 28. *The Unfortunate Death of Major André (Adjutant General to the English Army) at Head Quarters in New York, Oct*. 2. *1780, who was found within the American Lines in the character of a Spy.* ☆ *Hamilton delin. Goldar sculp. [From Edward Barnard, The New, Comprehensive and Complete History of England: From the earliest period of authentic information, to the middle of the year 1783 ... Embellished with upwards of 100 engravings. London, A. Hogg, [1783?] Opposite page 694.]*

Line engraving. 11¾ x 8 inches.

The blackest name in American history is Benedict Arnold. Arnold, late major general in the Continental Army and now brigadier general in the British Army, died in his bed in London on June 14, 1801. The principal victim of Arnold's foul treason, Maj. John André, died on a gibbet in the American camp at Tappan, N. Y., on October 2, 1780.

Benedict Arnold was a very untypical Connecticut Yankee: for shrewdness and patience he substituted ambition and rancor; for temperance and frugality he substituted extravagance and greed. The historian of his native town, Norwich, thought "it should excite but little surprise that an ambitious, extravagant man, with fiery passions and very little balance of moral principle, should betray his friends and plunge desperately into treason." Arnold was certainly a man of large abilities, whose services to the American cause on Lake Champlain in 1776 and at Saratoga in 1777 had been great. But his sense that these services were inadequately appreciated and rewarded led to increasing disgruntlement, which turned to violent resentment when, in 1779, he was reprimanded for having turned his position as Commander in reoccupied Philadelphia to private profit. The utter foulness of his treasonable course from this point has only been made finally clear by the laborious disentanglement of Mr. Carl Van Doren. In May 1779, Arnold began his negotiations with an influential loyalist looking toward contact with Sir Henry Clinton, the British Commander in Chief at New York. It was altogether his own idea; he was not seduced by any British agent. In the course of the following year, in order to increase his bargaining power, and largely by parading his three-year-old wound, Arnold hoodwinked

Washington, who had always been his friend and advocate, into putting him into command of the all-important American stronghold on the Hudson, West Point, the "key to America."

With West Point thrown in, Arnold could not be passed over by Sir Henry, who deputed his Adjutant General, Major André, long in charge of Clinton's secret agents and correspondence with Americans who volunteered information, to complete the transaction. After "Gustavus" (Arnold) and "John Anderson" (André) had exchanged enough letters, a personal interview became desirable in order to arrange the final betrayal of West Point to Clinton's army and the rewards which would accrue to Arnold. On September 20, 1780, André sailed up the Hudson in the sloop *Vulture,* and from this point whoever watches over America saw to it that everything went wrong. Washington having protested against Arnold seeing André, even on the spurious pretext that had been given, the interview had to be secret; the *Vulture* was fired on and driven down the river; André had to put on civilian attire and make his way through the American lines with a pass from Arnold in his pocket, and incriminating documents in his boot; and finally, André was so little at home in the role of a spy that when at last stopped by an American patrol at a point in sight of the British lines, he gave himself away. The officer before whom he was taken sent the evidence to Washington but notified Arnold, who made a dash for his life into the British camp.

The tragic aspect of the situation now became apparent. The Adjutant General of the British Army in America, young, handsome, capable, talented, and charming, beloved by his fellow soldiers and respected by his enemies, had been taken in the character of a spy, which he had no intention of assuming and into which circumstances had driven him at the last moment. He must hang, while the traitor who had sought to ruin his country's cause would still receive the rewards which British honor felt bound to give. André was tried by a board of major generals and brigadier generals of the Continental Army with Nathanael Greene presiding, and including, by a curious turn of fate, that Robert Howe whom André had lampooned in one of his verses—it is not often that we are privileged to sentence the man who has satirized us to hang by the neck until dead. Clinton sent a delegation to reason with Washington, who permitted their leader to talk with Greene; the British indignantly rejected Greene's suggestion that André might be exchanged for Arnold, and the only result was to postpone the execution from October 1 to October 2. André was nauseated, not by death, but by the thought of a felon's ending, and all that can be offered against his viewpoint is that a man who has encouraged espionage and treason in others late his countrymen should not be too revolted when he finds himself in a spy's position. The final scene took place on schedule on Tuesday, October 2; André, in spite of his disgust, died like a brave man; and we may hope that the spectators were not swayed by their own wishes when they thought that his neck was broken in the first fall from the high gibbet.

On the morning of the first André wrote to Washington a brief letter, still moving in spite of the formal diction of its period, asking that he might not have to die on a gibbet. It was at the same time and doubtless with the same pen and ink that he dashed off, without the aid of a mirror, a little sketch of himself seated at a table in his guardroom. It was merely a form of releasing his pent-up energies, and he turned the result over to the officer of the guard, Ensign Jabez H. Tomlinson of the Ninth Connecticut Line. Tomlinson was still alive 52 years later when the sketch, which he had carefully preserved, was presented to the President of Yale College, who graciously and gratefully accepted in a letter of August 10, 1832. It is a good drawing, able in its general expression if careless in detail—which carelessness, at the moment, can surely be forgiven to the artist—but its greatest interest arises from the circumstances of its creation. Our second plate is a contemporary attempt to image the execution. One Edward Barnard brought out at London in 1783 a *New Comprehensive and Complete History of England,* from earliest times to that very year, in thick folio, and sought to compensate for its completely derivative text by embellishing it "with upwards of 100 engravings more highly and curiously finished than those given in any other work of the kind whatsoever." Four members of the Royal Academy furnished the designs, which were executed by 16 copper-plate engravers, but, as usual, the result was less impressive than the fanfare. The designer of the André plate was probably WILLIAM HAMILTON (1761–1801) who had studied in Italy and was at the time extensively employed in book illustration, "both to the approbation of his employers, and the admiration of the public;" the engraver was JOHN GOLDAR (1729–95), who is credited with several humorous prints and at least one naval view. The André plate is evidently based on no special knowledge; the rope is certainly far too short, but there is an element of truth in the averted face of the American who has gone up the ladder.

PLATE NO. 29. *The British surrendering their Arms to Gen: Washington after their defeat at York Town in Virginia October 1781.* ☆ *[Names under fifteen figures.] Drawn by John Francis Renault. Engraved by Tanner, Vallance, Kearny & Co. and Wm Allen. To the Defenders of American Independence, this Print is most respectfully inscribed by their Fellow Citizen, J^r. F^cis Renault, Assistant Secretary to the Count de Grass, and Engineer to the French Army at the Siege of York.* ☆ *Entered according to Act of Congress, the 25th day of January, 1819.*

Line engraving. 24½ x 34 inches.

On October 17, 1781, "about 10 o'clock the Enemy beat a parley"; notes flew back and forth between Charles, Earl Cornwallis and General Washington; hostilities were suspended; British terms were offered, rejected, surrender demanded, accepted, the Definitive Capitulation signed; and from his headquarters near York, on October 19, the Commander in Chief of the Continental Army had "the Honour to inform Congress, that a Reduction of the British Army under the Command of Lord Cornwallis, is most happily effected."

At two o'clock of that bright day the British regiments, 7,073 men, marched out of Yorktown on the Hampton road. To the left the French allies lined the roadside, while before them "gorgeously paraded" their rich standards of white silk, embroidered with the golden fleurs-de-lis of His Most Christian Majesty. Their drummers, fifers and the band, "which played delightfully," stood in front, just behind Rochambeau and his glittering staff. The troops behind, tall, handsome men, wore white regimentals faced in color. On the right of the road

General Washington sat his white charger, his generals, Gates, Steuben, Anthony Wayne, and Lincoln beside him, and behind them the American army. "They were paraded in three lines, the first composed of the regulars, who had also a band playing moderately well. They looked passable, but the militia from Virginia and Maryland, forming the second and third lines, were but a ragged set of fellows and very ill-looking" (Diary of an Anspach sergeant, John Conrad Doehla).

The British army marched in platoons, wearing new uniforms, their arms shouldered, and their colors cased. Their drums, according to the terms of surrender, were beating "a British or German march"; it was a popular English tune, "The World Turned Upside Down." Lord Cornwallis had pleaded illness and the Irish General O'Hara led the conquered army, carrying Cornwallis' sword. As he reached the head of the line, he turned to the left and offered the sword to the Comte de Rochambeau. Rochambeau waved him toward Washington, across the road. Washington pointed to the officer designated to receive it, and the sword was handed to General Lincoln, who the year before had rendered up his own sword at Charleston. According to Rochambeau, Washington, as O'Hara put his hand to the hilt, "fit un signe negatif et dit: 'Never from such good a hand, jamais d'une aussi brave main.'"

The British regiments marched by; according to two American witnesses, they "appeared to be much in liquor." They filed into the open field beyond, surrounded by a circle of mounted French dragoons. The cased standards were handed over and the privates grounded their muskets, many of them "throwing their arms on the pile with violence, as if determined to render them useless." They turned and marched back, prisoners of war, between the two lines of allies, and the prejudiced sergeant Doehla reported that "the American part of our conquerors jeered at us very insultingly." Then the couriers mounted, among them Col. Tench Tilghman with Washington's special dispatch to Congress, and to Philadelphia and the north sped the news that Cornwallis was taken.

For JOHN FRANCIS RENAULT, the only claim to immortality is the painting from which the present print, a blend of mass portrait and French eighteenth-century allegory, was made. Fielding's *Dictionary of American Artists* speaks of Renault as having exhibited the original painting throughout the United States previous to 1824, possibly in anticipation of Lafayette's visit in that year. We find nothing about Renault and can only guess that the assistant secretary to the Comte de Grasse, who could also turn his hand to engineering at the siege of Yorktown, became so enamored of the country whose independence he had helped to win that he either obtained his discharge and stayed on after the war, or returned later, perhaps during the French Revolution. Obviously he had before 1819 taken out citizenship papers and foresworn his native tongue insofar as his given names were concerned. He had not lost the Versailles touch evidenced in the neo-classical columns, funeral urn surrounded by draped muses, and overturned chariot and victims of the lightning shafts shot by the goddess from her cloudtop machine in the background.

The engraving from Renault's canvas was made by a Philadelphia engraving company, TANNER, VALLANCE, KEARNY & CO., which had their offices at 10 Library Place from about 1819

48

to 1823. In 1821 Cornelius Tiebout was also associated with them. Their primary interest was the engraving of banknotes. Mr. Henry S. Tanner, brother of the engraver Benjamin Tanner, managed the financial concerns, so ingeniously that *he* realized a large profit. But Francis Kearny came out a complete loser, making nothing on his labor of three years. John Vallance, an excellent script engraver, whose name appears on good early banknotes, died in 1823, at the age of 53. With his death the firm seems to have broken up, probably in a row, if we may read between the lines of Dunlap's note on Kearny. The "Surrender of Cornwallis" must have been among the early productions of Tanner, Vallance, Kearny & Co. Its cost to subscribers was $12, with an additional $3 for the accompanying "Plan." To nonsubscribers it would be sold after publication only for $15 and $5 for the "Plan." The stock must have been turned over to Benjamin Tanner, to be sold from his engraving shop at 74 South Eighth Street, after the break-up of the partners, for on February 10, 1824, he was advertising it in a newspaper, the *New England Palladium & Commercial Advertiser*. The banknote influence is to be seen in the style of engraving, not unsuited to the formal pageantry of the plate, in which each figure is presented according to his official importance.

PLATE No. 10. *The Bloody Massacre Perpetrated in King Street, Boston, March 5, 1770. Engraving by Paul Revere, 1770.*

The Battle of Lexington, April 19th 1775. Plate 1.

1. Major Pitcairn at the head of the Regular Granadiers.
2. The Party, who first fired on the Provincials at Lexington.
3. Part of the Provincial Company of Lexington.
4. Regular Companies on the road to Concord.
5. The Meetinghouse at Lexington.
6. The Public Inn.

A. Doolittle Sculpt.

PLATE No. II. I. *The Battle of Lexington, April 19, 1775. Engraving by Amos Doolittle, 1775.*

Plate II. A View of the Town of Concord

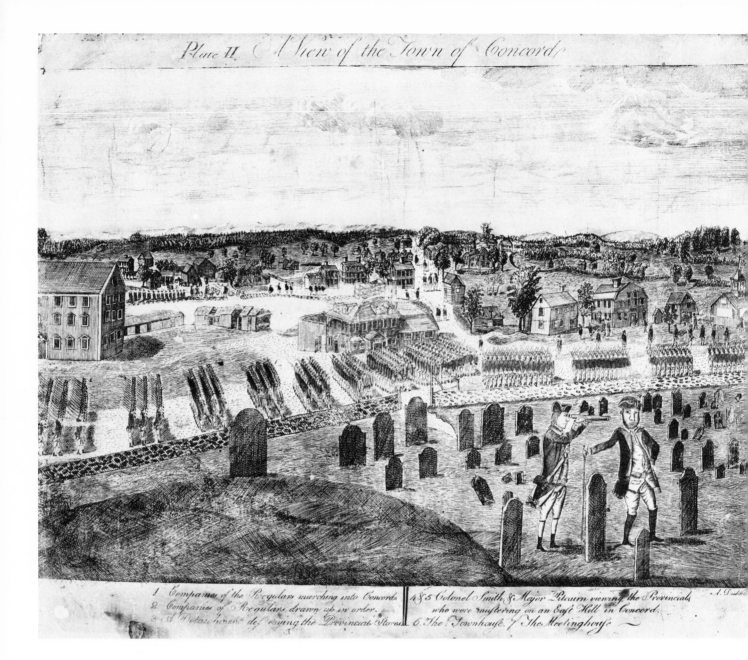

1. Companies of the Regulars marching into Concord.
2. Companies of Regulars drawn up in order.
3. A Detachment destroying the Provincial Stores.
4 & 5 Colonel Smith & Major Pitcairn viewing the Provincials who were mustering on an East Hill in Concord.
6. The Townhouse. 7 The Meetinghouse.

A. Doolittle

PLATE NO. 12. *II. A View of the Town of Concord, April 19, 1775. Engraving by Amos Doolittle, 1775.*

52

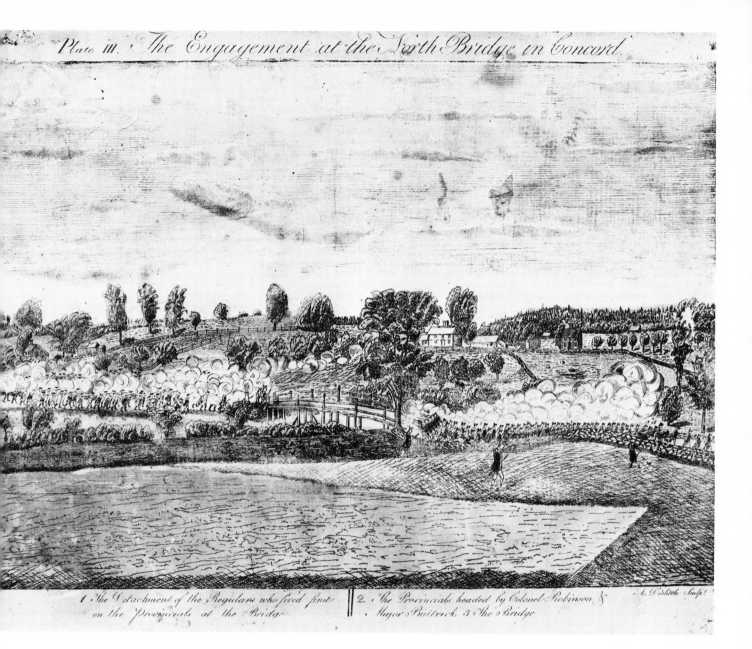

Plate III. The Engagement at the North Bridge in Concord.

1 The Detachment of the Regulars who fired first on the Provincials at the Bridge 2. The Provincials headed by Colonel Robinson & Major Buttrick. 3 The Bridge

A. Doolittle Sculp.t

PLATE No. 13. III. *The Engagement at the North Bridge in Concord, April 19, 1775. Engraving by Amos Doolittle, 1775.*

53

1. Colonel Smith's Brigade retreating before the Provincials.
6. & 7. The Flanch-guards of Piercys Brigade.
2. Earl Piercy's Brigade meeting them.
8. A Fieldspiece pointed at the Lexington Meetinghouse.
3. & 4. Earl Piercy & Col. Smith.
5. Provincials.
9. The Burning of the Houses in Lexington.

PLATE No. 14. *IV. A View of the South Part of Lexington, April 19, 1775. Engraving by Amos Doolittle, 1775.*

AN EXACT VIEW of THE LATE BATTLE AT CHARLESTOWN June 17th 1775.
In which an advanced party of about 700 Provincials stood an Attack made by 11 Regiments, & a Train of Artillery, & after an Engagement of two hours Retreated to their Main body at Cambridge Leaving Eleven Hundred of the enemy Killed and Wounded upon the field.

PLATE No. 15. *An Exact View of the Late Battle at Charlestown, June 17, 1775. Engraving by Bernard Romans, 1775.*

55

PLATE No. 16. *The Battle of Bunker's Hill, June
17, 1775. Engraving by Johann G. von Müller,
after John Trumbull, 1798.*

56

eprésentation du feu terrible à nouvelle Yorck, que les Américains ont allumé pendant la nuit du 19. septembre 1776. par lequel ont été brulés tous les Bâtimens du coté de Vest

droite de Borse, dans la rue de Broock jusqu'au collége du Roi, et plus de 1600. maisons avec l'Église de la St. Trinité la Chapelle Lutherienne, et l'école des pauvres.

Paris chez Basset Rue S. Jacques au coin de la rue des Mathurins.

PLATE NO. 17. *Représentation du feu terrible à nouvelle Yorck, September 19, 1776. Engraving by André Basset.*

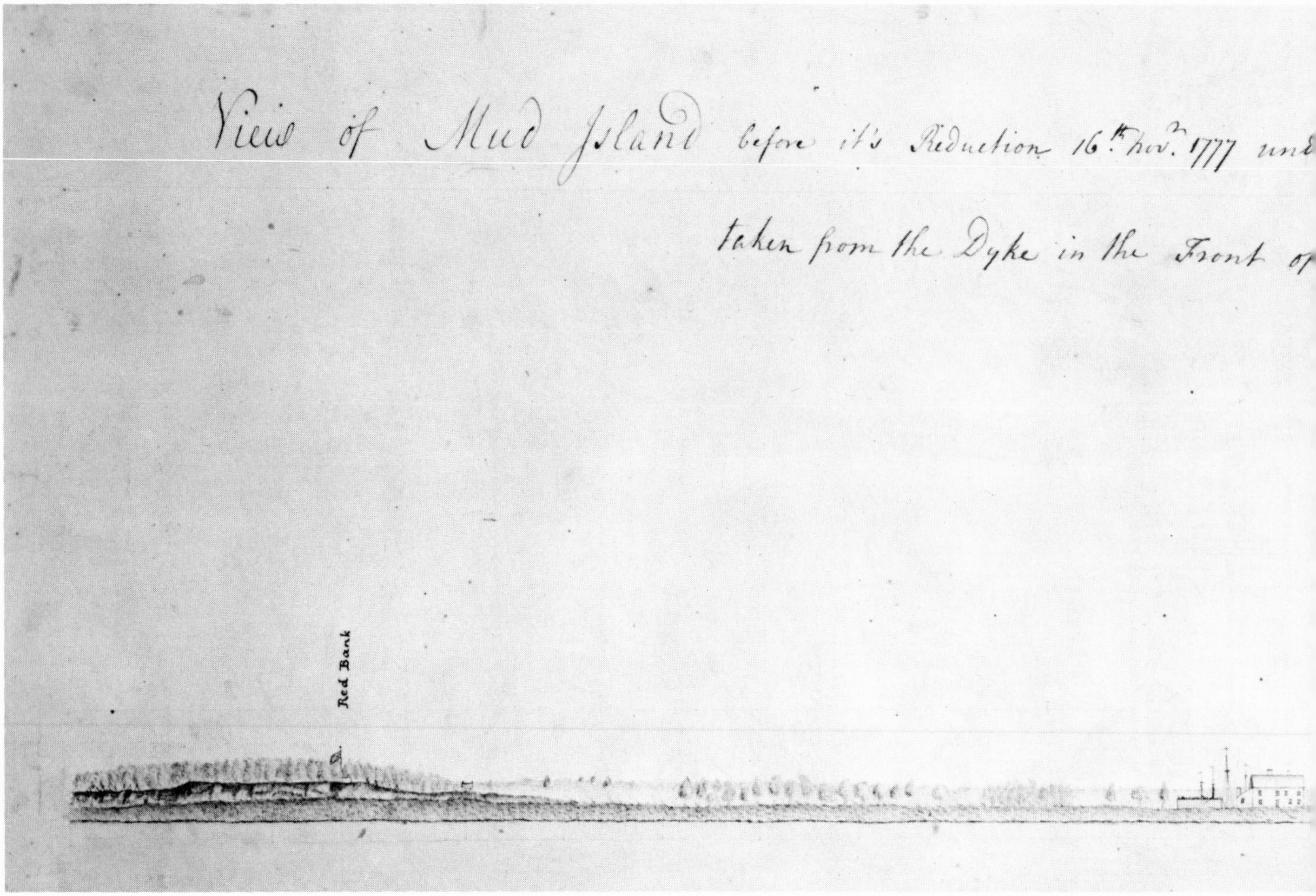

View of Mud Island before it's Reduction 16th nov. 1777 und

taken from the Dyke in the Front of

Red Bank

PLATE NOS. 19–20. *View of Mud Island before its Reduction, November 16, 1777. Topographical drawing by Pierre Nicole, 1777.*

PLATE NO. 18. *The Landing of the British Forces in the Jerseys, November 20, 1776. Watercolor by Thomas Davies, 1776.*

58

Direction of John Montrésor Esq.r Chief Engineer in America

Gun Battery on Carpenter's Island.

FORT

Mc Colloch's Leap.

On Stone by G. W. Fasel.

Print by Nagel & Weingärtner.

PLATE NO. 21. *McColloch's Leap into the Wheeling Creek, Virginia, 1777. Lithograph by G. W. Fasel, 1851.*

60

Stone by G. W. Fasel

Entered according to act of Congress in the year 1851 by G. W. Fasel in the Clerk's Office of the District Court of the Southern District of N.Y.

Print by Nagel & Weingärtner

Benjamin Logan saving Harrison from being scalped

...was one of a party of three men guarding the women while milking the cows, outside the station, when they were suddenly attacked by Indians and fired upon, two were killed instantly and Harrison disabled, when Logan seeing his friend writhing in agony, sprang forward at the risk of his own life, and lifting him in his arms, regained the Fort in safety. May 1777.

New-York, Published by Emil Seitz, 253 Broadway.

PLATE No. 22. *Benjamin Logan Saving Harrison from being Scalped, May 1777. Lithograph by G. W. Fasel, 1851.*

61

Das merckwürdige See Gefecht zwischen Capitain Pearson und Paul Jones welches 1779 den 22 September sich eraugnet wo der Cap. das Schiff den Serapis, und der Paul Jones, den guten Mann Richard genañt commandurte.

Combat memorable entre le Pearson et Paul Jones doñe le 22 7bre 1779 le Capitaine Pearson comendant le SERAPIS et Paul Jones commandant le Bon home Richart et son Escadre.

Se vend à Augsbourg au Negoce commun de l'Academie Imperiale d'Empire des Artstibereaux avec Privilege de Sa Majesté Imperiale et avec Défense en son Sens in de l'ordre des Copies.

PLATE No. 23. *Combat mémorable entre le Pearson et Paul Jones, September 23, 1779. Engraving by Balthasar F. Leizelt.*

62

Capt. PAUL JONES ſhooting a SAILOR who had attempted to ſtrike his COLOURS in an Engagement.

PLATE NO. 24. *Capt. Paul Jones Shooting a Sailor Who had Attempted to Strike his Colours. English mezzotint, 1780.*

PLATE No. 25. *General Marion in his Swamp
Encampment Inviting a British Officer to Din-
ner. Mezzotint by John Sartain, after John B.
White, 1840.*

64

PLATE. No. 26. *Peter Francisco's Gallant Action
with Nine of Tarleton's Cavalry, Amelia
County, Va., 1781. Engraving by David Edwin,
1814.*

PLATE NO. 27. *Maj. John André's Self-Portrait
on the Eve of his Execution, 1780. Drawing.*

66

The Unfortunate DEATH of MAJOR ANDRE

Hamilton delin. *Goldar sculp.*

(*Adjutant General to the English Army*) *at Head Quarters in New York, Oct.ʳ 2. 1780, who was found within the American Lines, in the character of a Spy.*

PLATE No. 28. *The Unfortunate Death of Major André, October 2, 1780. Engraving by John Goldar, 1783.*

The British surrendering their Arms to Gen: Washington after their defeat at York Town in Virginia October 1781.)

TO THE DEFENDERS OF AMERICAN INDEPENDENCE, THIS PRINT IS MOST RESPECTFULLY INSCRIBED BY THEIR FELLOW CITIZEN.

PLATE No. 29. *The British Surrendering their Arms to General Washington, October 17, 1781. Engraving by Tanner, Vallance, Kearny & Co., 1819.*

68

III

The New Navy: Frenchmen and Barbary Pirates 1797-1804

THE frigate *Alliance,* flagship of Capt. John Barry and last survivor of the tiny Continental Navy to engage British sea power in the War of the Revolution, was sold in 1785. The adoption of the Constitution found the United States of America without a ship at her command. The merchant ships of New England, Philadelphia, and Baltimore carried guns of their own, and at need could turn privateer, but there was no American Navy.

In a few years it became evident that naval protection was needed for our commerce, not only against the piratical Barbary Powers in the Mediterranean, but also against our late allies. The French Revolution brought in its wake a wave of lawlessness at sea, and French warships as well as privateers freely captured or plundered American merchantmen. In 1794 Congress authorized the construction of a new Navy, six frigates, rendered necessary by "the depredations committed by the Algerine corsairs." But after four years none was ready for service, and war with France loomed very near. Congress was authorized by the Constitution "to provide and maintain a navy." By the act of April 30, 1798, the Navy Department was created, and President Adams placed its affairs in the capable hands of Secretary Benjamin Stoddert. In June and July the new frigates put to sea, equipped for war, the *United States,* 44 guns, Commodore Barry, the *Constellation,* 36 guns, Captain Truxton, and the *Constitution,* 44 guns, Capt. Samuel Nicholson.

The "quasi-war with France," more properly a limited naval war, had already begun. Though no formal declaration was ever made, Congress on May 28 had authorized our ships to take French armed vessels which might be found hovering on our coasts. Two small frigates, the converted Indiaman *Ganges* and the *Delaware,* were watching the Atlantic coast. The *Delaware* won the first prize, *La Croyable,* off Egg Harbor, New Jersey on July 7. Then came the authorization by act of Congress on July 9 to capture French armed vessels at sea, and the squadron was ordered to the West Indies. Through nearly three years of undeclared war the fleet, cruising in the Caribbean, and gradually increased to a total of over 50 vessels, searched for privateers and escorted convoys of merchantmen, going home for repairs when it became necessary. A total of 85 French vessels were captured, mostly privateers, but some warships of the regular navy as well. Only one American naval vessel was taken, or rather retaken, the schooner *Croyable,* now named *Retaliation,* but several hundred American merchant ships were seized by France, some in European and some in American waters.

The "Franco-American Misunderstanding" ended with the ratification late in 1801 of a "Convention of Peace, Commerce and Navigation," which had been signed on September 30, 1800.

PLATE NO. 30. *Frigate United States. T. Clarke Sculp! Philad? For the American Universal Magazine.*

Line engraving. $3\frac{5}{16}$ x $5\frac{1}{16}$ inches.

The frigate *United States* was the first vessel completed for the United States Navy. She was laid down in Philadelphia, in the shipyard of Joshua Humphreys, the great shipbuilder, whose designs had been accepted for the new frigates authorized by Congress. He was later appointed naval constructor in the Navy. He planned the *United States,* the *Constellation* and the *Constitution,* longer and broader than the frigates of the Royal Navy, but lower, carrying as many guns on one deck as some ships of the line bore on two, fast sailing so as to fight or to run at choice. Humphreys' frigates are considered the best of his time.

The *United States* was launched on May 10, 1797, and in July of the following year put to sea as the flagship of Commodore John Barry, commander of the squadron in the Caribbean. During the Naval War with France she took seven prizes, and in 1800, reversing her role, carried to Europe the three commissioners who made peace with Bonaparte. She was then laid up until the War of 1812. Her great moment came on October 12, 1812, when under the command of Capt. Stephen Decatur she captured the British 38-gun ship *Macedonian.* Then for the rest of the war she lay under blockade at New London, Conn. Her subsequent career, while long and honorable, was not combative. On April 12, 1861, she was burned at the Norfolk Navy Yard to prevent her falling into the hands of the Confederacy.

The *American Universal Magazine,* which pursued the policy of giving its readers a plate with each number, embellished its issue of July 24, 1797, with a view of the frigate *United States,* launched 10 weeks earlier. Whether the frigate was actually armed and under sail at this time may be questioned. The *American Universal Magazine,* which lasted about a year and a half, was an enterprise of Samuel Harrison Smith, who was brought to Washington by President Jefferson a few years later as official journalist and printer for the Democratic Party. No text or explanation accompanies the plate. The engraver, THOMAS CLARKE, worked in both Philadelphia and New York from 1797 to 1800. William Dunlap, who is not always reliable, tells us that he was an English engraver specializing in stipple (this is line), and that he went south, became deranged, imagined that he was constantly pursued by a negro without a head, and finally cut his own throat to escape from this phantasm—an unworthy fate for the first man to depict the new American navy!

PLATE NO. 31. *Huzza for the Constellation. Sung by Mr Fox at the Theatre. Printed & sold at B:Carr's Musical Repository Philadelphia J:Carr's Baltimore & I:Hewitt's NYork (Price 32C^{ts}) Secured according to Law. [Two bars of music, Allegro]*

Sheet music, first page, with line-engraved vignette, [1799]. $10\frac{3}{4}$ x $7\frac{3}{4}$ inches.

ORIGINAL IN THE MARYLAND HISTORICAL SOCIETY, BALTIMORE. ANOTHER COPY, A LATER AND WEAKER IMPRESSION FROM THE SAME PLATE, IS IN THE LIBRARY OF CONGRESS.

On February 9, 1799, off the Island of Nevis in the West Indies, the most exciting action of the Naval War with France took place. The

French frigate *Insurgente*, 38 guns, was captured by the *Constellation*. Bold Commodore Truxtun ran in a rough sea under the lee of the *Insurgente* and in an hour's close and successful engagement forced the Frenchman to strike his colors. Thomas Truxtun, an old Revolutionary privateersman and junior among the six captains of the new Navy appointed on June 5, 1794, was the principal hero of this naval war. A year after his capture of the *Insurgente,* on February 1–2, 1800, Truxtun on the *Constellation* pursued, brought to action, and captured the large French frigate, *Vengeance,* of 54 guns. The victor had already been celebrated, after his first triumph, in a song:

Come join my hearts in jovial glee
    While I sing strains of victory
And boast our prowess on the sea
        In the brilliant Constellation.
A Frigate fine Commander brave
As ever cut Atlantic wave
        With Sailors bold
        And hearts of gold
Who conquer with Columbian stripes
And shout whene'er the boatswain pipes
        All hands in the Constellation.

We left our Wives our Sweethearts dear
    Each jolly Tar a volunteer
Resolv'd our much lov'd coast to clear
        Or die in the Constellation.
The ninth at noon a sail in view
My eyes we thro' the ocean flew
        To pass the word
        Brave Truxton roar'd
Your studen sails display to view

Skyscrapers, Royals, Sweepers too
    Boys shew 'em the Constellation.

The sea ran high a sweeping swell
    The Monsieur yaw'd her main top fell
The wind convey'd a distant yell
        Huzza—cried the Constellation.
At three P.M. to hail she tried
We answer'd with a full broadside
        Which she return'd
        Both for conquest burn'd
We rak'd her thrice boys fore and aft
At four P.M. her flag abaft
        Was struck to the Constellation.

By virtue sway'd by wisdom blest
    May no rank fears on shore infest
At sea no foe shall e'er molest
        In sight of the Constellation.
No matter if one deck or two
Brave Truxton and his gallant crew
        Columbians like
        Will never strike
While we've a man to stand on deck
Or while our pumps can float the wreck
        Huzza—for the Constellation.

GILBERT FOX (1776–1807?) was born in England and apprenticed to the London engraver Thomas Medhard, with whom he learned the art of line engraving. The American engraver James Trenchard, on a visit to London, bought off Fox's time so that the young man might come to Philadelphia and give him instruction, "his reward to be liberty and good wages." Fox came to America in 1795 and introduced the art of etching; though he had been brought only to instruct Trenchard, "it soon spread and everyone became etchers," said a contemporary. Gilbert Fox "did not like confinement and work," and so became a drawing master in a young ladies' boarding school. "He was a pretty young man, had a sweet voice, and an irresistible lisp, and taught 'love's dream' to one of his pupils, who became Mrs. Fox." The school ousted him as a result, and the versatile youth went on the stage as a singer at the Chestnut Street Theatre in Philadelphia. He was so successful that Joseph Hopkinson wrote "Hail, Columbia" for him, to be sung at his benefit in 1798. "Poor Fox, he had some excellent qualities, but prudence was not one of them" (William Dunlap). He was always in debt, and down to 1807 continued to supplement his theatrical earnings by engraving. While he may not have engraved the musical notation of "Huzza for the Constellation," which he sang at the theatre, it is highly probable that this singer-engraver—an extraordinary and perhaps unique combination of gifts!—produced the excellent and vigorous little vignette of single combat between warships which heads the score. There was no vignette on the New York version of the song, *Captain Truxton,* which was "sung by Mr. Tyler at the Theatre with the greatest applause."

In 1804 he went to Boston and became a member of the Boston Theatre Company. He is said to have been "a versatile, pleasant actor, good in tragedy, comedy, or comic opera." We lose all trace of him after 1807, although Dunlap suggests that he received an inheritance and went back to England.

PLATE No. 32. *A perspective View of the loss of the U. S. Frigate Philadelphia in which is represented her relative position to the Tripolitan Gun-boats when during their furious attack*

upon her she was unable to get a single gun to bear upon them. ☆ *C⁵ Denoon del:*

Line engraving. 14½ x 20 inches.

For centuries the Mohammedan pirates of the Barbary coast had been the scourge of the Mediterranean Sea. The day of the galley-slave was past when American merchant ships began to be seen in these waters, but vessels were still seized on occasion by the corsairs of Morocco, Algiers, Tunis and Tripoli, and their crews carried into slavery. In Algiers between 1784 and 1796, 130 Americans, the survivors in 13 vessels, had been held as slaves, and few more than half of them were finally ransomed, at a total cost of about $525,500. The European nations engaged in the carrying trade had adopted the humiliating policy of buying off the Barbary powers, and in her first years of commerce under the stars and stripes the United States was forced to the same expedient. Treaties, for which huge sums must be set down, annuities, and particularly "presents" to Moslem officials with strange and outlandish titles were the necessary order between 1784 and 1801, when difficulties of long standing finally came to a head with the so-called Tripolitan War.

William Bainbridge was the unfortunate captain upon whom fell the greatest misfortune of the war, the loss of the frigate *Philadelphia*. He had already suffered in connection with the Barbary States; in 1800 he had been sent with his first command, the frigate *George Washington*, 24 guns, first American man-of-war to enter the Mediterranean, on the painful errand of carrying tribute to Algiers. There, to his great embar-

72

rassment, he was forced by the Dey, who regarded tribute-bearers as his slaves, to carry an Algerian ambassador, with a suite of 200 persons, "4 horses, 150 sheep, 25 cattle, 4 lions, 4 tigers, 4 antelopes, 12 parrots," and other regalia, to the Ottoman Porte—worst of all, flying the Algerine flag. Bainbridge conducted the difficult business with skill and dignity, and wrote that he hoped never again to deliver tribute save "from the mouth of our cannon."

In 1801 the Pasha (or Bashaw, as the Americans sometimes called him) of Tripoli found himself slighted in the matter of blackmail, and cut down the flag of the consulate, declaring war on the United States. A "squadron of observation" was already on its way to the Mediterranean, under Commodore Richard Dale, but with orders too vague to allow much action. A blockade of Tripoli was set up, and Dale attempted to stop the little pirate barks in their constant attacks on American merchantmen. A second squadron in 1802 did little but continue the fitful blockade of Tripoli, which had incensed the Emperor of Morocco into declaring war in his turn. Finally in August 1803, Commodore Edward Preble sailed with the frigate *Constitution,* his flagship the *Philadelphia,* Captain Bainbridge, and several brigs and schooners, for a more vigorous prosecution of the war. Preble's first move was an impressive demonstration before the port of Tangier, which frightened the Moroccan ruler out of the affair and into prompt renewal of his treaty.

Meanwhile (October 31, 1803) the *Philadelphia,* commanded by the unlucky Bainbridge, was alone in the blockade of Tripoli. From a stone prison in that barbaric stronghold the captain wrote the next day "a communica-

tion the most distressing of my life," informing the Secretary of the Navy with deep regret of the loss of the U. S. frigate *Philadelphia,* by going aground on rocks between four and five miles to the eastward of Tripoli. Bainbridge had chased a small Tripolitan craft into the harbor and had struck an uncharted reef. Every expedient had been tried, all the resources of splendid seamanship. Among his officers and in the subsequent court of inquiry there was unanimity in the belief that everything possible had been done. Bainbridge even went so far as to heave his forward guns overboard in an effort to lighten the ship. Throughout the day the little Tripolitan gunboats had been gathering about the helpless *Philadelphia,* becoming increasingly bold as her plight worsened. At sunset, after a hopeless struggle of half a day, Bainbridge surrendered. He and his officers and crew, 307 men, were carried ashore and held miserably in prison till the war's end in 1805. Even then, $60,000 was required for their ransom. The generous solicitude of the Danish consul in Tripoli had provided them with a few comforts beyond the usual lot of slaves, but little could be done to mitigate their sufferings. To add to their first overwhelming mortification, two days after their capture a heavy tide floated the stern of the *Philadelphia,* and a host of Tripolitans, with tiny boats, anchors and cables, got her off the reef and triumphantly moored her in Tripoli harbor.

Charles Denoon, the artist who designed the engraving, was a seaman aboard the *Philadelphia* and went with Bainbridge into captivity. While confined in Tripoli he evidently witnessed the highly successful attack made on the harbor by Commodore Preble's squadron on August 3, 1804; an interesting engraving of this action from a sketch by Denoon, showing the ships and fortifications, also was printed, and is reproduced in the Grolier Club's catalog, *The United States Navy, 1776–1815* (1942), opposite page 24. In its extreme left foreground Denoon, perhaps to the memory of the *Philadelphia,* has placed a wicked reef. The officers of the *Philadelphia* watched the assault from the windows of their prison; the seamen, Denoon probably among them, "were employed in carrying ammunition to the Tripolitan batteries and were severely beaten and maltreated" (Gardner W. Allen). No engraver is named in either print. With respect to our plate this is not surprising, inasmuch as it is a routine job with the methodology of engraving only too visible—art having failed to conceal art.

PLATE NO. 33. *The burning of the American Fregate the Philadelphia in the Harbour of Tripoli happily executed by the valiant Cap: Decatur to whom this Plate is respectfully dedicated by his Obedient Servant John B: Guerrazzi ☆ Sold in Leghorn 1805.*

Line engraving. 12⅛ x 15⅞ inches.

ORIGINAL IN THE PEABODY MUSEUM, SALEM, MASS.

Commodore Preble was a skillful and bold commander, and in his squadron there sailed, as junior officers, a galaxy of some of the brightest stars in American naval annals, Lts. Stephen Decatur and James Lawrence, Midshipmen Thomas Macdonough and Thomas A. Anderson, to name a few. Of all the brave exploits of the Barbary Wars, most conspicuous for its audacity was the burning of the *Philadelphia* in Tripoli harbor under the very noses of the enemy. On the night of February 16, 1804, Lt.

Stephen Decatur, Jr., sailed into the crowded and well-defended port where the *Philadelphia* lay at anchor. The plans had been well laid, with some help from letters smuggled through from Bainbridge giving intelligence about the position of Tripolitan batteries and gunboats. A Tripolitan ketch, the *Mastico,* with a lateen rig, had been captured and rechristened the *Intrepid.* A Sicilian pilot, Salvatore Catalano, familiar with the waters and the languages of the Mediterranean, had been found; he remained for many years a sailing-master in the American navy. When Decatur, at the Syracuse base, had mustered the crew of his own ship, the *Enterprise,* and called for volunteers, "every officer, man, and boy" stepped forward. Eighty men were chosen, from Decatur's ship and from the *Constitution.*

With the brig *Siren* standing by to cover his retreat, Decatur sailed boldly, late at night, into the dark harbor of Tripoli. His vessel was to all appearances Tripolitan; at her helm stood the pilot, beside him, Decatur and six or eight men in the masquerade disguise of Maltese dress. The rest of the crew was in concealment below. Catalano hailed the *Philadelphia,* running under her port bow; he had, he said, lost his anchors in the gale just over, and would like to tie up to the frigate for the night. Permission was granted, and the deluded Tripolitans on the *Philadelphia's* deck caught and hauled on the rope which drew the ketch against the side of the condemned frigate. As they made contact the Tripolitans guessed the truth, "and the cry of 'Americanos!' resounded through the ship. In a moment we were near enough, and the order 'Board!' was given; and with this cry our men were soon on the decks of the frigate." Morris, whose words are quoted, was first on

74

the *Philadelphia's* deck, his sword drawn. In five minutes the American boarding party had cleared the decks, with their swords and cutlasses only, no shot having been fired. Then, in squads, they set their carefully prepared combustibles, and the *Philadelphia* burst into fierce flames. Morris' squad, in the cockpit, had barely time to get away; Decatur was the last man to leap into the rigging of the ketch. The affair had taken 20 minutes.

As the flames burst out and as the escaping Tripolitans shouted from the water, the harbor and town were aroused. The ketch might still have made her escape unobserved in the darkness, but her crew could not resist three huzzas as they pulled away. A general discharge thundered from the shore batteries and from the gunboats, but only one shot struck the *Intrepid,* passing through the top-gallant sail. She ran to the entrance of the harbor where she was met by the *Siren's* boats, and got off safely to Syracuse. "The most bold and daring act of the age," said the great Admiral Nelson, then blockading Bonaparte's ships in Toulon.

The flame and smoke-filled print by the Ital-ian engraver Guerrazzi was inspired by the narrative of these events, and was undoubtedly executed for the specific purpose of sale to the American crews. For that reason the legend was put in English, and Guerrazzi's given name—probably Giambattista—turned into a good Yankee "John B." Guerrazzi is not a well-known engraver, but it is not improbable that he may have been the father of the Leghorn writer and patriot, Francesco Domenico Guerrazzi. Francesco was born in 1804, and the *Enciclopedia Italiana* relates that his father was a wood engraver, and a severe man, of whom the writer left a "Plutarchian portrait." If our artist was the Plutarchian father, his business sense must have made profit out of the tourist trade, for in 1819 the son was provided with funds to study law. Copper was perhaps an unfamiliar medium, since Guerrazzi did not succeed in this plate in producing anything better than good journalistic engraving. Guerrazzi made another print, one of the bombardment of Tripoli on Aug. 3, 1804, which, as we saw, was likewise sketched by Denoon, and respectfully dedicated it to the commander of the American squadron, Commodore Preble.

FRIGATE UNITED STATES

T. Clarke Sculp P

PLATE NO. 30. *Frigate United States. Engraving by Thomas Clarke from American Universal Magazine, 1797.*

76

PLATE No. 31. *Huzza for the Constellation, February 9, 1799. Sheet music with vignette engraved by Gilbert Fox, 1799.*

A perspective View of the loss of the U.S. Frigate Philadelphia in which is represented her relative position to the Tripolitan Gun-boats when during their furious attack upon her she was unable to get a single gun to bear upon them.

PLATE No. 32. *A Perspective View of the Loss of the U. S. Frigate Philadelphia, October 31, 1803. Engraving after Charles Denoon.*

78

PLATE No. 33. *The Burning of the American Frigate the Philadelphia in the Harbour of Tripoli, February 16, 1804. Engraving by John B. Guerrazzi, 1805.*

79

IV

The War of 1812

THE War of 1812, properly considered, is one of the most dismal passages of American history, redeemed only by the valiant skill of our sailors and the ultimate emergence of some commanders who could and did fight. Britain had given us more than sufficient cause for going to war in the preceding decade, most scandalously in 1807 when the *Leopard* attacked the unready and unoffending *Chesapeake;* when we did fight it was not in defense of the Freedom of the Seas, but because some southern and western Congressmen had fixed covetous eyes on Canada. Our invading hosts of partially trained militia led by superannuated and inept survivors of the Revolution came to such uniform and total grief that it would have been comic had it not led to results so tragic. The theoretical pacifism of Jefferson had seen to it that under his chosen successor we were totally unprepared for a war which President Madison did not have sufficient spine to keep out of. On the sea, our ships and sailors were as good as could be found, but our handful of frigates had little more than a nuisance value against the mighty fleets of Britain, while Mr. Jefferson's gunboats proved to be a liability. When Napoleon collapsed in 1814 and left the British armaments free to go where they would, the United States, with New England on the verge of secession, was in a condition of peril not incomparable to 1941. From this critical situation we were res-

cued by some splendid soldiers and sailors whom the course of the war had brought to the fore: Jacob Brown, Winfield Scott, and Eleazar Ripley on the Niagara Frontier, Thomas Macdonough and Alexander Macomb at Plattsburg, the defenders of Baltimore, and Andrew Jackson at New Orleans. Britain was weary of war after over 20 years of it in Europe, and was not inclined to press her advantage against so stout a defense. By the time Jackson administered the last and worst repulse at New Orleans, the Treaty of Ghent had already been signed and the *status quo* restored.

PLATE No. 34. *Constitution's Escape from the British Squadron after a chase of sixty hours [Names of ships:] Africa Constitution Shannon AEolus Guerrière Belvidera ☆ M. Cornè p. W. Hoogland Sc ☆ Entered according to Act of Congress Nov. 25, 1815 by A. Bowen ☆ Engraved for the Naval Monument.*
Line engraving. 4¾ x 8⅛ inches.

PLATE No. 35. *This Representation of the U. S. Frigate Constitution, Isaac Hull, Esqr. Commander, Capturing His Britannic Majesty's Frigate Guerrière, James R. Dacres, Esqr Commander; Is respectfully inscribed to Capt. Isaac Hull, his Officers and Gallant Crew; by their devoted humble Servant, James Webster. ☆ Painted by T. Birch, A. C. S. A. ☆ Fought August 19, 1812. ☆ Engraved by C. Tiebout, A. C.*

S. A. ☆ [*Medallion of Hull, surmounted by legend "Veni, Vidi, Vici." Five lines of small type.*] ☆ *Printed ᵃ Published 19ᵗʰ Augᵗ 1813 by James Webster.*

Stipple engraving. 21¾ x 27¾ inches.

The 44-gun frigate *Constitution,* the most famous ship in the history of the United States Navy, was already a veteran when the War of 1812 broke out. She was authorized by Congress in 1794, and launched in Boston in 1797. Through the Naval War with France and the Tripolitan War she had served as a flagship. When the declaration of war on England came, in June, 1812, she was in Chesapeake Bay under the command of Capt. Isaac Hull. He hurried out to avoid blockade and sailed toward New York, looking for Commodore Rogers and the American squadron.

At 2 p. m. on July 17, progressing slowly up the New Jersey coast, Hull sighted four sails. He thought they were the American ships and made way toward them; as he counted a fifth sail the wind failed. The ships lay becalmed out of range of one another. Toward evening came a faint breeze, and Hull headed toward the fifth ship, which happened to be His Majesty's frigate *Guerrière,* 38 guns, Capt. James R. Dacres. Not recognizing her he cleared for action before displaying secret signals, which were not answered. Darkness fell, and at dawn the *Constitution,* drifting in an idle wind, found herself in the thick of the British squadron. The chase went on almost without respite for 36 hours. The *Constitution* was under fire at long range again and again. By ingenious seamanship and occasional pieces of luck with the winds, Hull on the night of the 19th managed to escape unharmed, leaving the enemy hull down to leeward. He headed for Boston and made port on the 27th of July. Plaudits were vigorously forthcoming, and Hull inserted a notice in the Exchange Coffee-House books, asking the transfer of good wishes from himself to his officers and crew.

The famous fight of the *Constitution* and the *Guerrière* took place on August 19, 1812. Captain Hull, watching for enemy merchant shipping southeast of Halifax, again sighted the *Guerrière* and gave chase. The British frigate was far inferior in gun power to the *Constitution,* the relative weight of shot in her broadside being 570 pounds to the 736 pounds of Hull's ship. However, she carried all the prestige of the invincible British navy; and Captain Dacres had written on the register of the brig *John Adams,* which he had boarded a few days before this combat, his invitation to any American frigate for "a few minutes' tête-à-tête."

The chase began at three, and for three hours the frigates manoeuvred, exchanging occasional fire. At six the *Constitution* drew up on the left-hand side of the *Guerrière,* within pistol shot, and the main battle began. During the first 20 minutes, broadsides from the *Constitution's* guns carried away the *Guerrière's* mizzen mast. An English shot rebounded from the hull of the American ship, and a seaman shouted—so runs the legend—"Huzza, her sides are made of iron!"

Hull steered across the enemy's bow to reach a position where his guns could rake her side, but overshot. As "Old Ironsides" turned, the British bowsprit fell foul of the American rigging. Boarding parties gathered on both decks, and a heavy exchange of musket fire resulted in many casualties. But there was to be no boarding; in a few minutes the British fore and main masts gave way, and "she lay a helpless hulk in the trough of a heavy sea, rolling the muzzles of her guns under" (A. T. Mahan). The *Constitution* hauled off, returning in half an hour to receive the *Guerrière's* surrender. Too badly cut up to be taken to port, the prize was burned, and Hull returned in triumph to Boston. The American victory over the pride of His Majesty's navy was hailed with exultation by the entire United States.

The first of the two *Constitution* pictures reproduced is from *The Naval Monument,* a volume published by Abel Bowen, Boston 1816, commemorating the deeds of the Navy in the late war. The text compiled out of *Niles' Register* was illustrated with 25 engravings on wood and copper, all but two from the designs of MICHELE FELICE CORNÉ. This Italian artist, born in 1752, had come to America in 1799, to escape compulsory service in the Neapolitan army. He settled first in Salem, Mass., then in Boston, where he decorated interiors, the best known of which is Hancock House. In his spare time he painted ships and marine views. From Boston he went in 1822 to Newport where he died ten years later.

Bowen specialized in wood engraving, and so got other hands to make his copper plates. This one was done by WILLIAM HOAGLAND, a competent engraver whose earliest work, a series of vignettes, was done at New York in the previous year. He was one of the earliest engravers of American bank notes.

THOMAS BIRCH (1779–1851), who painted the design for the second print, was the son of a London miniaturist and engraver. He emigrated to America in 1793 and established himself in Philadelphia about 1800. In 1807 he started painting marine views, and after the war began, turned his interest to pictures of battles at sea. At the instance of the publisher, James Webster, he painted four phases of the fight between the *Constitution* and *Guerrière,* which now hang at the Naval Academy in Annapolis. It is from one of these that a splendid stipple engraving, published by Webster, was executed by CORNELIUS TIEBOUT (c. 1744– c. 1830), whom the principal authority declares to have been "the first American-born professional engraver to produce really meritorious work" (Stauffer). Supposed to have been born in New York, he supplemented the inadequate training which was all that was to be had at home by a residence in London from 1793–96, when he learned the art of stippling, and produced an engraving of John Jay which is a landmark in the history of American portraiture. First in New York, until 1799, and then in Philadelphia until 1825, Tiebout conducted a large and profitable engraver's business. It is sad to have to record of so worthy an American pioneer that he lost the whole of his life's earnings in some speculation, and in 1825 left Philadelphia for the West, where he died in complete obscurity.

PLATE No. 36. *This View of his Majesty's Ship Shannon, hove too, & cooly waiting the close approach of the American Frigate Chesapeak, who is bearing down to the Attack, with all the confidence of Victory; with its Companion the Capture of the Enemy; is with all due respect, & admiration of their intrepid conduct, most respectfully inscribed to Captain P. B. V. Broke and his gallant Ships Company, by their Obed.ᵗ Servant Rob.ᵗ Dodd. ☆ Painted by R.*

Dodd from the information of Capt. Falkinir. ☆
Published August, 1813, by R. Dodd, N° 3,
Lucas Place, Commercial Road and G. An-
drews, N° 7, Charing Cross.

Aquatint, colored by hand. 14¾ x 19¼ inches
(trimmed within the plate-mark).

PLATE No. 37. *To Captain P. B. V. Broke*
commanding his Majesty's Ship Shannon, his
Officers, Seamen, & Marines, this representa-
tion of their gallantly boarding the American
Frigate Chesapeak, being 110 Men superior
in force and hauling down the Enemy's Colours
in fifteen Minutes from the commencement of
the Action Is most respectfully Inscribed by
their Ob.ᵗ Servant Rob.ᵗ Dodd. ☆ *Painted by Rob.ᵗ*
Dodd from the information of Capt.ⁿ Falkinir. ☆
Published August, 1813, by R. Dodd, N°. 3,
Lucas Place, Commercial Road and G. An-
drews, N° 7, Charing Cross.

Aquatint, colored by hand. 14½ x 19¼ inches
(trimmed within the plate mark.)

On June 5, 1813, the Baltimore news magazine, *Niles' Weekly Register,* published a note:
"A letter from *Boston* says—'that captain
Lawrence of the *Chesapeake* having received
a challenge from commodore Brooke, commanding the *Shannon,* had accepted it, on the
single condition that the commodore should
pledge his honor that he would be alone. The
condition is said to have been accepted, and our
frigate was to sail on Sunday last. *We are will-*
ing this may be true."

It was true in that the *Shannon* was alone.
It was true also in that Broke had written a
challenge to Lawrence, couched in the delib-
erately provocative terms of the golden age of

dueling. But Niles' confident anticipation of a
"glorious result" was unjustified, as his next
issue witnesses:

"Alas! by some uncommon incident not yet
explained, the event has terminated in the loss
of that ship, and in all probability, (which is
of much more consequence) the destruction of
many of her gallant officers and crew."

Commodore Bainbridge, the commanding
officer of the squadron in Boston, breaking the
"unpleasant intelligence" to the Secretary of the
Navy, wrote: "We have lost one frigate, but in
losing her, I am confident we have lost no reputation." That was not true. Lawrence's daring
had outrun his prudence. He had not waited to
receive Broke's note of challenge, which reached
Boston after he had put to sea. He had taken
command of the frigate only 11 days before,
bringing his first lieutenant with him. His crew
was for the most part enlisted within the
month; his third and fourth lieutenants were
midshipmen with "acting" appointments, and
had joined ship on May 27th. His adversary
had commanded his ship and crew for 7 years;
"no more thoroughly efficient ship of her class
had been seen in the British navy" in 20 years,
opines Admiral Mahan. It was the primary duty
of Lawrence, as of the American sea-going navy
in general, to destroy enemy commerce, not to
seek glory in combat. The historians have ever
since been discussing the mistake and the les-
sons of warning to be gained therefrom. One
commodity Lawrence and the crew of the
Chesapeake did not lack, bravery; one contribution outweighed the humiliation of the defeat, a slogan. As Lawrence lay for three days
dying in the hold, he repeated over and over

the words which, on Perry's flagship at Lake Erie, and in every textbook of American history, have sounded with a magical inspiration: "Don't give up the ship."

Captain Broke, blockading Boston Harbor in the early summer of 1813, not only had sent his note of challenge; he had run in close to Boston Light and showed his colors in defiance. Nothing could have been more satisfactory to him than to see the *Chesapeake,* at noon of June 1, lift her anchor and make sail to meet the challenge. The British ship stood out to sea and hove-to on the starboard tack. The *Chesapeake* followed under full sail. At 5:30 she hauled up her courses in fighting trim. Broke, "cooly waiting the close approach" of the American ship, allowed the choice of position to Lawrence, who took the windward for an artillery duel. But, overeager, he came up under too great headway. At 5:50 the *Shannon* opened fire, and the *Chesapeake* answered. In the first exchange of broadsides, which lasted six minutes, Lawrence was wounded, and his sailing master killed. At the same time the ship's forward canvas was shot away; she became uncontrollable, and lay paralyzed 70 yards from the *Shannon,* her guns out of range, her stern, quarter and decks raked by the British fire. Lawrence saw she must drift foul of the enemy, cried, "Boarders away," and then fell mortally wounded. First lieutenant, master, marine officer, boatswain, fourth lieutenant, had all fallen, and the midshipman acting third lieutenant, the only officer left on the gun deck, went to carry his captain below. The gun crews ran forward, probably for their weapons to board the Britisher, but it was the *Shannon's* men led by Broke himself who leaped over the side of the *Chesapeake* as the two ships locked. Broke declared in his report:

"The enemy made a desperate but disorderly resistance." By 6:15 the American crew was driven forward, and an English sailor hauled down the Stars and Stripes and ran up the Union Jack.

The *Shannon* towed the *Chesapeake* triumphantly into Halifax harbor. There Lawrence and his dead officers were borne in solemn procession on shore and buried with the honors accorded to a brave enemy. Says Admiral Mahan: "To the accusation of his country and his service that he brought upon them a mortification which endures to this day, the only reply is that he died 'sword in hand.' This covers the error of the dead, but cannot justify the example to the living."

Meanwhile, British morale, stunned by a succession of utterly unanticipated defeats in frigate duels, received a tremendous uplift. And to this day, any British book which gives brief notice to the War of 1812 at sea, mentions the *Shannon-Chesapeake* battle and little else.

In the first of the two British prints the men in the rigging of the *Chesapeake* are clearly to be observed, as well as the streamer on her mast, "Free Trade and Sailors Rights," the slogan of the war. In the second print the ships have become entangled, and the forward rigging of the *Chesapeake* hangs helplessly.

ROBERT DODD, like Richard Paton, was an English marine painter who specialized in the sea fights of the British Navy, although he could also do storms at sea. He was active from about 1781, and made paintings of Parker's victory over the Dutch, of Rodney's great victory in the West Indies, and of the crowning triumph of Trafalgar. The *Shannon's* victory was important enough to get a pair of aquatints,

85

which was then the favorite form of reproducing naval scenes. Dodd's work, on the basis of these prints, may be described as somewhat routine but entirely competent. These prints must have been made toward the end of his life, since the principal English work of reference loses sight of him after 1809.

PLATE No. 38. [*In box on plate:*] *Plan of Fort Meigs' and its Environs Comprising the Operations, of the American Forces, under Genl. W. H. Harrison, and the British Army and their Allies, under Genl. Pro*^c*tor, and Tecumseh. By an Officer of the Kentucky Militia. "O blest Columbia! Long thy sons shall be, A grand example, for the world to see." [4 stanzas of verse, etc.]* ☆ [*Second box in rectangle:*] *Scale—1 mile to the foot. Fort—50 yd*^s *to the inch: By 35 do.* ☆ [*On plate: Verses, indications, references, account of siege, etc.*]

Figurative map, largely hand-drawn; descriptions in hand-set type, by Captain William Sebree. Undated. 23½ x 37¾ inches.

This pictorial map, full of little men on horseback, ships, Indians in canoes, and such-like decoration, is one of the most extraordinary pieces in the Division of Maps of the Library of Congress, to which it was presented in 1934 by the granddaughter of its maker, Capt. William Sebree. Its indications and references, hand-printed in most fancifully used type, cover practically the entire course of the famous siege. After the disasters of Detroit and the River Raisin, the American forces in the West were thrown on the defensive. Gen. William Henry Harrison built Fort Meigs on the south bank at the rapids of the Maumee River, Ohio, in early 1813, and from April 28 to May 9 defended it against a mixed force of British regulars, Canadians, and Indians. A relieving force of Kentucky militia under General Green Clay came up on May 5. Orders were got through to them to spike the enemy's guns, a task in which they were successful. Unfortunately part of them, under Col. William Dudley, ignored Harrison's orders and failed to withdraw after the spiking. The 800 untrained men were surrounded and over 80 percent were killed or captured by General Proctor's unrestrained allies. Harrison could now do no more than await the result of a passive defence. Fortunately, Tecumseh's warriors were wearied with siege operations and four days later withdrew, to the amazed relief of the Americans in the fort.

Captain Sebree, of the Kentucky riflemen, was mentioned by Harrison in his despatches from Camp Meigs on May 9, 1813. In his own explanations on the map he speaks of its genesis: "The original sketch, and notes were prepared in my tent, subject to many inconveniencies with ill health." It is partially dated by his declaration, "The transaction is a recent one." He was evidently a man of parts and fond of poetry, for among the verses scattered over the map he quotes the whole of Tom Moore's Irish Melody, "Remember the Glories of Brien the Brave," published in 1797. Information regarding Sebree is slight. He was born in 1776, and died at Pensacola, Fla. His name is not in the register of officers of the United States army, and he was presumably a militiaman. In later years he is said to have served in the navy.

PLATE No. 39. *Perry's Victory. on Lake Erie, Sept*^r *10*th *1813.* ☆ *Drawn by J. J. Barralet. Engraved by B. Tanner.*

Line engraving. 21⅝ x 27½ inches.

"We have met the Enemy and they are ours, two ships, two brigs, one schooner and a sloop," read the laconic despatch from Commodore Oliver Hazard Perry at Put-in-Bay, Lake Erie, to Gen. William Henry Harrison, commander of the armies of the Northwest. Perry's own fleet consisted of one captured brig, the *Caledonia,* and eight vessels built at Erie, two 500-ton brigs and a half-dozen schooners. Perry's flagship, the *Lawrence,* bore at her head a streamer on which were written the hero's dying words, "Don't give up the ship."

In his famous victory of September 19, 1813, against the British commander Capt. Robert H. Barclay and his squadron of the Great Lakes, Perry's six smaller vessels outnumbered the British light craft two to one, and both small and large American ships were more powerfully armed than their opponents, although the guns of the British offset the disadvantage in weight by their longer range. Perry had planned his line of battle with ship opposing ship, but in the critical center, the *corps de bataille,* he made a last-minute change when he saw the British line, and placed the *Caledonia* after the *Lawrence,* rather than her sister ship. The result was that the brig *Niagara,* Capt. Jesse D. Elliott, failed to engage closely the *Queen Charlotte* as Perry had intended—the controversy has never been settled as to whether Elliott did right or wrong—but in consequence the *Lawrence,* unsupported, sustained the fire of the two major British ships, *Detroit* and *Queen Charlotte,* for 2½ hours. At last, when four-fifths of the *Lawrence's* crew had been killed or wounded, and the brig badly damaged, Perry left her and was rowed through a dangerous fire to the *Niagara.* As he boarded her the *Lawrence* struck her colors.

But the commodore's flag was now on the *Niagara,* and Perry, who before battle had reenforced his orders "by quoting to his subordinates Nelson's words, that no captain could go very far wrong who placed his vessel close alongside those of the enemy" (Mahan), immediately bore down upon his late opponents, the *Detroit* and *Queen Charlotte,* pouring in broadsides at close range. The British surrender came almost at once.

JOHN JAMES BARRALET was the artist responsible for the fine drawing of massed sails from which this print was engraved. Barralet, born in Dublin of French parentage about 1747, had come to Philadelphia, the center of American engraving, in 1796, and lived there until his death in 1815. For a time he was associated in business with the engraver Alexander Lawson; and his funeral took place from the house of the print publisher, W. H. Morgan, who reissued our Plate 49. Barralet was primarily a portrait painter and is said to have been a highly irritable and eccentric individual, difficult to manage. He would probably have said the same of his subjects. He may have been more amiable when engaged on water-color landscapes, in which noses did not have to be handsome as well as like their original. His work for the engravers consisted mostly of designs, though he himself turned out a few competent plates. He is said to have invented a ruling machine for work on bank notes.

BENJAMIN TANNER, one of the best Philadelphia engravers of the early century, was born in New York on March 27, 1775, and died in Baltimore, November 14, 1848. By 1792 he had begun his engraving career in New

York, probably as an apprentice of Peter R. Maverick. In 1805 he removed to Philadelphia, where he stayed till three years before his death, and set up as a general engraver and map publisher. His engraving shop was a city landmark, from 1811 to 1830 at 74 South Eighth Street, from 1831 at 75 Dock. He may have had some connection with the firm of his brother, Henry S. Tanner, and his partners, Vallance and Kearny, 1819–23, for in 1824 he was advertising their prints for sale. Like that firm, he engaged in the profitable labor of engraving bank notes. He kept up with technological progress, and in 1837 opened a new shop, calling himself a stereographer, making steel plates for commercial firms. His engravings are in both line and stipple, and include some excellent large plates of portraits and historical subjects. In particular his naval prints are notable; in 1812 he published the *Engagement between the Constitution . . . & the Guerrière,* and perhaps also the *Explosion of the British Frigate Guerrière,* which was, like *Perry's Victory,* designed by Barralet. His *United States and Macedonian* is undated, but is probably of the next year. On March 9, 1814, he advertised in the *Boston Columbian Centinel* the plate of *Perry's Victory.* Its cost was $5, but anyone who had bought the *Capture of the Macedonian* might buy it for $4—a good bargain for Tanner collectors. He was still interested in warships in 1819, when he published the fascinating *Launch of the Steam Frigate Fulton the First, 29th Oct.ʳ 1814.*

PLATE No. 40. *Battle of the Thames. 5th Oct.ᵗ 1813. Respectfully Dedicated to Andrew Jackson Esq. President of the United States.* ☆ *Drawn on Stone. Clay. J. Dorival Lith. 52 Ann Sᵗ* ☆ *En-tered according to Act of Congress 9th of August 1833 in the clerks Office of the district, Court of the S. D. of New York, by [written in] Wᵐ Emmons- [Eleven references, in small print]*

Lithograph. 13¾ x 20⅝ inches.

PLATE No. 41. *Death of Tecumseh. Battle of the Thames Oct 5.ᵗʰ 1813.* ☆ *J. E. M.ᶜGee del: et lith.* ☆ *Entered according to act of Congress in the year 1841 by N. Currier in the Clerks office of the District Court of the Southern Distrit of New York.*

Lithograph. 11½ x 9 inches.

Tecumseh's Shawnee name, which meant Falling Star, symbolized his historical position among the Indians of the eastern United States. He was the last of the great chieftains of the Old Northwest, whose passing ended all hope of Indian resistance to the westward sweep of the whites. A warrior distinguished in the border wars, even his enemies, the white settlers, granted that he was humane and that his word might be trusted. About 1808 he settled, with Tenskwatawa, "the Prophet," who was known as his twin brother, at "Prophet's Town," on the Wabash near the mouth of the Tippecanoe. This became the center of his efforts for a confederacy of the tribes which should put a stop to further land cessions and establish an Indian buffer state in the old Northwest. The Prophet was leader of a mystical revival, and preached a doctrine of return to primitive living, above all of avoidance of the white man's rum, the ruin of the Indians.

Gen. William Henry Harrison in 1801 was appointed the first governor of Indiana Territory, and from then until Tecumseh's last battle, the Thames, was the great chief's worst enemy, symbol of white encroachment on the red man's sovereignty. Year after year Harrison negotiated the treaties by which the tribes shamefully abandoned their heritage. Tecumseh, fighting in vain against superior power, made league with the British in Canada, visiting them constantly and receiving sympathetic advice and supplies from the royal warehouses. In 1811 he went south, hoping by his magnificent oratory to enlist recruits for his confederacy from the Five Nations. In his absence, and directly contrary to his warnings, the Prophet allowed himself to be manoeuvered by Harrison into fighting the battle of Tippecanoe. Indian magic did not prevent disaster, and all serious hope for the confederacy was lost. When the War of 1812 began, Tecumseh with his few remaining followers entered the British army, in which he was given the rank of brigadier general. He participated in the capture of Detroit and the siege of Fort Meigs, constantly but uselessly urging the British commander, Proctor, to decisive actions.

In the fall of 1813 General Harrison was able to gain the initiative which Hull had lost at the beginning of the war. His 1,400 regulars, supplemented by five or six thousand Kentucky recruits, were collected on the southern shore of Lake Erie, and after Perry's victory of September 10, were convoyed to the Canada side by the fleet. General Proctor determined to abandon the Lakes and retreat eastward through Canada. In a scathing speech, Tecumseh reproached the British "Father": "You always told us, that you would never draw your foot off British ground . . . We must compare our father's conduct to a fat animal, that carries its tail upon its back, but when

affrighted, he drops it between his legs and runs off . . . Our lives are in the hands of the Great Spirit. We are determined to defend our lands, and if it be his will, we wish to leave our bones upon them." Nevertheless, as Proctor and his 800 soldiers retired at full speed toward Lake Ontario, Tecumseh with his 1,500 Indians covered the British retreat. At the Thames River on October 5, General Harrison caught up with the hopelessly outnumbered enemy, who took up a defensive position of Tecumseh's choosing between the banks and the marshes. Colonel Richard Mentor Johnson, later Vice President of the United States under Van Buren, was in command of the 1,500 mounted Kentuckians. They charged the British left, and the redcoats promptly surrendered. The Indians fought on from ambush, but Tecumseh had foretold the will of the Great Spirit. In about 20 minutes he fell—shot, claimed Johnson, by his own hand—and with him died the last statesman of the eastern Indians. His hunted followers dispersed in the forest.

Plate 40, which is dedicated to the great Indian fighter, Andrew Jackson, was drawn on stone by the New York lithographer, JOHN DORIVAL. He flourished from 1826 to 1835 or 1838, producing competent work of an intelligent sort. Propaganda for Colonel Johnson ("Humpsy, Dumpsy, Colonel Johnson killed Tecumseh," ran an irreverent campaign couplet) was apparently one of his interests, for he did a large portrait lithograph of the Kentucky soldier statesman, as well as the view of his celebrated victory. The artist from whose design the lithograph was taken was EDWARD W. CLAY (1799–1857), a Philadelphia caricaturist and engraver of portraits in stipple. In 1837 he went to New York and took up lithography, becoming one of its most brilliant artists; "his work is always of interest and technically excellent." In the late forties he went to Europe and studied the higher aspects of art for five years, but his eyesight failed and he was forced to give up his career. He spent his last days as a minor judicial officer of the State of Delaware.

PLATE No. 42. *Gen. William Henry Harrison* ☆ *Lith: of Endicott.* ☆ *Entered according to act of Congress, in the year 1840, by G. Endicott, in the Clerk's Office of the District Court for the Southern District of New York. [Small panels surrounding central portrait:] Scene at North Bend. The Patriots Hall. Senator and Statesman. Battle of the Thames. Defence of Fort Meigs. Treating with Indians. Pardoning the assassin. Quelling a mutiny at Fort Defiance. Harrison at Wayne's Victory. Welcome of a fellow Soldier. Battle of Tippecanoe. Making hard Cider.*

Lithograph. 17 x 14¾ inches.

The log cabin and hard cider campaign of 1840, with its memorable slogan of "Tippecanoe and Tyler too," was the first national victory of the Whig party, and unique in its utilization of organized advertising. The only Whig platform was to beat the Democrats. The Endicott print is a typical campaign production. The election of Jackson had pointed out the political path for the military hero. The ugly lithograph portrays the warlike candidate on his battle charger, with no less than four battles, one mutiny and an Indian treaty in the surrounding panels. The notion of Harrison living in a log cabin was fantastic, but enough enfranchised citizens were convinced by it or some other phase of the ballyhoo to elect him.

The ENDICOTTS of New York were actually the first American firm to print machine-made lithographs in mass production. Their company was founded in 1828, originally as Endicott & Swett. Moses Swett had previously been with William S. Pendleton in Boston, the fountainhead of American lithography. In business before Currier and Ives, the firm lasted almost as long, passing through the hands of a succession of business-minded Endicotts—George and William and Francis. In the hands of the second George, after 1887, lithography gave way to—insurance! They always employed able craftsmen—Charles Parsons among others—but, as Mr. Peters deplores, in spite of the volume and competence of their output, they never achieved real individuality of style; and as time passed, of course, the case grew worse. Mere longevity and quantity, however, assure them a very important place among American lithographers.

PLATE No. 43. *Dress, the most distinguishing mark of a military Genius. Designed and Engraved by James Akin Philad.*

Line engraving. 5¼ x 2¼ inches.

In 1782 there appeared at London an anonymous satire, *Advice to the Officers of the British Army: With the Addition of Some Hints to the Drummer and Private Soldier.* It has been attributed to Capt. John Williamson and to Lord Townshend, but is in all probability the work of Francis Grose (1731–1791), adjutant in the Hampshire and captain in the Surrey militia. Captain Grose, "immensely corpulent, full of humour and good nature, and an inimitable boon companion," was an antiquarian and a miscellaneous scholar as well as a militiaman, whose *Provincial Glossary* (1787) and *Classical Dictionary of the Vulgar Tongue* (1785) are still well known in their respective fields. His *Advice to the Officers* was a trenchant and amusing castigation of the foibles and pretensions of the less admirable portion of the military profession, and proved so popular as to run through a number of editions. One of the later London editions added *Some Advice to the Officers of Ordnance and the Secretary at War,* whether by Grose or not is impossible to say. By 1813 some Americans were ready to retaliate upon the brass hats of their day, and a partial adaptation of Grose's work for American readers was published at Philadelphia, under the title, *Advice to the Officers of the Army,* and at Baltimore, under the title, *The Military Monitor: or, Advice to the Officers and Soldiers of the American Army.* The nature of the adaptation can be briefly illustrated: whereas the English editions advised you, if you should be appointed adjutant to a regiment of militia, to "talk of your campaigns in Germany, and America, of the roasting you have experienced in the East and West Indies, and the cold of Newfoundland and Canada," the American editions substituted, flatly enough, "talk of your campaigns during the revolutionary war, and of your services in the North-Western Territory, and Canada." The English editions carried a rough engraved frontispiece, a satyr holding a mirror up to a group of dismayed military men, the design for which was probably supplied by Grose himself, who had studied art in his youth, and exhibited drawings at the Royal Academy. The Baltimore edition of 1813 carried an even cruder version of Grose's original frontispiece, but the Philadelphia one included a new engraving by James Akin which was a much finer and wittier piece of work than the original. It illustrated a passage from the chapter of advice "to Young Officers":

The first article we shall consider is your dress; a taste in which is the most distinguishing mark of a military genius, and the principal characteristic of a good officer.

Ever since the days of Antient Pistol, we find, that a large and broad-rimmed beaver has been peculiar to heroes. A hat of this kind worn over your right eye, with two large dangling tassels, and a proportionate cockade and feather, will give you an air of courage and martial gallantry.

The fashion of your cloaths must depend on that ordered in the Corps; that is to say, must be in direct opposition to it; for it would show a deplorable poverty of genius, if you had not some ideas of your own in dress.

Your cross belt should be broad, with a huge blade pendent to it—to which you may add a dirk and a bayonet, in order to give you the more tremendous appearance.

It is only necessary to glance at the plate to see how well Akin has carried out Grose's idea. The fan, however, was out of his own head!

JAMES AKIN (*c.* 1773–1846) is one of the most interesting of our early engravers. Born in South Carolina, he is supposed to have engraved there and to have received some education in the craft in old England before setting up business in New England, at Salem and Newburyport, from 1804–08. It was in New England, apparently that he developed his most original vein, of caricature and satire. His vigorous "Infuriated Despondency" is supposed to be a caricature of a Newburyport publisher who, aiming a skillet at Akin, sent it through a window and struck one of the worthies of the town; Akin printed it not only upon paper, but upon at least one earthenware pitcher! It is probably not surprising that he left New England after four years. The last four decades of his life were spent in Philadelphia, where he evidently did not prosper too well at his art, since he appears also as a druggist and an eating-house keeper. He mastered the new art of lithography and drew caricatures on stone. Stauffer has tagged him as a "jack of all trades," but it is certainly as one of our earliest masters of graphic humor that he excelled and deserves further study.

PLATE No. 44. *Macdonough's Victory on Lake Champlain, and Defeat of the British Army at Plattsburg by Gen! Macomb, Sept! 11ᵗʰ 1814.* ☆ *Painted by H. Reinagle. Engraved by B. Tanner.*

Line engraving. Undated. 19 x 24½ inches.

HUGH REINAGLE, the artist from whose painting comes this spirited print of Macdonough's victory, was well known as a landscape, *genre* and scene-painter. He was born in Philadelphia in 1790, the son of Frank Reinagle, "a professor of music and partner with Wignell in the Chestnut Street Theatre," according to William Dunlap. "Hugh was a pupil of John J. Holland. He painted landscape both in water color and oil. A panorama of New York was painted by him, which was exhibited in Broadway. [Other well known pictures are of Niagara Falls, and views on the Hudson River.] For many years he was principal scene painter at the New York theatres; and in 1830 went to New Orleans, in consequence of offers from Mr. Caldwell, man-

ager of the American Theatre at that plate, and there died of Asiatic cholera in 1834. Mr. Reinagle was a man of amiable disposition, correct conduct, and unblemished reputation. He left a widow and a large family, I fear slenderly provided for."

The sea battle on September 11, 1814, was of the greatest importance in deciding the outcome of the war of 1812. Commander Thomas Macdonough's flagship *Saratoga* and his other strong vessel, the *Eagle,* forced the newly built and powerful 37-gun British flagship *Confiance* and her mate, the *Linnet,* to strike their colors in an engagement fought off Plattsburgh. The American fleet had lain in the bay waiting for weeks, anchored in a defensive alignment. The small American army under General Macomb had been forced to withdraw from Plattsburgh on September 5 by the advance of the British general Prevost with between 11 and 14,000 men, most of them veterans of Wellington's army recently arrived. Macomb had taken up a prepared position across the Saranac River, on some bluffs overlooking the bay. Prevost, occupied, the artist would lead one to believe, in burning the town, decided not to cross the Saranac, where, if he disposed of Macomb, he could attack Macdonough from the shore. The British, therefore, did not even get well started on the route which Burgoyne had traced in 1777.

In Reinagle's picture, four of Macomb's officers are presumably galloping with despatches past a group of interested local spectators, men and boys, whose gestures proclaim their excitement. A realistic dog turns tail, afraid of the guns, and three boys are to be made out in grandstand seats, high in the branches of the big stage-set tree at the right. Warfare, Reinagle and Tanner believe, can be fun, especially if our side wins.

PLATE No. 45. *Camp Dupont. From The Martial Music of Camp Dupont, Philadelphia, G. E. Blake*, circa 1816.

Aquatint. 6⅜ x 10 inches.

Camp Dupont was the encampment of the Pennsylvania volunteers who in the spring of 1814 rushed to the defense of Delaware when the news came of British forces in the Chesapeake. The first volunteers left Philadelphia on May 13. The site originally planned was at Staunton below Wilmington, known as Camp Bloomfield, which is spoken of by Scharf and Westcott in their account of the "State Fencibles" (Plate 53). But a rumor came of impending attack on the Dupont powder mills above Wilmington, and the camp was moved near the Brandywine, to the spot called Oak Hill, or Camp Dupont. Here the Pennsylvanians trained, imbibing with their music the martial spirit. But they were not forced to put their bravery to proof; the British, repulsed at Baltimore, left the Chesapeake, and the troops went home to Philadelphia before the end of July.

According to the third page of this volume of pianoforte music, "the forces at Camp Dupont under Brig. Gen. Thomas Cadwalader, were designated as the *advance Light Brigade.*" There were 3,428 men, all Pennsylvania militia except for 600 detached regulars. The largest element was the First Regiment of Pennsylvania Volunteers, which had been recruited in Philadelphia. It included the aforementioned "State Fencibles," and their original captain, Clement C. Biddle, was promoted to colonel in command of the regiment. His name is down as subscriber for one copy of the "Martial Music"; General Cadwalader, in keeping with his exalted rank, subscribed for five copies. The music was arranged by R. Taylor, possibly the bandmaster. The Introduction contains the following:

"The following are the regular beats in camp.
1. The Reveille—
2. The Drummer's call—
3. Pioneer's march—
4. The Breakfast call—

[and so to]

12. The General.

There are several other beat's in camp, which are adapted only for the drum, such as the Adjutant's call, the first sergeant's call, . . . the whiskey call, the assembly &c."

GEORGE E. BLAKE, who graced his volume with this anonymous aquatint, was a music publisher of considerable importance. In 1793 he had come over from England as a teacher of flute and clarinet. He established himself in Philadelphia, and in 1803 or 1804 opened his music publishing business at 1 South 3d Street, where he or his successors remained until 1871. We have no indication of who sketched the scene or made the plate; but while the result is no great matter as art it is of considerable interest as the earliest camp view we have found.

PLATE No. 46. *A View of the Bombardment of Fort McHenry, near Baltimore, by the British fleet, taken from the Observatory under the Command of Admirals Cochrane, & Cockburn, on the morning of the 13th of Sepr. 1814. which lasted 24 hours, & thrown from 1500 to 1800 shells. in the Night attempted to land by forc-*

*ing a passage up the ferry branch but were re-
pulsed with great loss.* ☆ *J. Bower, sc. Phil.ª* ☆
Copy Right, Secured. ["References," naming
locations]

Aquatint, colored by hand. Undated. 12¼ x
17⅛ inches.

Fort McHenry stood on a small island in
Baltimore harbor, where it had been constructed in fear of the French in 1799. On the
night of September 13, 1814, Admiral Sir
George Cockburn, leaving behind him the city
of Washington ravaged and in flames, sailed
with the British fleet up the Chesapeake Bay
and bombarded the fort. A gentleman of Baltimore, the young lawyer Francis Scott Key, had
been sent on an embassy and detained during
the battle. All night he watched from the deck
of a British ship. The dawn's early light showed
him the scene here depicted, in the center of
which, over the brave little fort, still waves the
Star-Spangled Banner.

JOHN BOWER, a map-engraver who worked in
Philadelphia from 1810–19, was responsible for
this aquatint of the bombardment of Fort Mc-
Henry. Little is known about him. He did a
few poorly executed plates for Collins' Quarto
Bible in 1816, and made stipple portraits of
Washington and Adams, both in one plate, in
two circles set in a rectangle. Our plate is strictly
a homespun production, and it is curious that
one so little gifted as Bower should attempt the
complex process of aquatint at all (it is, by the
way, the only American aquatint we present—
there were some good ones!) But it is spirited
in its rough way, and it is the only contemporary representation of the scene which **gave**
birth to our national anthem.

PLATE No. 47. *Defeat of the British Army, 12,
000 strong, under the Command of Sir Edward
Packenham in the attack of the American Lines
defended by 3,600 Militia commanded by Maj.
General Andrew Jackson January 8ᵗʰᵉ 1815, on
Chalmette plain, five miles below New Orleans,
on the left bank of the Mississippi* ☆ *Drawn on
the Field of Battle and painted by Hᵗʰᵉ Laclotte
archᵗ and assisᵗ Engineer in the Louisiana Army
the year 1815.* ☆ *Défaite de l'Armée* [same in
French] ☆ [Seal; above] *To the United States'
Glory.* ☆ *Gravé par P. L. Debucourt.*

Aquatint. 21½ x 27 inches.

PLATE No. 48. *Battle of New Orleans and
Death of Major General Packenham On the 8ᵗʰ
of January 1815.* ☆ [Portrait bust of Jackson on
crossed flags, swords and cannon, etc., in center]
J. Yeager Sc ☆ *Copy Right Secure'd Accordᵍ to
Law Published and Sold by J. Yeager Nº 103
Race Sᵗ Philadª*

Line engraving, colored by hand. 14¾ x 20½
inches.

The battle of New Orleans was fought and
won two weeks after the signing of the treaty
of peace at Ghent (December 24, 1814). The
news of the treaty did not reach the United
States until February 11, 1815, by which time
the defeated British force had retired to its ships
and departed. Its leader, Sir Edward Pakenham, brother-in-law of the great Duke of Wellington, was left dead on the field. The Mississippi Valley was saved from invasion, and the
hero, Gen. Andrew Jackson, had won the rep-

utation which was to carry him to the White House 14 years later.

When the British fleet of 50 ships, carrying 7,500 veterans of the Napoleonic wars, appeared in the Gulf of Mexico in the autumn of 1814, the energetic Governor Claiborne undertook what defenses he could for New Orleans, and General Jackson, commander of the American army in the Southwest, hurried to the city. His army was chiefly militia, about six or seven thousand raw recruits from Kentucky, Tennessee, and Louisiana. Knowing their lack of training, Jackson realized his only hope lay in securing a defensible position. Pakenham aided him by making no attempt to maneuver the Americans out of their entrenchments; instead he prepared a frontal assault. Jackson had bent all his energies toward making impregnable a spot between the river and a cypress swamp, cut by a deep canal that lay like a moat before his redoubt, reinforced by cotton bales. Behind stood the fine plantation house of the rich Creole sugar planter, Chalmette, whose two-storied porticos rise in the left of Laclotte's picture. The artist shows only one small portion of the upper balcony shot away, but after the battle the building was a charred ruin. The moat, full of drowning redcoats, runs across the foreground of this picture.

Jackson's riflemen were drawn up behind the parapet, and so disposed that they could alternately load and discharge their pieces, keeping up a continuous fire against the headlong British attack. West's quaintly rugged picture gives a vivid idea of the heroic and suicidal British advance against the powerful redoubt, from which big guns and muskets pour forth a sea of fire and smoke. In the foreground the leader himself has fallen, surrounded by his weeping

staff, while the Union Jack droops alongside his thoroughly dead horse. Because of the protection of the breastworks, Jackson's army suffered only 13 killed and 58 wounded. In the course of a few minutes the British suffered over 2,000 casualties, including the three ranking officers.

Little is known about the painter HYACINTHE LACLOTTE, "architect and assistant engineer in the Louisiana Army," and presumably a Creole volunteer. However, the Paris engraver, LOUIS-PHILIBERT DEBUCOURT (1755–1832), was one of the great masters of the colored aquatint, surpassed in reputation only by his immediate predecessor, Jean-François Janinet. Debucourt was a pupil of J. M. Vien, an associate of the Académie in 1781, and a full member in 1782. Under the *Ancien Régime* he had great success with his *genre* painting, but after 1785 he worked exclusively in aquatint. "Ce fut le graveur de l'élégance française"; he left more than 558 plates. His powers declined in his later years, during which he worked in part from the designs of others. In the print from Laclotte's painting, however, it is still the master's touch which, in spite of the tremendous panorama, centers the composition on the two figures fighting with swords at the rampart.

The artist of the second plate, WILLIAM EDWARD WEST (1788–1857) was born in Lexington, Ky., the son of a watchmaker and inventor. He evidently became a painter at an early age, and for several years painted miniatures in the West. About 1807 he went to Philadelphia to study under the great Thomas Sully, "the friend and refuge of all who applied to him." He worked in Philadelphia until 1819, and, presumably, during this period made the design for Yeager's print; whose is the crudity and

95

whose the vigor, it is hard to say. In 1819 he went to Natchez where a Mr. Evans became his patron and sent him to Europe. He painted Byron and Shelley in Italy, distinguished Frenchmen in Paris in 1824, and the celebrities of London for 15 years. In 1839 he returned to the United States and established himself in New York where he painted until 1855. He left to end his days in Nashville.

JOSEPH YEAGER, another Philadelphia engraver, who did general work in line engraving and etched portraits, flourished from 1816–45. Among his productions are close copies of Cruikshank's etchings, executed for American editions of English novels.

PLATE No. 49. *Major General Andrew Jackson. President of the United States. ☆ Painted by Thomas Sully. Engraved by James B. Longacre. ☆ Published by Wm H. Morgan N° 279 Market Street Philad^a ☆ Published & Entered according to Act of Congress November 2nd 1820 by Joshua Shaw. Samuel Kennedy & James B. Longacre. of the State of Pennsylvania. Managers & Trustees for the Association of American Artists. Philadelphia.*

Stipple engraving. 18¼ x 13¼ inches.

THOMAS SULLY, the "Sir Thomas Lawrence of America," never painted a homely man, woman or child, as countless portraits of early nineteenth-century American ancestors testify. His portrait of Maj. Gen. Andrew Jackson, hero of New Orleans, is no exception. The general, in this three-quarters' length presentation, stands beside his battle charger, with his left hand on the reins and his right on the hilt of his sword. The painting was done in the master's Philadelphia studio after 1815, and repro-

duced in a splendid stipple engraving by Longacre, one of the finest examples of that process.

JAMES BARTON LONGACRE was born of English and Swedish ancestry in 1794, in Delaware County, Pennsylvania. John F. Watson, the Philadelphia annalist, discovered the boy's talents and placed him with George Murray of Philadelphia to learn engraving. By 1819 Longacre was sufficiently well known to set up his own business. His earliest work under Murray had been illustrations for S. F. Bradford's Encyclopedia, "but he first attracted attention by his admirable large plate of Andrew Jackson." His place as the leading stipple engraver of the country was established in 1820 by John Binns' publication of a facsimile of the Declaration of Independence, for which Longacre had engraved portraits of Washington, Jefferson, and Hancock, on a plate 35 x 25 inches in size, "the largest engraving that had been made in the United States up to that time."

Longacre was commissioned to engrave portraits for many biographical works of the period. The most important was an ambitious undertaking, *The National Portrait Gallery of Distinguished Americans,* published by him and James Herring of New York in four octavo volumes from 1834–1839. There were a number of reissues, and on these engravings, some from his own portraits, rests Longacre's chief claim to fame.

In 1844 Longacre was appointed chief engraver of the United States Mint, and as such was responsible for the design and engraving of the first double-eagle, 1849, the first $3 gold piece, 1854, and the gold dollar of that period. In addition, he remodeled the coinage of the new republic of Chile. He died in Philadelphia in 1869.

96

The process of *stipple engraving,* of which Longacre was one of the principal American masters, differs from line engraving in that, after the outline has been etched on the plate, a downward-curving graver is used, picking out dots and flicks. By their size and position these small impressions produce tones of light and shade, making for greater flexibility than is possible in line engraving—if also for less directness and strength. In such an example as Longacre's portrait of Jackson, we have what is known as heavy stipple, in which the tones of black "rise to a richness that is of a resounding sonority" (Frank Weitenkampf). It has been objected that such a use of stipple usurps the work of mezzotint, but a masterpiece like this justifies its own technique. Attention may be called to the remarkable use of light and shade in the modelling of the face.

According to the legend of the plate, it was originally published under a copyright of 1820, held by Joshua Shaw. Our reproduction is of the second "state" of the plate. Such a second or later state contains additions or deletions not to be found in prints made from the plate as originally completed. It was published by William H. Morgan, who added his own name and address, and the legend, "President of the United States," some time after the election of 1828.

Africa   CONSTITUTION   Shannon   Æolus   Guerriere   Belvidera

Constitution's Escape from the British Squadron after a chase of sixty hours

PLATE No. 34. *Constitution's Escape from the British Squadron after a Chase of Sixty Hours, July 17, 1812. Engraving by William Hoogland, 1815.*

98

REPRESENTATION OF THE U.S. FRIGATE CONSTITUTION, ISAAC HULL, ESQ? COMMANDER, CAPTURING HIS BRITANNIC MAJESTY'S FRIGATE GUERRIERE, JAMES R. DACRES, ESQ? COMMANDER and Gallant Crew by their devoted humble servant. James Webster.

PLATE No. 35. *The U. S. Frigate Constitution Capturing His Britannic Majesty's Frigate Guerrière, August 19, 1812. Engraving by Cornelius Tiebout, 1813.*

This View of his Majesty's Ship SHANNON, hove too, & cooly waiting the close approach of the American Frigate CHESAPEAK, who is bearing down to the Attack, with all the confidence of Victory; with its Comp...
the Capture of the Enemy, is with all due respect, & admiration of their intrepid conduct, most respectfully inscribed to CAPTAIN P. B. V. BROKE and his gallant Ships Company, by their Obed.t Servant Rob.t Dodd.

PLATE NO. 36. *H. M. S. Shannon coolly Waiting
the close Approach of the American Frigate
Chesapeake, June 1, 1813. Aquatint after Robert
Dodd, 1813.*

100

CAPTAIN P. B. V. BROKE *commanding her Majesty's Ship* SHANNON, *his Officers, Seamen & Marines, this representation of their gallantly boarding the American Frigate* CHESAPEAK, *being so Men superior in force and hauling down the Enemy's Colours in fifteen Minutes from the commencement of the Action Is most respectfully Inscribed by their Ob.t Servant — Rob.t Dodd.*

PLATE No. 37. *H. M. S. Shannon's Crew gallantly Boarding* the *American Frigate Chesapeake, June 1, 1813. Aquatint after Robert Dodd, 1813.*

101

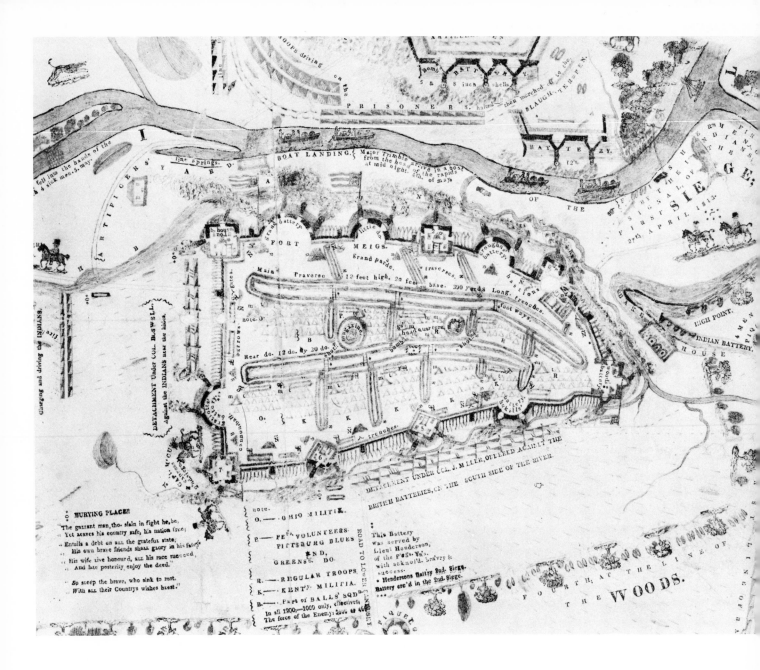

PLATE No. 38. *The Siege of Fort Meigs, April 28–May 9, 1813. Figurative map by William Sebree.*

Drawn by J.J.Barralet.   Engraved by B. Tanner.

Perry's Victory
on Lake Erie Sep. 10 1813

PLATE NO. 39. *Perry's Victory on Lake Erie,*
September 10, 1813. Engraving by Benjamin
Tanner, 1815.

103

PLATE No. 40. *Battle of the Thames, October 5,*
1813. Lithograph by Edward W. Clay, 1833.

104

DEATH OF TECUMSEH,

PLATE No. 41. *Death of Tecumseh, Battle of the Thames, October 5, 1813. Lithograph by John L. McGee, 1841.*

GEN. WILLIAM HENRY HARRISON

PLATE No. 42. *Gen. William Henry Harrison.*
Lithograph by George Endicott, 1840.

Designed and Engraved by James Akin Philad.a

DRESS,

the most distinguishing mark of a military Genius.

PLATE NO. 43. *Dress, the most Distinguishing Mark of a Military Genius. Engraving by James Akin, from "Advice to the Officers of the Army," 1813.*

Macdonough's Victory on Lake Champlain

PLATE No. 44. *Macdonough's Victory on Lake Champlain, September 11, 1814. Engraving by Benjamin Tanner, 1816.*

CAMP DUPONT

PLATE No. 45. *Camp Dupont, near Philadelphia.*
Aquatint, from Blake's Martial Music of Camp
Dupont, c. 1816.

A VIEW of the BOMBARDMENT of Fort Mc.Henry, *near Baltimore, by the British fleet taken from the Observatory, under the Command of Admirals Cochrane & Cockburn, on the morning of the 13th of Sepr 1814 which lasted 24 hours, & thrown from 1500 to 1800 shells, in the Night attempted to land by forcing a passage up the ferry branch but were repulsed with great loss.*

References.
A. Fort Mc Henry
B. Lazaretto
C. Saltmore River
D. Admiral Ship & North Point
E. Ferry and Fort

PLATE No. 46. *View of the Bombardment of Fort McHenry, September 13, 1814. Aquatint by John Bower.*

110

PLATE No. 47. *Defeat of the British Army under the Command of Sir Edward Packenham, January 8, 1815. Detail from aquatint by Louis-Philibert Debucourt.*

111

PLATE No. 48. *Battle of New Orleans and Death
of Major General Packenham, January 8, 1815.
Engraving by James Yeager.*

112

Published by Wm H. Morgan No 279 Market Street Philad.ª

MAJOR GENERAL ANDREW JACKSON.

PRESIDENT of the UNITED STATES.

PLATE No. 49. *Maj. Gen. Andrew Jackson. Engraving by James B. Longacre, after Thomas Sully, 1820.*

113

V

Indian Wars and Volunteer Companies
1832-1845

PLATE No. 50. *Battle of Bad Axe.* ☆ *Schlacht von Bad Axe. H. Lewis pinx. Lith. Jnst. Arnz & Cº Düsseldorf.*

Lithograph, printed in color. 5¾ x 7¾ inches.

"Why did the Great Spirit ever send the whites to this island, to drive us from our homes, and introduce among us *poisonous liquors, disease, and death?* They should have remained on the island where the Great Spirit first placed them." This pathetic lament of Black Hawk, the last noble red man of the East, echoes the futility of the last attempt at armed resistance on the part of the tribes east of the Mississippi. The word "battle" lends an unwarranted dignity to the pitiful massacre which ended the Black Hawk War.

HENRY LEWIS, born in Kent, England, about 1819, was a carpenter by trade. About 1836 he emigrated with his elder brother to St. Louis, where he became a stage carpenter at the Ben De Bar Opera House. In 1841 a St. Louis artist, Banvard, produced a canvas 440 yards long, a panoramic view of the Mississippi River, which was exhibited widely in the United States, and was soon flattered by a number of imitations. It is claimed that the idea of the panorama had been Henry Lewis' and that the two men had planned to collaborate, but failed to agree. However, Lewis realized the possibilities of river views for a wide public, and in 1847–49 he di-

vided his time between trips in a crude house boat in the Mississippi and long days in his studio painting his own panorama. This measured 12 feet by 1,325 yards, twice the size of any competitive work. Eight hundred and twenty-five yards were given to the region between St. Anthony and St. Louis, and 500 to the distance from St. Louis to New Orleans. Congressmen, generals, and governors gave him letters of commendation. After a tour in eastern America, Lewis displayed his canvas in England and in Germany. In 1851 he settled at Düsseldorf and there, in 1854–57, lithographic plates were made from his original sketches and published, with a substantial text by his friend and companion on the river trips, George B. Douglas. The text had been translated into German—*Das illustrirte Mississippithal*—and the plates were printed in full color.

In the print of the Black Hawk fight, the steamer *Warrior* puffs down the river, between close-hanging banks which rise in the background to sizeable cliffs. On her deck stand four or five blue-uniformed soldiers, firing a cannon point-blank at the enemy. Fire issues from the cannon's mouth, first red, then yellow, and then a smoke cloud, and its effect on the Indian raft in the river is that of a well-bowled ball on a row of skittles. A swarm of Indian canoes are hastening to put out from the farther tree-lined shore, on whose bank a few figures still stand in stiff attitudes of terror.

The accompanying chapter may have been based on the classic *Life of Black Hawk*, which the old chief, in confinement at Jefferson Barracks, Iowa, dictated to the Indian interpreter of the Sac and Fox Agency, and which was edited and published by J. B. Patterson of Rock Island, Ill., in 1834. Douglas' sympathy is definitely with the poor remnants of the tribe, turned away from their beloved island, where for a hundred and fifty years they had planted their corn and held their feasts, and where lay the bones of their ancestors.

The Sac [Sauk] and Fox Indians of Illinois, Missouri, and eastern Wisconsin were comparatively docile, and as early as 1804 had ceded title to 50 million acres of land. Black Hawk, who was, as he explains, a civil chief, not a war chief, had been leader of the village at Rock Island. The treaty was not understood by the tribe; they could not believe that the good Father in Washington had meant them to leave their homes in exchange for a few medals and presents or promises of presents. In 1831 squatters invaded the Rock Island village, and the young men of the tribe could not resist a few shots and scalps. When the Sixth Infantry under Gen. Henry Atkinson and 900 Illinois militia were called out, Black Hawk and his followers withdrew to the Iowa shore. But they longed for their own fields of corn, and early in 1832 they drifted back. Atkinson ordered Black Hawk to return to Iowa, but he did not go, and the "Black Hawk War" began. The Indians, outnumbered and hopeless, retired slowly up Rock River, with Atkinson in pursuit. Black Hawk said that orders were to refrain from killing the whites, but there were a few accidents. On August 3, 1832, the little band was penned up against the Mississippi at

the mouth of the Bad Axe River in Wisconsin. The Indians were trying desperately to cross to the western side; Black Hawk and Douglas in the German book say that he sent out a white flag. But the captain of the steamer fired, the braves resisted, and that was the end. The women, swimming the river with their children on their backs, were shot in the water.

A few reached the other side, among them Black Hawk himself. They went to a Winnebago village, with whose chief Black Hawk left the medicine bag of his tribe. The squaws made him a white dress of deer skin (the British dress uniforms at Yorktown, Lee's new gray uniform at Appomattox!) and he went to the agent at Prairie du Chien to give himself up. He was taken to Jefferson Barracks, where he "met the great war chief, White Beaver [Atkinson] who had commanded the American army," and who "received us kindly, and treated us well." Actually they were kept in confinement and in irons! In the spring, Black Hawk was sent to Washington where he had an audience with President Jackson, and was shown (or shown off in) the great cities. On his return to Jefferson Barracks he called for the interpreter and, as a last service to his race, dictated his memories.

PLATE No. 51. *Massacre of the Whites by the Indians and Blacks in Florida. The above is intended to represent the horrid Massacre of the Whites in Florida, in December 1835, and January, February, March, and April 1836, when near Four Hundred (including women and children) fell victims to the barbarity of the Negroes and Indians.*

Wood engraving, colored by hand. From "An Authentic Narrative of the Seminole War",

116

Providence, D. F. Blanchard, 1836. 6½ x 20 inches.

The *Authentic Narrative of the Seminole War,* "communicated for the press by a gentleman who has spent 11 weeks in Florida, near the scene of the Indian depredations, and in a situation to collect every important fact relating thereto," is a 24-page pamphlet which serves mainly as explanatory text for the hair-raising representation of scenes from the "Massacre" which is the folding frontispiece.

The crude wood-engraving whose designer discreetly omitted his signature, presents the conventional idea of Indian warfare. The "war-whoop" is sounded, the redskin warriors burst with brand, tomahawk and scalping knife upon the helpless settlers, and then dance around their victims whom they have tied to the stake. The Gentleman's *Narrative* is filled with circumstantial case histories of unfortunate families who, fleeing from their blazing houses, had all been brutally murdered or had miraculously escaped. On one occasion the Indians surrounded Major Dade and a small force of regulars and killed them all. Many of the Indian assailants were "well mounted, naked, and painted"—which hardly justifies the little skirts modestly worn by the warriors of the frontispiece.

The Seminole Wars differed from other Indian frontier troubles chiefly in that the tribes in the swampy lands of Florida Territory had become a haven for runaway slaves, so that there was a considerable intermingling of "Blacks." The first Seminole War, in 1816–18, had been brought to an end by Andrew Jackson, and treaties in 1832 and 1833 had provided for the westward removal of the Seminoles,

along with the Creeks, Cherokees and others of the Five Civilized Tribes. The Indians procrastinated, and in 1835 Osceola, who was leading the resistance, was arrested. After his release the Indians broke out with the war-whoop and the "horrid Massacre" depicted by our plate. Volunteer forces were raised to supplement the regulars, and the war was pursued relentlessly on both sides, with many hand-to-hand skirmishes in the swamps. Our Gentleman describes the Indian leader, "Osciola, otherwise called Powell," in one such attack: "He wore a red belt, and three large feathers, and would step boldly out from behind his tree, take a deliberate aim, and bring down his man at every fire!" Osceola's capture in 1837 brought organized resistance to an end, but the final process of seizing, bargaining with, and deporting the Seminole groups continued until 1842.

PLATE No. 52. *The National Lancers with the Reviewing Officers on Boston Common. Taken from the Original Painting (as designed and executed by C. Hubbard) on the Standard, which was presented to the Company by His Excellency the Governor of Massachusetts, on the 30th of August, 1837. This Print, published by request, is respectfully dedicated to the Corps. Boston, Sept. 1837. ☆ C. Hubbard del. On stone by F. H. Lane. Moore's Lithography, Boston [Copyright notice]*

Lithograph. 16¾ x 21¼ inches.

Under the Militia Act of 1792, which was not repealed until 1903, all able-bodied male citizens of the respective States, between the ages of 18 and 45, were to be "severally and respectively enrolled in the militia," and each to "be constantly provided with a good musket or firelock, a sufficient bayonet and belt, two spare flints, and a knapsack," as well as other accouterments. From colonial days militia had been subject to general musters once or twice a year. The annual muster day could easily become an annual spree. The militia which was called out for the Whiskey Rebellion in Pennsylvania in 1794, for frontier defense, and during the War of 1812, was volunteer. It early became obvious that training was needed for an efficient citizen force, and volunteer companies, precursors of the National Guard, were organized during times of stress. In the years of peace they held frequent drills and displayed their resplendent uniforms in parades on public occasions.

The National Lancers had not been long organized in 1837, when C. Hubbard made the painting which was placed on the standard, and from which the lithograph was made. In the print they are being reviewed by Gov. Edward Everett upon Boston Common, under the gilded dome of the State House. The young trees that line the walks in the print were blown down in the great hurricane of 1939.

The corps of Lancers was Boston's only cavalry troop, and traditionally escorted the Governor to Cambridge for Harvard commencements. They were occasionally called upon to quell riots. Their motto was "Liberty, Union and the Laws." They wore double-breasted coats of green, with "collar, cuffs, turnbacks, linings and stripe on the trowsers, red, and the length of the skirts to be what is called three-quarters; ornament on the skirts, cross sabres." On their heads they bore a "Cap—black leather, seven and a half inches deep," ornamented with gilt crossed sabres and a "drooping white horsehair pompom, with a stripe of red hair to

show in front." We have reproduced an uncolored copy; another, handsomely colored by hand, is reproduced in H. T. Peters' *America on Stone*.

The National Lancers is the first wholly superior *lithograph* that we have reproduced in this Album, and we therefore pause to comment upon this highly important process. A lithograph is, as its Greek name indicates, a print made from stone, but a very special sort of stone was required, namely, a kind of calcareous slate, 97 percent carbonate of lime, quarried in the neighborhood of Solenhofen, Bavaria, and hardly anywhere else. Nowadays we have become so technologically expert that lithographs—or prints indistinguishable from lithographs—can be made from zinc or aluminum, but this development did not come until the last decade of the Nineteenth Century. The method of treating such a stone so as to turn it into a plate was discovered by a Bavarian, Alois Senefelder (1771–1834), who was driven by the necessity of supporting a large and needy family into the desperate exercise of his ingenuity, and so at last invented a graphic process which was neither *intaglio,* such as engraving, nor *relief,* such as woodcut, but has been called *planographic,* from the flatness of surface in the finished stone. The essential discovery was made in 1798; Senefelder received an English patent in 1801 and a French one in 1802, but still made little direct profit from a process which became so universal. His *Complete Course of Lithography* (1818) was a full exposition of all the basic techniques; within a year or two lithography had been attempted in the United States. Some of the earliest American firms called themselves "Senefelder Lithographic Companies."

Senefelder himself called his invention "chemical printing," and the entire process, in Mr. Peters' acute phrase, "depended on so simple a principle as the natural antipathy between grease and water." Senefelder's first experiments were made with oil, acid, and water on paper; he could get one impression from the paper but it was not strong enough to go on printing from; and his inspiration came when he thought of transferring the method to a porous stone. A carefully ground and polished stone plate could be drawn on with a lithographic *grease-crayon*. After applications of gum arabic mixed with acid, and of water, a special greasy ink was applied to the stone; the ink was absorbed by the parts originally covered by the crayon, and repelled by those uncovered, which were already saturated with water. Printing could now take place. The whole process, if somewhat cumbrous in the description, was so much more direct and rapid than existing graphic methods—engraving a hard copper plate, for example—that it at once opened up a field of copious and inexpensive popular illustration.

In Germany, where it was invented, the process was for long chiefly used as a means of reproducing existing works of art. The possibilities of so facile and flexible a medium were first realized in France, whose "Golden Age of Lithography" lasted for two decades, from about 1820 to 1840. Such mighty names as Daumier and Delacroix brought out original works in the new medium, while a host of lesser men applied it to every form of illustration, particularly to the romantic taste for medieval remains which was then universal. Contemporary with the beginning of this French Golden Age, the first American experiments were made—

Bass Otis printed a lithograph in the *Analectic Magazine* for July 1819—but the craft naturally took longer to develop in a country where there was relatively less demand for art than in France. In the course of the 1820's a number of commercial firms took hold, the earliest and most important being that of the brothers Pendleton in Boston, and, according to Mr. Drepperd, "the year 1830 may safely be set down as that which marks the birth of lithographic production on a large scale in America." People who have been interested exclusively in fine art have usually been rather condescending toward the early age of American lithography; but this is the wrong approach. It is as popular art and as general illustration that it should be regarded, with, however, this important proviso: there is absolutely no line of demarcation. Many of the best American artists engaged in lithography, and there was no reservation of special subjects, inferior workmanship, and second-rate people for this field. All that belongs to the later age of completed industrialization and mass minds. The early American lithograph was often as good as it was popular. To be sure, it had to represent something, and something recognizable.

Curiously, however, lithography as a popular art has been extinct for decades, but it survives—flourishes would be a better word—as a fine art. After the Civil War, when as a popular art it was in decay, it was taken up by a number of notables, William Morris Hunt, Whistler, and Joseph Pennell among others. In the Third National Exhibition of Current Prints held last year (1945) at the Library of Congress, over 150 lithographs were exhibited, fully half of the whole.

The artist, C. HUBBARD, was a Bostonian.

This is his best known work and is sufficient to prove his ability to subordinate details to a coherently conceived design. It is warmly praised by Mr. Peters, who mentions also his drawing for the lithograph of Charles Carroll of Carrollton published by Endicott.

FITZ HUGH LANE, who transferred Hubbard's painting to stone, was first interested in lithography, like so many others, by William S. Pendleton. He was for a time in partnership with John W. A. Scott, another Pendleton apprentice contemporaneous with Nathaniel Currier, in the 1840's. He later won fame as a marine painter. THOMAS MOORE'S LITHOGRAPHY, at 204 Washington Street, Boston, from 1835-41, was the successor of the Pendleton firm at their last address. Moore was an Englishman who had been bookkeeper for Pendleton, and in 1836 bought out his business. He is said to have been a bibulous, flirtatious dandy, and succeeded in keeping his business going for only six years. The "National Lancers" is the finest print known to have come from his presses.

PLATE No. 53. *The Company of State Fencibles Commanded by Col: James Page. Entered according to act of Congress in the year 1845 by F. Mahan, 211, Chestnut St: in the Clerk's Office of the District Court of the Eastern District of the State Of Pennsylvania.*

Lithograph colored by hand. 8¾ x 7½ inches.

On May 26, 1813, a volunteer company was organized in Philadelphia by Capt. Clement C. Biddle. The "State Fencibles," as they came to be known, were a proud outfit and succeeded in lasting into the next century. *Fencible,* by the way, is an old term meaning a soldier enlisted for home service only. In 1814 they saw active service for the first time, marching in August to Camp Bloomfield below Wilmington, where an army was gathered for the defense of Delaware against the British. At this encampment the first full regiment of Pennsylvania volunteer infantry was organized, and Captain Biddle selected as colonel. Captain Hartman Kuhn took over command of the Fencibles, in which there were enrolled 16 officers, 112 privates, and one musician. Among the privates was James Page, one of Biddle's original group, who succeeded Kuhn as captain and was for many years—until 1860—in command of the company. "The organization was spirited and popular. It was effective on many occasions when the presence and support of military force was necessary for the preservation of the public peace" (Scharf and Westcott).

About 1830 the State Fencibles, jointly with another volunteer company of long standing, the Washington Blues, used for armory the third story of a tavern on Library Street, between Fourth and Fifth Streets, which was known as "Military Hall." Before the Civil War they moved to a large building belonging to the owner of the *Public Ledger,* on the north side of Chestnut Street opposite the State House. By the time of the Mexican War they had divided into two companies, both of which were among the 102 Philadelphia companies answering the call for volunteers. Similarly in the Civil War, they were among the earliest volunteers for the first three months' enlistment. In 1913 the Fencibles celebrated their centennial, and published a book to commemorate it: *The State Fencibles, 1813-1913,* by Thomas S. Lanard (Philadelphia, 1913).

The work of FRANCIS MAHAN was exhibited at Franklin Institute in 1847. It probably included the handsomely colored lithograph of the State Fencible in his fine uniform. Not only the drawing, but the uniform itself was undoubtedly of Mahan's design and from his own hand, for he was a master tailor of Philadelphia. He opened his tailoring shop at 215 Chestnut Street in 1829, and in 1837 he added to his title in the City Directory the words, "publisher of Philadelphia fashions." His shop which, when it moved, moved only to other addresses on Chestnut Street, appeared in the Directory until 1870. By 1860 he had dropped the term "tailor," and was variously a "publisher of fashions," a "fashioner," a "fashion reporter," and at the end simply a "publisher." In his last years he made his residence in Camden. The prestige of the State Fencibles was such that it was only natural that they should have themselves outfitted by Philadelphia's self-appointed arbiter of fashion.

H Lewis pinx.

Lith.Jnst Arnz & Cº Düsseldor

PLATE No. 50. *The Battle of Bad Axe, August 2, 1832. Lithograph by Arnz & Co., Düsseldorf, from Lewis's "Das illustrirte Mississippithal," 1857.*

122

Massacre of the Whites by the Indians and Blacks in Florida.

The above is intended to represent the horrid Massacre of the Whites in Florida, in December 1835, and January, February, March and April 1836, whe near Four Hundred (including women and children) fell victims to the barbarity of the Negroes and Indians.

PLATE No. 51. *Massacre of the Whites by the Indians and Blacks in Florida, 1835–36. Wood engraving from "An Authentic Narrative of the Seminole War," 1836.*

123

THE NATIONAL LANCERS WITH THE REVIEWING OFFICERS ON BOSTON COMMON.

Taken from the Original Painting (as designed and executed by C. Hubbard) on the Standard, which was presented to the Company by His Excellency the Governor of Massachusetts, on the 30th of August, 1837.

This Print published by request, is respectfully dedicated to the Corps.   Boston, Sept. 1837.

PLATE No. 52. *The National Lancers with the
Reviewing Officers on Boston Common. Lithograph by Fitz Hugh Lane, 1837.*

124

THE COMPANY OF STATE FENCIBLES
Commanded by Col. James Page.

Entered according to act of Congress in the year 1845 by F. MAHAN, 211, CHESNUT ST: in the Clerk's Office of the District Court of the Eastern District of the State of Pennsylvania.

PLATE No. 53. *The Company of State Fencibles Commanded by Col. James Page. Lithograph by F. Mahan, 1845.*

VI

The Mexican War
1845-1847

WHEN in 1821 Mexico finally established her independence of Spain she inherited the northern borderlands, those outposts of Texas, New Mexico, and California which had been planted by Spanish imperialism in order to keep the other colonizing powers away from the strategic approaches to her choicest provinces. They remained in 1821 much as they had been at the time of their founding, decades or centuries earlier: sparsely settled by white men, and tenuously connected to the centers of administration by long and difficult lines of communication. Upon these outposts the advancing American frontier now threatened to impinge, when Mexico in 1823 committed the supreme unwisdom of admitting into Texas a Trojan Horse in the form of Stephen F. Austin's colony of 200 American families. The natural clash of racial temperaments united with the chronically chaotic state of Mexican administration to bring about a Texan Revolution in 1835, sustained by the victory of San Jacinto in the following year. The United States made no haste to receive Texas as a sister, but finally, after James K. Polk won a presidential campaign on the platform of "reannexation," Congress resolved, on February 18, 1845, to admit Texas as a State of the Union. Mexico had been willing to come to terms with Texas, but not to swallow the fact of annexation, and now, after threatening war, broke off diplomatic relations with the United States. The Texan frontier was in dispute and Polk naturally sent General Taylor with an army to secure the American side, at the same time attempting to reopen negotiations not only for its settlement, but for the purchase of New Mexico and California as well. He took the further precaution of fomenting a revolution among the Americans in California. When Polk's emissary, Slidell, was not received either by the original Mexican government or by the new one which shortly dispossessed it, the President sent Taylor forward from the Nueces to the Rio Grande, over the zone of dispute. The Mexicans attacked on April 25, 1846, and Polk had his war, "by the act of Mexico." It was not, however, war that he had been seeking, but expansion, to be achieved by peaceful means if possible, by warlike ones if necessary. Many Europeans, remembering 1812, expected another piece of military bungling from the Americans, and were quite astonished by the business-like war of conquest which followed. In less than a year and a half an American army was in Mexico City, and the Mexican Republic was prostrate.

PLATE No. 54. *Birds-eye view of the Camp of the Army of Occupation, Commanded by Gen! Taylor. Near Corpus Christi, Texas, (from the North) Oct. 1845. ☆ D. P. Whiting Capt. 7ᵗʰ Inf. Del. Lith. and Printed in Colors by G. & W. Endicott N. York. On Stone by C. Parsons. ☆*

Entered according to act of Congress in the year 1847 by D. P. Whiting in the Clerk's Office of the district Court of the Southern district of New York. [Designations of troops]

Tinted Lithograph. 19½ x 15 inches.

In June 1845, following the break in diplomatic relations with Mexico, Gen. Zachary Taylor was ordered to proceed with that part of our small army which was then concentrated at Fort Jesup, La., to the frontier of newly annexed Texas. In July he established camp 25 miles north of the Rio Grande at Corpus Christi, at the mouth of the Nueces. Here through the fall and most of the winter he watched and waited, while other troops assembled from Florida, Missouri, Mississippi, and Texas, until the entire strength numbered 3,900 men. The camp, although it suited Taylor, was uncomfortable and unsanitary, the men idle, and the higher officers principally concerned with wrangling over precedence. The junior officers alone kept the little army from complete demoralization.

Capt. Daniel Powers Whiting, of the 7th Infantry, was one of these junior officers. Born in Troy, N. Y., in 1808, he had graduated from West Point in 1832, and went to serve on the frontier, and later in the Seminole Wars. For two years of the Second Seminole War he had trained backwoodsmen and recruits at Newport, Ky. At the Military Academy he had received an excellent training in topographical drawing, an important auxiliary to an officer's training, and one for which he had a considerable inclination and talent. In 1848 he published "The Army Portfolio," a series of five lithographs illustrating his Mexican War ex-

perience, printed in color by the lithographic house of Endicott in New York. The drawing of the Camp of the Army of Occupation is the first of the series; the others show later stages in Taylor's campaign, three in Monterey, and one in the valley leading toward Saltillo.

Whiting was brevetted major in April 1847 for gallant and meritorious conduct in the battle of Cerro Gordo, but spent the last year of the Mexican War on recruiting service. He was still a major, 10th Infantry, when the Civil War broke out. On February 15, 1862, he became lieutenant colonel of the 6th Infantry. On November 4, 1863, he was retired from active service for disability resulting from his long service and from exposure in the field. Through most of 1864 he was in command of Fort Mifflin, Pa. He died in 1892.

The artist who drew the design on stone, CHARLES PARSONS (1821–1910), is one of the great names in American lithography. He was brought over as a small boy from England and apprenticed to George Endicott. After the fashion of the day he was taken into Endicott's house, and in two years, by the time he was 14, was promoted to the lithographic department. Eventually he became a partner in the firm. In 1863, after 30 years as a practicing lithographer, during which he had made important contributions to the development of the art, he went to Harper and Brothers as Superintendent of the Art Department. On the staff when he arrived was Alfred R. Waud. Here Parsons gathered around him a group of brilliant young artists as illustrators, such men as Edwin Abbey, Howard Pyle, and Joseph Pennell. To all of them he was both teacher and friend. His own oils and water colors, chiefly marine views and

128

landscapes, have distinction. Joseph Pennell believed that "the growth of real and vital American art started in the department of Mr. Parsons in Franklin Square."

PLATE No. 55. *Battle of Palo Alto, May 8th 1846. ☆ [Above:] Battle of Resaca de la Palma, May 9th 1846. ☆ From Drawings Taken on the Day of the Respective Battles by Ange Paldi 5th Inf. U S A and Respectfully Dedicated to the Colonel of His Regiment General Geo. M. Brooke. ☆ [Designation of troops] ☆ Lith by Klauprech & Menzel Corner of Fifth & Vine St. Cincinnati Published by W. Wiswell.*

Lithograph. Undated. 14⅞ x 19¼ inches.

The soldier artist, ANGE PALDI, is known only as one of the 2,200 Americans of Taylor's command who met the Mexican army at Palo Alto, May 8, 1846, in the first real engagement of the war. Palo Alto lay across the Rio Grande from the fortress of Matamoras, whence the enemy had come in force over the river. The artillery opened the battle and the American batteries were so prompt and effective that great swaths were cut in the Mexican lines even while they were forming. The dry prairie grass was set on fire, and its smoke combined with that of the guns to prevent the armies from getting a clear view of each other. Main honors went to the flying batteries of Ringgold and Duncan, and darkness came down on a field in which Mexican casualties were seven times the American. We had lost only nine killed, 44 wounded, and two missing.

On the morning of May 9th the enemy withdrew on the road to Matamoras, and Taylor, encumbered by his wagon trains—some of the

wagons may be seen in the foreground of Paldi's lower drawing—was able to meet them only after they had taken up an excellent defensive position behind an old river channel. The Resaca Guerrero, from which the battle took its name of Resaca de la Palma, was densely overgrown with chaparral and mesquite, and the Americans, attacking with the bayonet, had to hack their way through the undergrowth to get at their foes. Once through, they attacked so furiously that the less disciplined Mexicans broke and fled in panic. Many drowned as they tried to cross the Rio Grande to Matamoras, whose towers loom in the distance of the upper drawing.

The German-American lithographers, KLAUPRECH AND MENZEL, flourished in Cincinnati during the 'forties and 'fifties. Adolphus Menzel seems to have been the senior partner, though Emil Klauprech's name precedes his in the title of the firm. They very properly specialized in views of Ohio, and their work is appraised by Mr. Peters as "extremely good and interesting"; he laments that no one as yet has made their prints a subject for collection. The placing of the two views one above the other is unusual, and the prints would seem to have been very literal transcriptions of Paldi's sketches.

PLATE No. 56. *Death of Major Ringgold, of the Flying Artillery, at the Battle of Palo Alto, (Texas) May 8th 1846. ☆ Entered according to Act of Congress in the Year 1848, by J. Baillie, in the Clerk's Office of the Dist of N. Y. [In plate:] Nagel del*

Lithograph colored by hand. 8⅝ x 12¼ inches.

Maj. Samuel Ringgold was in command of one wing of the flying artillery which was so largely responsible for the success of Palo Alto. The horse-drawn guns were rushed almost instinctively into the position where they were most needed, and it was against them that the main enemy strength was directed. "Here Ringgold received his death wound. He was mounted at the time, and the shot struck him at right angles, entering the right thigh, passing through the holsters and upper part of the shoulders of his horse, and then striking the left thigh in the same line." So we are told by John Frost, whose highly popular *Pictorial History of Mexico and the Mexican War* was published in 1848. Our lithograph could have been made as an illustration of Frost's sentence. He continues with a high tribute to the dead artilleryman: "Major Ringgold, who fell at the battle of Palo Alto, is entitled to the perpetual remembrance and gratitude of his countrymen, for his exertions in contributing to bring into so high a state of discipline this efficient arm of the service" [the flying artillery.] The dashing Marylander and West Point graduate (class of 1818) who served faithfully in the regular army for many years, and had been brevetted Major in 1838 for meritorious conduct and activity and efficiency in the Seminole War, was accounted one of the best artillery officers in the service. Contrary to the legend of the print, he did not die on the field, but was carried back to Point Isabel, where he lingered for 60 hours. His last words were of his pride in his battery and joy in the victory. He died on the 11th, and was buried next day with full military honors.

The signature *Nagel* appears in the stone; this may have been the Louis Nagel who later

130

had his own lithographic house in partnership with Adam Weingärtner (Plates 21 and 22). The lithograph was printed and issued by JAMES S. BAILLIE, who, after coloring prints for Nathaniel Currier and others, set up in New York a business of his own which derived most of its ideas and methods from Currier. The present one, in the most melodramatic style conceivable—"Grand Opera!," one person exclaimed on first looking at it—is obviously an attempt to out-Currier Currier. But Baillie did not succeed in carrying away the custom of the older firm, and went out of business in 1849 or soon after.

PLATE NO. 57. *Battle of Buena Vista. View of the Battle-Ground and Battle of "The Angostura" Fought near Buena Vista, Mexico February 23ʳᵈ 1847 (Looking S. West.)* ☆ *From a Sketch Taken on the Spot by Major Eaton, Aid de Camp to Genˡ Taylor.* ☆ *Lith. Pub. & Printed in Colors by H. R. Robinson, 142 Nassau Sᵗ N. York. [In plate:] T. Palmer* ☆ *[Copyright notice, 1847].*

Lithograph, printed in color. 18½ x 27⅞ inches.

After Resaca de la Palma Taylor was in a position to invade Mexico, but his progress was slow. In September 1846 he marched inland and took Monterrey, but with heavy losses; and then concluded two months' armistice. On its expiration he moved on to Saltillo, capital of Coahuila. As Santa Anna with a large Mexican force approached, the main army retreated to the heights of Buena Vista, where the Mexicans, 20,000 strong, attacked on February 22 and 23, 1847. Taylor had the advantage of position, with strong batteries posted at La Angostura, a pass in which a creek had caused a network of high gullies, beyond which extended the plateau of Buena Vista. But the vastly superior force of the Mexicans made progress on the first day, and on the second, defeat was averted only by the light artillery of the junior officers, Braxton Bragg and William T. Sherman, and the charge of the Mississippi infantry, under Capt. Jefferson Davis, against the Mexican cavalry.

General Taylor had returned to Saltillo to prepare its defenses, leaving the American command to General Wool. On the late afternoon of the 22d, however, Taylor arrived on the battlefield, presumably accompanied by his aide, Maj. Joseph H. Eaton, from whose sketch of the following day the lithograph was made. It was on the second day that General Taylor seems not to have said, "Give them a little more grape, Mr. Bragg," preferring, according to one who was present, the more persuasive, "Double-shot your guns and give 'em hell!"

JOSEPH H. EATON, of Massachusetts, was a West Pointer (1835) who had served on the frontier in Louisiana, and as an assistant instructor of infantry tactics at West Point. He took part in the military occupation of Texas, and was General Taylor's aid-de-camp throughout the Mexican War. Promoted to captain at the beginning of the war, he was brevetted major for gallant and meritorious conduct at Monterrey, and again rewarded for gallantry at Buena Vista, issuing from that engagement a lieutenant-colonel. For a time after the war he was attached to the Adjutant-General's office, compiling returns, and was later detailed to frontier duty in New Mexico. In 1856 he resigned and made his residence in Chicago, where he supervised the construction of the new U. S. Custom House and Post Office.

There is no record of other works of art from his hand, and although his was presumably an amateur talent, it certainly issued in a very handsome lithograph. The corrugated surface of the mountain presents a tremendous contrast to the activity on the battlefield.

HENRY R. ROBINSON, successively a carver and gilder, caricaturist, and lithographer, was in business in New York from 1833 to 1851. His chief production was political cartoons, of which he turned out a great number—spirited caricatures, usually with long speeches in "balloons" proceeding from the mouths of the subjects, interesting but difficult to understand without close study of contemporary politics. Besides the cartoons Robinson published some interesting and important views. He was a precursor of the tabloid in his prints of crimes and disasters. His first, the pioneer undertaking in the field, was that of the murdered Ellen Jewett in her bed. His example led Nathaniel Currier to produce cartoons on current events.

Robinson rarely mentioned the names of his artists, and it was probably his flair for news that made him wish to attribute the battle print to a military authority whose name would give a flavor of authenticity; otherwise Major Eaton's artistic talent might have remained forever hidden under a bushel.

PLATE No. 58. *General Zachariah Taylor, (Old Rough and Ready.) As he appeared at the battle of Palo Alto: from a sketch by a lieutenant of Artillery.* ☆ *Lith. & Pub. by T. W. Strong 98 Nassau St. N. York.* ☆ *Entered according to Act of Congress, A.D. 1846. by C. J. Pollard, in the Clerk's Office of the District Court of N. York.* [On plate:] *N.º 15.*
Lithograph colored by hand. 9⅞ x 9 inches.

Zachary Taylor, "Old Rough and Ready," after many years of inconspicuous service with the regular army, rose on the tide of his success at Palo Alto, Monterrey, and Buena Vista to become a national hero and was swept into the presidency of the United States at the next election. Some military historians characterize him as inactive, but Justin H. Smith, the historian of our war with Mexico, describes his cool courage as the inspiration of his troops. At Palo Alto, when he was notified of the tremendous Mexican advance, he kept on writing and merely said, "Keep a bright lookout for them." More glowingly still, Smith writes of Buena Vista: "Huddled rather than mounted, a great part of the time, on Old Whitey, with arms folded and one leg unconcernedly thrown across the pommel of his saddle, the conspicuous target of the Mexican artillery yet utterly unmoved even when his clothes were pierced, he was a fountain of courage and energy. In other words, the victory of Buena Vista was due primarily to Taylor's prestige, valor and gift of inspiring confidence."

In spite of the bitter criticisms of most of the regular officers, who thought the general totally incompetent to handle so large an army, his men had faith in Taylor. Such confidence was doubtless felt by the unnamed lieutenant of artillery who sketched with loving detail the general, top hat, epaulettes, spurs, and all, perched on Old Whitey against the background of chaparral.

THOMAS W. STRONG was in business as a lithographer in New York from 1842 to 1851. C. J. POLLARD, who held the New York copyright, may at this time have been associated with Strong. A few years later the gold rush lured him to California, where about 1852 he formed a lithographic partnership with James Britton in San Francisco. A well-known view of San Francisco from Rincon Point is from "C. J. Pollard's Lith."

PLATE No. 59. *A Camp Washing Day.*
Wood engraving. From "The Journal of William H. Richardson, a Private Soldier in the Campaign of New and Old Mexico", Baltimore, John W. Woods, 1848. Frontispiece. 3½ x 5¼ inches.

Col. Alexander W. Doniphan and his First Regiment of Missouri Mounted Volunteers formed part of the separate army group under General Kearny's command, which marched westward from Fort Leavenworth in the summer of 1846 to take possession, peacefully or by force, of northwestern Mexico. Fighting rough country rather than enemy opposition, they reached the old settlements and raised the American flag over Santa Fe on August 22. Kearny with the larger body moved on toward California, and Doniphan's command was detached for an expedition southward. The peaceable Pueblo Indians had come in and submitted to the Great White Father, but Doniphan had to subdue the warlike tribes above Taos, the Eutaws and Navahoes. On December 12, his troops reinforced to 856 men, he began his march from Valverde on the Rio Grande. At El Brazito, near El Paso, he defeated a thousand Mexicans, routed 3,000 across the river at Sacramento, and took and held for two months the capital city of Chihuahua. In the spring the expedition turned eastward through Mexico, joined General Wool at Saltillo, and then embarked for the United States, having completed in 15 months a victorious march of 3,500 miles.

132

Even more than with the hopelessly outclassed foe, their strife had been with mountain, desert and climate.

The young Marylander, William H. Richardson, who is known only through the diary he left of the expedition, had gone from his home in Ann Arundel County for a southern tour. Staying in Carroll County, Missouri, he found his young men acquaintances eagerly signing up as volunteers. "This, together with the enthusiasm which prevailed at a public meeting on the Fourth of July (when the ladies of Carrollton presented the company a beautiful flag, and many speeches were made)—caused me to decide to join the company." They marched to Fort Leavenworth, where they went about learning "the duties of a soldier, such as cooking, drilling, etc." On August 15th young Richardson wrote:

"This was our washing day. I went with the rest of the b'hoys to the branch, where we kindled three large fires, and put up our camp kettles to boil the clothes. I never boiled any before, and I felt pretty much as I did when I began to cook breakfast. I went to work awkwardly enough, as my scalded hands bore witness. But a man can even wash his clothes when he is obliged to do it, the opinions of the ladies to the contrary notwithstanding. In the evening we ceased our labors as washers of clothes, and went into the branch and washed ourselves. After bathing we returned to camp quite refreshed."

Richardson, if we may suppose him to be the awkward laundryman in the foreground of his picture, was then a dapper soldier. His description of himself as he landed on the wharf in New Orleans the next year warrants inclusion:

Upon my head there was no hat, having lost my last remnant overboard in the Gulf. My pants I had thrown away three days before, because (being composed of deerskin, worn into tatters), I despaired of making them look decent. A pair of drawers, rather the worse for wear, and an old overcoat, constituted my dress. If, to this description of my person I add that my hair, beard, and mustachios, had been left to vegetate undisturbed ever since I left Fort Leavenworth, then some idea may be formed of the accomplished soldiers of Colonel Doniphan's command.

PLATE No. 60. *The Island of Lobos. Rendezvous of the U. S. Army under General Scott, previous to the Attack on Vera Cruz, February 9ᵗʰ 1847. Drawn on the spot by Lieut. C. C. Barton U. S. Navy. Published by P. S. Duval, Nᵒ 7 Bank Alley, Philadelphia. ☆ [Inset, centered, with map & description of island] ☆ On stone by H. Dacre. P. S. Duval, Lith. Philadᵃ Entered according to act of Congress in the year 1847, by P. S. Duval, in the Clerk's Office of the District Court of the Eastern District of Pennsylvᵃ ☆ [Designation of ships]*

Lithograph. 16½ x 25¼ inches.

While Taylor at Saltillo in the winter of 1846–47 was marking time—and consenting to his candidacy for the Presidency—the general in chief of the Army, Winfield Scott, prepared the expedition he had planned, with very lukewarm support from the Polk Administration, to strike at the heart of Mexico through Vera Cruz. In February he sailed for Tampico, and assembled his ships and troops at Lobos Island, a dot in the Gulf of Mexico, some two hundred miles north of Vera Cruz. During the last week of February most of the expeditionary force landed on the tiny island and a fleet of nearly a hundred vessels collected within the anchorage.

Lt. Charles C. Barton, whose sketch formed the basis for the Duval lithograph, wrote his description beside the map in the inset:

"Lobos is about one mile round, and a quarter of a mile wide. Covered with Gum and Lime trees, and hugged up on the Southern side by pretty creeping Vines and wild Gourds. The Reefs abound with all sorts of beautiful Fish, the Red Groupa [i. e. grouper], Rock Cod, and a Species of Porgee being prominent."

Smallpox had broken out among the troops, and only the greatest care prevented it from spreading through the tightly packed assemblage, during the week or more spent on the hundred-acre coral strip.

One of Philadelphia's best known lithographers was PETER S. DUVAL, a Frenchman who in 1831 had been "imported" by Childs & Inman, the city's pioneer lithographic company, to superintend their processes. In 1835 he went into business for himself in partnership with the landscape painter and engraver, George Lehman. Lehman left him in 1840, and the firm went on under his name alone until 1893, although he retired in 1879. He was the first lithographer to make a color plate, *Grandpapa's Pet,* for Miss Leslie's Magazine, a work which set a style that, in the calendar line, is still in questionable vogue. The Franklin Institute awarded him prizes for color work in 1850 and 1851. Many of his views are excellent, and

he is considered to hold an important place in American lithography. H. DACRE, one of his workmen, is also highly praised for his drawing on stone. He is responsible for the highly finished reproductions of Lieutenant Barton's two views of the Vera Cruz expedition.

Little information is available about the naval officer, CHARLES C. BARTON, who made the sketches. He had gone into the service as a midshipman in 1824, probably at a very early age, for it was not until 1834 that he achieved the rank of Passed Midshipman. In 1841 he received his lieutenancy. We have no record of his service other than in the Mexican War. He died in 1851.

PLATE NO. 61. *Landing of the U. S. Army under General Scott, on the Beach near Vera Cruz March 9ᵗʰ 1847. Drawn on the Spot by Lieutenant Charles C. Barton, U. S. Navy. ☆ On Stone by H. Dacre. P. S. Duval, Lith. Philadᵃ Published by P. S. Duval, Nº 7 Bank Alley, Philadelphia. ☆ Entered according to act of Congress in the year 1847, by P. S. Duval, in the Clerk's Office of the District Court of the Eastern Dist. of Pᵃ*

Lithograph. 13⅜ x 24 inches.

On March 9, 1847, Scott landed his army of 10,000 men, without a single accident, about three miles southeast of Vera Cruz on the sheltered beach of Mocambo Bay, where the sand reef of Sacrificios Island formed an anchorage. Commodore Conner with the American squadron had arrived on March 5 at Antón Lizardo, a dozen miles beyond Vera Cruz, where the troops had been moved by transport three days before. The Commodore offered his larger ships rather than the clumsy transports, which coördination of navy and army Scott wisely accepted. On the morning of a perfect day the soldiers marched aboard the frigates *Raritan* and *Potomac* and the smaller vessels. The *Massachusetts* with Conner's flagship took the lead. In two hours the fleet was off Sacrificios, where "in close quarters, but without mishaps or even the least confusion, each dropped anchor in its allotted space." The anchorage was full of European vessels; gentlemen and lady travelers with spy-glasses on a British packet, crews of foreign men-of-war, viewed the landing with such interest as our movie-going public has lent to the beachhead operations on Pacific islands.

As the signal flags rose to the main truck of the *Massachusetts,* seven gunboats formed a line within range of the beach and cleared for action. Sixty-five surf boats were rowed by naval crews to the transports and took on 50 to 80 soldiers apiece, the whole of Worth's brigade. A shell whistled overhead from the beach, where Mexican cavalry had been seen and artillery was suspected. The gunboats raked the shore with shells, breaking up the cavalry, and at the flash of a signal gun "the surf boats cut loose, faced the shore abreast in the order of battle, and struck out for land."

Justin Smith's description is vivid:

"Here was the chance of the enemy, for our vessels could not fire without endangering Americans; but no enemy was to be seen. Led by their color-bearers the regulars quickly splashed ashore, formed in a moment, charged to the crest of the first dune, planted their standards and burst into cheers; the men on the ships, tongue-tied for some time by an excitement and anxiety that made their brains reel, answered with huzza after huzza till they made the bay 'seem peopled with victorious armies', wrote one of the soldiers, and the strains of 'Star-Spangled Banner' broke from the bands."

PLATE No. 62. *Landing of the Troops at Vera Cruz. ☆ Lith. & Printed in Colours by Wagner & McGuigan, 116 Chestnut St. Phila.*

Lithograph printed in color. From John Frost, "Pictorial History of Mexico and the Mexican War", Philadelphia, Thomas, Cowperthwait and Co., 1848. Frontispiece. 13½ x 18¼ inches.

John Frost, educator, born in Kennebunk, Maine, January 26, 1800, graduate of Harvard, 1822, schoolmaster in Boston and Philadelphia—principal of a girl's school in the latter place from 1827–36—professor of English literature in the Philadelphia Central High School, 1835–45, LL. D., Franklin & Marshall College, Pennsylvania, 1843, was a hack of the first order. His educational publications, begun in Boston with a compilation, *The Class Book of American Literature* (1826), followed in Philadelphia by *Elements of English Grammar* (1829), the *Youth's Book of the Seasons* (1835), *The Portfolio of Youth, by Robert Ramble* [*pseud.*] (1835), turned to historical themes as early as 1831, when he edited a *History of Ancient and Modern Greece.* In 1836 he wrote a *History of the United States; for the Use of Schools and Academies.* By 1845 he was well established as the author of histories of the Army, the Navy, Indian Wars, the *Heroes and Battles of the Revolution,* all popular subscription books, and retired from his school teaching to head a corps of writers engaged in historical research. Their labors amounted, according to Appleton's Cyclopedia, to "nearly 300 histories and biographies."

It was in 1848, the year of Taylor's presidential campaign, that Frost published his *Pictorial History of Mexico and the Mexican War*. In 1847 he had rushed into print a life of "Old Rough and Ready." It is understandable that the part played by Scott, the general in chief, discredited by the administration and the critical public, should be minimized by Frost. It is, however, a little surprising, in view of the few brief paragraphs devoted to the masterly assault and capture of Vera Cruz, to find as frontispiece of Frost's garishly illustrated book the colored panorama of the landing on the beach west of Isla Sacrificios.

PLATE No. 63. *Bombardment of Vera Cruz, March 1847. Attack of the Gun Boats upon the City, & Castle of San Juan de Ulloa. Commanded by Josiah Tatnall Esq. U. S. N. From a sketch taken on board the Steamer Spitfire, during the action, by J. M. Ladd U. S. N. ☆ [Designation of ships] Lith. & Pub. by N. Currier, 152 Nassau St. Cor. of Spruce N. Y. ☆ Entered according to Act of Congress in the year 1847 by N. Currier, in the Clerk's Office of the District Court of the Southern District of New York.*

Lithograph, colored by hand. 9 x 13¼ inches.

Vera Cruz, the old city founded in 1520 by Cortes, prided itself on being an impregnable fortress. Its great fort of San Juan de Ulloa had been built on a reef in front of the city after it had been twice sacked by pirates in 1653 and 1712. The fort had been greatly strengthened after its capture by the French in 1838, and its guns were formidable.

General Scott was pressed for time—in a month yellow fever would be due. His strategy,

which brought upon him the violent criticism of the young officers eager for an assault and of neutrals whose property was injured in the bombardment, is highly praised by students of war. In spite of orders placed months before, and obstructed from Washington—only 15 carts, a hundred draught horses and one-fifth the ordnance requisitions had arrived—and the fact that Scott was short of "almost every requisite for siege operations," he nevertheless made the best disposition of his limited resources, and on the 22d called on the city to surrender. When the refusal came, the guns of the "mosquito" fleet, two small steamers and five gunboats, and three army batteries on shore opened fire, answered by a blaze of fire from the heavier guns of the castle and the city wall. The bombardment went on through the 23d, day and night, in a continuous burst of flame. Then, unsuspected by the Mexicans, a new battery, constructed by Robert E. Lee, was placed behind an eminence some 800 yards from the city wall. It mounted heavy naval guns, borrowed, with sailors to man them, from the squadron, now commanded by Matthew C. Perry. The guns were unmasked by the morning of the 24th; by the 26th the city, hungry and in panic, surrendered with San Juan de Ulloa still intact. Destruction in the town was great, but deaths few. The British naval commander, critical as he was of Scott's course, reported Mexican casualties as only 80 soldiers killed or wounded, and not over a hundred civilians killed. "The surrender was really due . . . to the moral effect of Scott's artillery" (Justin H. Smith). Although the Mexicans had fired over 6,000 shot and 8,000 shells, to say nothing of bullets, there were only 82 casualties among the besiegers, 19 of them killed.

136

The artist of this Currier print, Midshipman JAMES M. LADD, a boy from the State of Maine, had received his appointment on March 2, 1839. He had seen service on the coast of South America in the suppression of the slave traders on the west coast of Africa, and with the Mediterranean Squadron. In 1844 he had been sent to the Naval School at Philadelphia, graduating as Passed Midshipman on July 2, 1845. In May 1846 he was ordered to the steam gunboat *Spitfire,* under Commander Josiah Tatnall. The action, during which he either made mental notes of the scene or actual sketches, was probably that of March 23, when the seven gunboats of the "Mosquito Fleet" made a sharp but brief attack to divert the Mexicans' attention from the construction of the naval battery on shore.

The *Spitfire* later led the attack against the port of Tuxpan, in which Tatnall was wounded. Ladd may have received a wound or fallen victim to the prevalent fevers. In any event, later in the year he returned to the United States and died in the Naval Hospital at Norfolk, Virginia, on November 26, 1847.

PLATE NO. 64. *[Above:] Naval Portfolio N. 8, Naval Scenes in the Mexican War By H. Walke Lieut. U. S. Navy.* ☆ *The U. S. Naval Battery during the Bombardment of Vera Cruz On the 24 and 25 of March 1847. The Battery was composed of heavy Guns From the U. S. Squadron under Com^{ore} M. C. Perry, and Commanded by the Officers in the following order opposite their respective guns. [Designation of officers and guns]* ☆ *Painted by H. Walke Lt U. S. N. Drawn on Stone by Pfau.* ☆ *Lith. of Sarony & Major N. York.* ☆ *Entered according to Act of Congress in the year 1848 by Sarony & Major*

in the Clerks Office of the district court in the Southern district of N. York.

Tinted Lithograph, colored by hand. 14½ x 22 inches.

H. Walke, Lieutenant, U. S. N., the young artist from whose "scine" of the Vera Cruz action this lithograph was made, was a distinguished naval officer who could tell Grant that he "had fought more for his country than any other officer in the Navy." Born on December 24, 1808, at his father's Virginia plantation, Rear Admiral HENRY WALKE's long life ended only four years before the century. From the academy of Chillicothe, Ohio, where the family had moved during his early childhood, he entered the navy as a midshipman on February 1, 1827. He retired as rear admiral in 1871. He died in Brooklyn, N. Y., March 8, 1896.

Twice during his first years at sea the young midshipman led his men aloft in a hurricane to furl the sails, a feat of bravery that won him some renown. In 1840–43, as lieutenant on the *Boston,* he took part in the round-the-world cruise of Commander Kearny designed to open Chinese markets to American trade. In the Mexican War he served as executive in the bomb-brig *Vesuvius,* and took part in the operations against Tuxpan, Vera Cruz, Alvarado, and Tabasco. During the bombardment of Vera Cruz the *Vesuvius* seems to have been inactive, so Lieutenant Walke presumably had leisure to execute the drawing here shown of the batteries commanded by his fellow officers. His next sketches in the series, those of the Tabasco Expedition, show his brig in action.

In the Civil War, Walke got off to a bad start by incurring censure for his conduct during the surrender of the Pensacola Navy Yard; but afterward redeemed himself by faithful service, first on the Mississippi and its tributaries, and later in pursuit of Confederate raiders on the high seas. He made some excellent pictures of naval operations during that war. In 1877, after his retirement, he published a book, *Naval Scenes and Reminiscences of the Civil War,* illustrated with 27 of his own skillful drawings.

PLATE NO. 65. [*Above:*] *Naval Portfolio. Naval Scenes in The Mexican War By H. Walke Lieut: U. S. Navy (N° 4.)* ☆ *The Attack of the Mexicans from the Chapperal. on the First Division of the Naval Expedition to Tabasco [Mexico.] Consisting of the U. S. Steamer Scorpion Com^{ore} Perry Capt Breese and Com^{er} Bigelo Bomb Brig Vesuvius. Coma^{er} Magruder. Brig Washington, Lieu^t Coma^{er} S. S. Lee. with a Detachment of Seamen and Marines in Barges from the Steam Frigate Mississippi; under, Coma^{er} Mackenzie and H. A. Adams, Marines Commanded by Capt Edson.* ☆ *Published by Sarony & Major 117 Fulton St. N. Y. Lith. of Sarony & Major* ☆ *Designed and Drawn on Stone by H. Walke Lt U. S. N.* ☆ *Entered according to Act of Congress in the year 1848 by Sarony & Major in the Clerks office of the district Court of the Southern district of New York.*

Tinted Lithograph, colored by hand. 14⅜ x 21⅛ inches. [See preceding print]

PLATE NO. 66. [*Above:*] *Naval Portfolio. Naval Scenes in the Mexican War by H. Walke Lieut. U.S.Navy. [N° 6.]* ☆ *The Landing, of the Naval Expedition, against Tabasco. [Mexico.] Com^{ore} M. C. Perry in Command.* ☆ *[Four lines of small type describing action]* ☆ *Painted by H. Walke Lt U. S. N. Drawn on Stone by Volmering &*

Davignon ☆ *Lith. by Sarony & Major Published by Sarony & Major 117 Fulton Street N. Y. Entered according to act of Congress in the year 1848 by Sarony & Major in the Clerks office of the district Court of the Southern district of N. York.*

Tinted Lithograph, colored by hand. 14¾ x 21⅝ inches.

After his brilliant cooperation with the land forces at Vera Cruz, Commodore M. C. Perry was left with no other duties than to blockade enemy merchant shipping. Mexico had no navy to be lured into combat, and almost no fortified ports. Her one other important port on the Gulf, Tuxpan, was taken after short resistance in April 1847. Perry now cruised for prizes. His best chance appeared to be in the southernmost province next to semineutral Yucatan, Tabasco. There contraband trade flourished. Already in the fall of 1846 Perry had sailed up the narrow Tabasco River to the capital city, San Juan Bautista, and had taken a number of prizes, but had not attempted to hold the town. In the summer of 1847 he decided on another Tabasco expedition.

With a flotilla of one brig, one schooner, four small steamers, three bomb-vessels, and rowboats—the ships are named in Walke's first picture—they started on June 14th up the winding jungle stream. The Mexicans had thrown up breastworks at several points along the thickly wooded banks, in the chaparral, that dense impenetrable thicket of thorny brush so characteristic of Mexico and the Southwest. Late next day as the fleet approached the curve called the Devil's Bend, where the river loops snakelike back on itself for several miles, and the chaparral comes down to the very shore, the alert Commodore looked for trouble. It came. From concealment in the brush a hundred muskets blazed a volley, followed by a dropping fire. Bullets pierced awnings, and one sailor on the *Vesuvius* was hit, but after a single burst from the small guns and one 10-inch shell from the big gun of the *Vesuvius,* the Mexicans "vamoosed." The watchful squadron pulled up to the bank and anchored for the night. Walke had time, one presumes, to make notes for his first sketch, a wildly tropical scene.

Next day they started early with more serious action ahead. Beyond the curve of the Devil's Bend and on the upward stretch, obstructions appeared in the stream. Perry dispatched survey boats, which reported fire from the shore and no observable channel. The Commodore decided to take all possible ambushes in the rear, and gave the order to land. The guns raked the shore in a clearing fire, and Perry in his own barge led the way, the first man to spring on the bank. In the second picture the Commodore himself, his sword valiantly drawn, is just in front of the flag planted on top of the slope. The legend below the title on the plate says:

"The landing was effected in 5 minutes, after the Com^ore gave the order (in the face of the enemy, intrenched,) by about 1000. American Seamen and Marines, armed with muskets, and 10 Brass field pieces which were served upon the enemy, after they had been driven from their works by the heavy guns of the Steamer Scorpion Com^ore Bigelow, Steamer Spitfire Lieut. Coma^er S. S. Lee, Steamer Vixen, Lieut. Coma^er Smith, Steamer Scourge Lieut. Coma^ers. Lookwood, and the Schooner Bonita, Lieut. Coma^er Birrien, which covered the landing."

From the landing point Perry marched his men the remaining miles to San Juan Bautista. It was not very far—they were in sight of the town by two p. m., after a longish noontime rest—and the only opposition which they met was at an open space where about a hundred Mexicans had assembled behind a little fort. But they broke and fled at the first American shot, and the landing party found a breakfast of tortillas and corn abandoned in the breastworks. The worst enemy, however, was the heat, which was almost insupportable. The road was a trail through the brush and swamp, and they were taking with them field pieces for which they had to throw corduroy bridges across the streams. The exhausted seamen, many fainting from fatigue, staggered in the hot afternoon sun into the little city, only to find that it had already been taken, with a minimum of effort, by Lieutenant (later Admiral) Porter and the fleet. The landing party had hardly been necessary; the fleet had easily passed by all obstruction. Porter generously welcomed the footsore Commodore by bringing out the band, and to cheers and the strains of "Yankee Doodle" the force marched, "company front," on to the plaza. "A few citizens" welcomed them, and they stayed for six days, making, says Perry's biographer, "ample provision . . . for the honor of the American name."

PLATE No. 67. *The Storming of Chapultepec Sep^t 13th ☆ Drawn on Stone, Printed in Colours, and Published by Sarony & Major. 117 Fulton St. N. Y. ☆ From a Painting by Walker, in the Possession of Capt Roberts U. S. A. ☆ N. Currier 152 Nassau St. N. York [Copyright notice, 1848, by Sarony & Major]*

Lithograph, printed in color. 23½ x 35⅜ inches.

Chapultepec, a steep porphyritic hill rising from the thousand-year-old cypress grove at the southwest gate of the City of Mexico, had been from prehistoric times seat of the rulers of the country. There the Montezumas had their palaces; and there in September 1847 stood strong forts and redoubts surrounding the summer palace of the president of Mexican republic. That president, Santa Anna, had under arms at least twice the number of men at Scott's disposal. The invading army, reduced by battles—Cerro Gordo, Contreras, Churubusco—and still more by sickness, had, in spite of reinforcements, shrunk from its original strength of 10,000 to 7,000. Although the way to the city lay open before his armies, General Scott desired to spare the capital and attempted negotiations with Santa Anna. They had no result and on September 13th Scott gave the order to storm Chapultepec. It was a spectacular hilltop fortress, and was popularly considered to be impregnable; but the keen eyes of Scott's engineers, in particular those of Lieutenant-Colonel Lee, perceived a practicable method of assault.

On the previous day an artillery duel had prepared the way. In the early morning the heavy guns opened again. General Pillow led the van, Quitman and Worth on the flanks, and P. F. Smith in the rear. The infantry advanced and drove in the outlying Mexican troops, but under the fort there was a terrible delay—the scaling ladders had not arrived. The men lay down, helpless under a galling fire, and waited. When at last the ladders came the men surged with an ardor increased by their restiveness up the sides of the fort, and overcame the garrison in a short hand-to-hand struggle. The citadel of Chapultepec was taken, and Mexico City lay at the victors' feet.

The painter JAMES WALKER (1819–89), like a number of the artists represented in this work, was born in England and brought as a child to America. Most of his life was spent in New York, but as a young artist he set off on his travels to find new and exotic scenes for his painting. He was living in Mexico City when the war broke out. As Scott and his army advanced from Vera Cruz, Santa Anna issued an edict banishing all American residents from the city. Walker stayed in hiding for six weeks, and finally escaped to the American lines where he was welcomed and instantly set to work as an interpreter. He came back with the army into the city from which he had fled, and remained during the occupation. In 1848 he returned to New York, only to set off on a visit to South America. At last in 1850 he settled down, opened his New York City studio, and went to work on large canvases, mostly battle paintings. He had been with Scott at Chapultepec, and his impressive picture, from which the lithograph was made, hangs in the Capitol at Washington.

Among Walker's other important battle pictures are several of the Civil War period, including *The Battle of Lookout Mountain,* commissioned by Gen. Joseph Hooker, the hero of the occasion. When in 1884 Walker was asked to paint a large battle picture for a private gallery in San Francisco, he went out to the coast and ended his days there, dying at Watsonville in 1889. Four of his canvases were included in the Exhibition of American Battle Painting at the National Gallery of Art in 1944.

Walke's sketches and Walker's painting were lithographed and published by the well-known house of SARONY AND MAJOR. This was established by the secession from Nathaniel Currier's staff of NAPOLEON SARONY (1821–96) and HENRY B. MAJOR, who entered into partnership in 1846. The first-named was the inspiration and artistic genius of the firm, even after it had been joined by Joseph F. Knapp (1857) and become very large. Sarony, the child of an Austrian father and a French mother, was brought from Quebec to New York when still a child and began artistic work in his teens. He had a considerable talent but was content to exert it in the popular field where the remuneration was more certain. After a beginning with Henry R. Robinson he transferred to the famous shop of Nathaniel Currier where, at the age of 18 or 19, he transferred to stone W. K. Hewitt's drawing of the steamboat *Lexington* disaster, thereby spreading Currier's fame over the country and giving himself a secure standing in the craft. Six years later he and Major went into business for themselves, apparently with the entire good-will of their late employer, the affable Currier, who was associated with them in the publication of our Plate 67, their largest and most important single piece of work.

For decades Napoleon Sarony was one of the best-known and most colorful figures in New York City; in his later years he "delighted to show himself on Broadway in an astrakhan cap, flowing beard and mustache, calfskin waistcoat, hairy side out, and trousers tucked into highly polished cavalry boots." Such attire was the expression of an expansive, eccentric, and Bohemian personality, which found its natural associates among artists and actors, of whom he made dozens of portrait lithographs and hundreds of photographs. He was very successful as a lithographer—the reputation of Sarony and Major was established by their prints of Commodore Matthew Perry's expedition to open up

Japan, and their plant on Broadway was, after the addition of Knapp, one of the largest in the country. Nevertheless in the course of the 1860's he withdrew entirely from lithography, and, after a considerable stay in Europe, opened a photographic gallery on Broadway. His brother, Oliver, was conducting a successful gallery in England, and now Napoleon, one career behind him, made himself "the swell photographer of his day" (Robert Taft). He sought to introduce life and variety into his work by putting his subjects in original and striking poses.

The Walke series, a *Naval Portfolio* of eight prints, are, we believe, among the best lithographs reproduced in this book, and a historical record of great value. They were apparently unknown to Mr. Peters when he compiled *America on Stone;* he must otherwise have singled them out for special praise, both of Walke and of his printers. Of our three prints from this series, one was drawn on stone by Walke himself, who was a versatile naval officer indeed; one by GUSTAVUS PFAU, who also drew portraits for Nagel and Weingärtner; and one by VOLMERING AND D'AVIGNON, a temporary association of Joseph Volmering or Vollmering, a German who had come to New York only the year before and was apparently using this means of getting a start in his career as a painter, and Francis D'Avignon, a "portrait lithographer of very first rank," who came to New York from Paris, and was afterward killed fighting in the Civil War.

PLATE No. 68. *Gen! Scott's entrance into Mexico ☆ C. Nebel fecit. Bayot lith Imp. Lemercier, r. de Seine 57 Paris.*

Lithograph printed in color. From Geo. Wilkins Kendall, "The War between the United States

and Mexico Illustrated", New York, D. Appleton & co. 11 x 16⅞ inches.

On September 14, the day after Chapultepec's fall, the American army marched unopposed into the beautiful capital city from which
Santa Anna and his troops had fled. "As a tri-
umphal procession the command looked rather
strange. Quitman and Smith marched at its
head on foot—the former with only one shoe;
and behind them came troops decorated with
mud, the red stains of battle and rough bandages, carrying arms at quite haphazard angles"
(Justin H. Smith). The scene in the great Plaza
before the Palace and Cathedral was depicted
by the architect CARL NEBEL, who kindly
ignores any deficiencies in American appearances. General Scott, however, appeared in full
uniform on his bay charger, so brilliant a figure
that he won the involuntary applause of the
Mexican crowds. Nebel was an old hand at
Mexican scenes; he had made a five-year tour,
studying archaeology and sketching, in 1829–
34, and had published a book of 50 large lithographic plates with explanatory text, *Voyage
pittoresque et archéologique dans la partie la
plus intéressante du Mexique*, Paris, 1836. A
Spanish edition appeared in Paris and Mexico
City in 1839. The plates are mainly views; a
few, however, depict the natives, with special
attention to costume. About half are in color.
One of the views shows the Plaza, but from a
different angle from that of the present lithograph. Armed with this experience, Nebel accompanied the armies and was present at every
major battle of the Mexican War except Buena
Vista, when he was presumably preparing to
follow the campaign about to open to the southward. From his sketches was made another

lithographic picture-book, *The War between
the United States and Mexico Illustrated,* with a
text by G. W. Kendall, published at New York
in 1851. The plate which we have reproduced is
considerably the most handsome in the book,
which was not a very satisfactory production
from a technical point of view. Nebel eventually
returned to Germany and died at Frankfort in
1865.

ADOLPHE JEAN-BAPTISTE BAYOT (b. 1810)
was known in Paris as a *genre* painter and exhibited in the Salons in 1863–66. He was, however, more successful as a lithographer.

PLATE No. 69. *General Winfield Scott.* ☆ *Lith.
of G. & W. Endicott. N⁰ 59 Beekman Sᵗ N. Y.* ☆
*Entered according to Act of Congress in the
year 1846 by A. S. Barnes & Cᵒ in the Clerks
Office of the District Court of the Southern District of New York.*

Lithograph. 23¾ x 15⅝ inches.

Winfield Scott, whom a historian of the United
States army calls "second to no leader in
our history," was a Whig in politics and so not
persona grata to the Democratic administration.
The general in chief of the United States Army,
a national hero since Lundy's Lane in 1814, and
the successful pacificator of Indian nations and
of Canadian neighbors, had also been since 1839
a Whig Presidential possibility. Called "Old
Fuss and Feathers" for his punctiliousness in
dress and decorum, outspoken in beliefs and
rhetorical in speech, he was not well equipped
for political success in the post-Jacksonian era.
In that period of furious partisanship the President, James K. Polk, lost no opportunity to reduce Scott's prestige. In consequence, says

W. A. Ganoe, he was "hindered more by the administration at home than the enemy in front."

His brilliant Mexican campaign was conducted with little or no error, with minimum loss of life and time. His administration of the conquered nation, called "noble" by Mexican historians, was so firm and humane that after the capitulation a deputation approached him with the proposition that after the ratification of peace he proclaim himself dictator of Mexico. Reports of this offer did him no good at home. In spite of his generosity to the officers below him, Generals Pillow and Worth and Col. James Duncan tried to undercut him, and were placed under arrest by the commander. Justin Smith explains their motives. Worth, Pillow, and the others were convinced that the next President would be a military man, as indeed he was. " 'Since we cannot attain to greatness, let us revenge ourselves by railing at it,' said Montaigne . . . and many of the officers knew that greatness was beyond their power. None of them could monologue as Scott did; none could look in a cocked hat as he looked [he stood six feet five]; none had won the Mexican War; and moreover, he was the sole general-in-chief."

Polk, who also lacked largeness, peremptorily relieved Scott, and the general was called home in disgrace—having performed his task, commented Robert E. Lee, he was "turned out as an old horse to die." In spite of many public honors, an unprecedented ovation in New York City, congressional thanks, medals and a resolution to tender him the rank of lieutenant general, political opposition was such that he did not receive that office—which he was first to hold since Washington—until 1852. As Whig candidate for the presidency in that year, he was overwhelmingly defeated by Franklin Pierce.

PLATE No. 70. *The Sailor's Return. 15. ☆ Lith. & Pub. by N. Currier, 152 Nassau St. Cor. of Spruce N. Y. ☆ Entered according to Act of Congress in the year 1847 by N. Currier, in the Clerk's office of the District Court of the Southern District of N. Y.*

Lithograph, colored by hand. 11⅞ x 8⅛ inches.

PLATE No. 71. *Soldier's Return. 13. ☆ Lith. & Pub. by N. Currier, 152 Nassau St. Cor. of Spruce St. N. Y. ☆ Entered according to Act of Congress in the year 1847 by N. Currier, in the Clerk's office of the District Court of the Southern District of N. Y.*

Lithograph, colored by hand. 11½ x 8¼ inches.

We conclude our section on the Mexican War with a brace of Currier and Ives Sentimentals. Properly speaking, they are merely Currier Sentimentals, for JAMES MERRITT IVES (1824–95) did not become a partner in the firm of NATHANIEL CURRIER (1813–88) until 1857. But our term is nevertheless not misleading, for although Mr. Ives made substantial contribution to the firm's vigor and stability, he did not change its character or the nature of its output; and any print from the house which dominated American popular lithography for half a century can with propriety be referred to, from the name by which the firm came to be best known, as a Currier and Ives print. With equal propriety one should not speak of Currier and Ives without also speaking of that prince of lithograph-collectors, student and repopularizer of the once popular, Mr. Harry T. Peters. The original edition of his *Currier and Ives, Printmakers to the American People* (2 volumes, New York, 1929–31) contains all that you know or need to know about the firm; the popular edition (New York, 1942) makes available at a modest price a representative gallery of reproductions, as well as the essential facts. Mr. Peters' *America on Stone* (1931) is an indispensable compendium of information concerning all the other lithographers of America beside Currier and Ives; outside its covers there is practically none, and we are happy to acknowledge our indebtedness to this source for the greater part of what we have to say concerning American lithography. Finally, his *California on Stone* (1935) is a splendid album as well as catalogue of lithographic prints illustrating a particular region, and a particularly colorful one.

Nathaniel Currier got in on the ground floor of American lithography. Some four or five years after the first American experiments in the process, William S. Pendleton and his brother John began the first commercially successful production of lithographic prints in Boston, and four years later, in 1828, they hired Nathaniel, a boy of 15, as apprentice to their French pressman. Six years later, in 1834, young Currier entered business for himself in New York City. In the following year, he found his specialty, the journalistic print, with plates of the burnt-down Merchant's Exchange in New York and the collapsed Planters' Hotel in New Orleans; and in five years more, in 1840 when he was still only 27, he achieved nation-wide fame and assured success with the print of the steamboat *Lexington* disaster. In the great days of the firm, which may be taken as extending from shortly after 1840 through the 1870's at

least, its peddlers and agents spread the Currier and Ives prints, priced for all pockets from six cents to three dollars for the largest and most elaborate, through the city and through the nation. There were many lithographic houses in America, but, says Mr. Peters, "the fact remains that none of these houses, or indeed not all of them together, had a list that could be compared either in variety of subject or in quality of workmanship with that of Currier and Ives." But this deserved success and the business methods which made it possible contained within themselves the seeds of decay. The popular lithographic print, in Currier and Ives hands and out of them, as it became increasingly commercialized and mass-produced, lost first its individuality and finally all artistic quality whatever. From the end of the century we shall have some horrible examples to show, not for pleasure or truth, but as specimens and curiosities.

Currier and Ives are the acknowledged masters of American *genre,* but unless we are much mistaken, they achieved no peculiar excellence in the historical print. The very qualities of homeliness and gentle realism which made them unsurpassed reflectors of the ordinary, day-to-day life of America handicapped them in dealing with the tense moments of war and battle. Such scenes require a certain amount of dignity, elevation, concentration, and austerity, and such were not the ordinary stock in trade of Mr. Currier and Mr. Ives. We have reproduced a number of their prints (eight altogether; Plates 41, 63, 67, 73, 80, and 92 in addition to the present pair), and we do not think our readers will consider these to outshine the contemporary lithographs of other firms. One, indeed, The Second Battle of Bull

Run (Plate 80) we give merely as a horrible example, and it can be matched by another, equally characterless, print of the Battle of Fair Oaks reproduced by Mr. Peters in Plate 128 of his 1942 *Currier and Ives*.

We prefer, therefore, to offer the faded Victorian charm of these two "Sentimentals" as more characteristic contributions of the house of Currier and Ives to our subject. Of their pop-ularity in their day no doubt can be entertained. In Mr. Peters' album just cited there are four alternative renderings of the same not very subtle theme, three from the period of the Mexican War and one, with uniform altered but sentiment unchanged, from the Civil War (his Plates 5 and 6). Why should they not have been popular? Who is it that G. I. Joe in 1946 comes home to see?

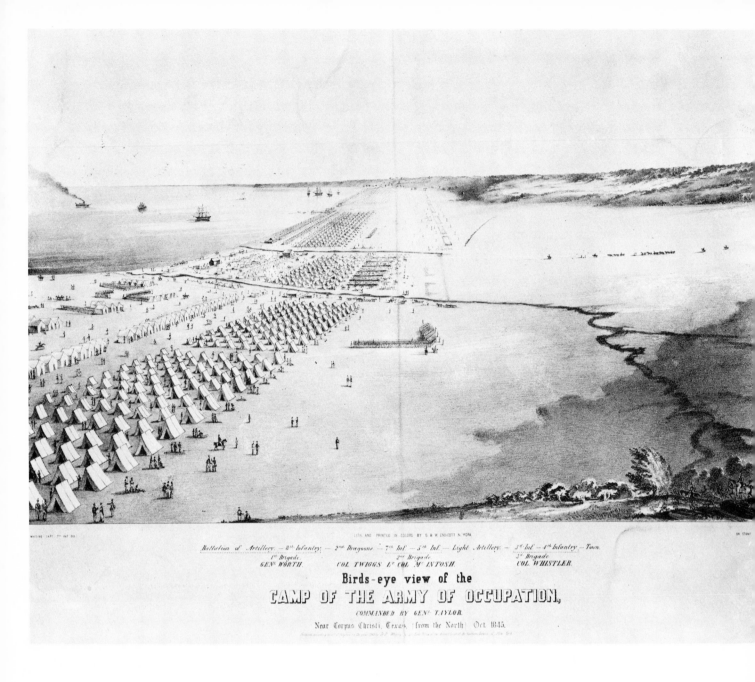

Battalion of Artillery. — 8th Infantry. — 2nd Dragoons. — 7th Inf — 5th Inf. — Light Artillery. — 3d Inf — 4th Infantry. — Town.

1st Brigade.   2nd Brigade   3d Brigade
GENL WORTH.   COL TWIGGS LT COL MC INTOSH.   COL WHISTLER.

Birds-eye view of the

CAMP OF THE ARMY OF OCCUPATION,

COMMANDED BY GENL TAYLOR.

Near Corpus Christi, Texas. (from the North) Oct. 1845.

PLATE No. 54. *Birds-eye View of the Camp of the Army of Occupation Commanded by General Taylor, October 1845. Lithograph by Charles Parsons, 1847.*

146

BATTLE OF RESACA DE LA PALMA,
MAY 9TH 1846.

BATTLE OF PALO ALTO,
MAY 8TH 1846

PLATE No. 55. *Battle of Palo Alto, May 8; Battle of Resaca de la Palma, May 9, 1846. Lithograph by Klauprech and Menzel.*

147

DEATH OF MAJOR RINGGOLD,
OF THE FLYING ARTILLERY, AT THE BATTLE OF PALO ALTO, (TEXAS) MAY 8th 1846.

PLATE No. 56. *Death of Major Ringgold, of the
Flying Artillery, at the Battle of Palo Alto, May
8, 1846. Lithograph by Nagel 1848.*

148

BATTLE OF BUENA VISTA.

VIEW OF THE BATTLE-GROUND AND BATTLE OF "THE ANGOSTURA" FOUGHT NEAR BUENA VISTA, MEXICO FEBRUARY 23.RD 1847. (LOOKING S. WEST.)

PLATE No. 57. *Battle of Buena Vista, February 23, 1847. Lithograph by Henry R. Robinson, 1847.*

GENERAL ZACHARIAH TAYLOR, (OLD ROUGH AND READY.)

As he appeared at the battle of Palo Alto: from a sketch by a lieutenant of Artillery.

PLATE No. 58. *Gen. Zachariah Taylor (Old Rough and Ready), as He Appeared at the Battle of Palo Alto, May 8, 1846. Lithograph by C. J. Pollard, 1846.*

150

A CAMP WASHING DAY.

PLATE No. 59. *A Camp Washing Day, August 15, 1846. Wood engraving from The Journal of William H. Richardson, 1848.*

On Stone by H. Dacre.

1 *Transport with Troops.* 2 *Transport with Troops.* 3 *Transport with Troops.*

THE ISLAND

Rendezvous of the U.S. Army under General Scott, previous

Drawn on the spot by

Published by P.S Duval, N°7

OF LOBOS.

to the Attack on Vera Cruz, February 9th 1847.

Lieut. C.C.Bartan U.S. Navy.

Bank Alley, Philadelphia.

4 *Transport with Troops.* 5 *St Marys.*

P.S. Duval Lith. Philad.ª

PLATE No. 60. *The Island of Lobos, Rendezvous
of the U. S. Army under General Scott, previous
to the Attack on Vera Cruz, February 9, 1847.
Lithograph by H. Dacre, 1847.*

152

LANDING OF THE U.S. ARMY UNDER GENERAL SCOTT, ON THE BEACH NEAR VERA CRUZ MARCH 9TH 1847.

Drawn on the Spot by Lieutenant Charles C. Barton, U.S. Navy.

Published by P.S. Duval, No. 7 Bank Alley, Philadelphia.

PLATE No. 61. *Landing of the U.S. Army under General Scott, on the Beach near Vera Cruz, March 9, 1847. Lithograph by H. Dacre, 1847.*

153

LANDING OF THE TROOPS AT VERA CRUZ.

PLATE No. 62. *Landing of the Troops at Vera
Cruz. Lithograph by Wagner and McGuigan,
from Frost's "Pictorial History of the Mexican
War,"* 1848.

154

PUB. BY N. CURRIER.
Falcon. L! Glasson.   Reefer. L! Sterett.   Entered according to Act of Congress in the year 1847 by N! Currier, in the Clerk's office of the District Court of the Southern District of New York.
Vixen. Comd. Sands.   Petrel. L! Shaw.   Bonita. L! Benham.   Spitfire. Comd. Tatnall.   Tampico. L! Griffin.   146 NASSAU ST. COR. OF SPRUCE N!

BOMBARDMENT OF VERA CRUZ, MARCH 1847

ATTACK OF THE GUN BOATS UPON THE CITY, & CASTLE OF SAN JUAN DE ULLOA.

COMMANDED BY JOSIAH TATNALL ESQ. U.S.N.

From a sketch taken on board the Steamer Spitfire, during the action, by J.M. Ladd U.S.N.

PLATE No. 63. *Bombardment of Vera Cruz, March 1847: Attack of the Gun Boats upon the City and Castle. Lithograph by Nathaniel Currier, 1847.*

155

PLATE No. 64. *The U. S. Naval Battery during the Bombardment of Vera Cruz, March 24–25, 1847. Lithograph by Gustavus Pfau, 1848.*

156

PLATE No. 65. *The Attack of the Mexicans from the Chapperal on the First Division of the Naval Expedition to Tabasco, June 15, 1847. Lithograph by Henry Walke, 1848.*

157

PLATE No. 66. *The Landing of the Naval Expedition against Tabasco, June 16, 1847. Lithograph by Joseph Volmering and Francis D'Avignon, after Walke, 1848.*

158

PLATE No. 67. *The Storming of Chapultepec,*
September 13, 1847. Lithograph by Sarony &
Major, 1848.

PLATE No. 68. *General Scott's Entry into Mexico City, September 14, 1847. Lithograph by Adolphe J.-B. Bayot, from Kendall's "War between the U. S. and Mexico, Illustrated," 1851.*

160

GENERAL WINFIELD SCOTT.

PLATE No. 69. *Gen. Winfield Scott. Lithograph by G. & W. Endicott, 1846.*

LITH. & PUB. BY N. CURRIER, *Entered according to Act of Congress in the year 1847 by N. Currier, in the Clerk's office of the District Court of the Southern District of N.Y.* 152 NASSAU ST. COR. OF SPRUCE N.Y.

THE SAILOR'S RETURN.

PLATE No. 70. *The Sailor's Return. Lithograph by Nathaniel Currier, 1847.*

SOLDIER'S RETURN.

PLATE NO. 71. *Soldier's Return. Lithograph by Nathaniel Currier, 1847.*

VII

The Civil War
1861-1865

APART from the recurrent Indian wars, which concerned only the outermost layer of the population, and the brief, triumphant interlude of the Mexican War, the United States had enjoyed nearly half a century of peace. But now the question became increasingly insistent whether the United States, in any real and national sense, existed. The grand problem of Slavery had always been troublesome in a nation that had established itself upon Jefferson's Declaration of Independence, and most of the Southern Founders had looked upon it as an evil that had to be presently endured, but ought to be progressively lessened and eventually done away with. After Whitney's cotton gin had led the South to change its mind on the subject, and brought it into an inconvenient dependence on a single staple, there did exist an irrepressible conflict, and the only question was whether statesmanship could prevent its taking a violent and military form. The Slavery issue was compromised in 1820 and again in 1850, but there was no easing of tension during the fifties. In 1854 a too clever presidential aspirant from Illinois destroyed the second compromise by his Kansas-Nebraska Act, and the North, aroused at last, became politically aggressive. Six years later the Democratic Party split, and "Black Republicans," led by an almost unknown attorney from Springfield, Ill., carried the national elections. Almost at once the fiery State of South Carolina met in convention and seceded from the Union, and the rest of the Southern States followed at intervals, while a bewildered President looked helplessly on at the dissolution of the Union he was sworn to protect.

There were to be four long and terrible years of a brothers' war. The South had a naturally military population and superior generalship, especially that of Robert E. Lee, one of the tactical geniuses of history. The Union, in army and administration alike, fumbled and stumbled. But, apart from the possibility of overwhelming defeat in battle, everything was on the side of the Union: numbers, industrial and food resources, transportation, sea power and communication with the rest of the world. After disasters such as First and Second Bull Run, Fredericksburg, and Chancellorsville, and disappointments and lost opportunities without number, the tide began to turn in July 1863. Meade inflicted a bloody check upon Lee at Gettysburg, and Grant captured the stronghold of Vicksburg on the Mississippi. Grant now came East, and, while directing a coherent forward movement of all the Federal armies, himself engaged Lee in mid-Virginia. The Confederacy struggled with a bravery and tenacity never surpassed on this planet, but its road lay steadily downhill to Appomatox.

In this section we present the greatest number of our plates from any single hand—16 pencil-and-wash drawings by ALFRED R.

WAUD. When Pvt. Lincoln Kirstein was making his survey of materials for the Battle Art Exhibitions, it at once became apparent to him, and has since been fairly obvious to everyone else concerned, that Alfred Waud is one of the most important illustrators of American history that we have, and that in its collection of his drawings the Library of Congress has a great and a singularly neglected treasure. But who has ever heard of Alfred R. Waud?—we do not even know his middle name. There are, we think, several reasons for his undeserved but almost complete obscurity. In the first place, Alfred Waud's drawings were made for publication in *Harper's Weekly,* in the course of which they were turned into wood engravings—commercial "quickies"—and lost, as a rule, every atom of their individuality and artistic value. Even the superior reproductions in *Battles and Leaders of the Civil War* retain almost nothing of the quality of the originals. In the second, Waud's style was not one likely to impress his contemporaries: instead of the mid-Victorian heavy finish, he employed a quick, light touch, an impressionism and even a shorthand which are thoroughly modern and are characteristic of drawings made 50 years later. We are not claiming, of course, that Waud's drawings are comparable to Raphael's or Michelangelo's; but we are certain that, considering their purpose and the conditions under which they were made, they are very, very good by any standards. Finally, the drawings came to the Library just after the First World War, and the twenties had their attentions focussed on a different sphere of art. In 1937, however, Prof. J. G. Randall used some of them as illustrations in that nonpareil among our historical textbooks, *The Civil War and Reconstruction;*

although he seems to have preferred Forbes.

The Alfred Waud drawings are a part of the J. Pierpont Morgan Collection, presented to the Library of Congress by the financier and connoisseur in 1918. The Collection also includes drawings by Alfred's brother, WILLIAM WAUD, likewise an able artist if less gifted than his brother, and by the much better known EDWIN FORBES. We reproduce three drawings by William Waud, two of which illustrate his characteristic and skillful use of wash; and two drawings (one a double plate) and one etching by Forbes. In spite of their greater reputation, Forbes' pencil drawings will not stand comparison with the Wauds'; in that light they appear as heavy, stiff, lifeless, and uninspired. Nevertheless, he remains an important illustrator, and occasionally rose above himself, as in Plate 99.

At present we know little about Alfred Waud's life and career, although it is a subject which the Library proposes to investigate further. *Appleton's Annual Cyclopedia* for 1891 carried an obituary from which we learn that he was an Englishman, born in London in 1828, and that he received his artistic education there. Coming to New York in 1858, he exhibited at the National Academy of Design, but made his living as an illustrator of periodicals and books. After the war broke out came the great opportunity of his life, as "special artist" or pictorial correspondent for *Harper's Weekly.* We have a letter (July 5, 1862) written by him soon after the Peninsular Campaign. He has barely recovered from a "billious remittent fever—brought on by exposure to the damned climate in the cussed swamps," but outlines the dreadful hardships of the Seven Days' Battles: "Only think of it, seven days almost without food or sleep, night and day being attacked by overwhelming masses of infuriated rebels, thundering at us from all sides . . ." From this letter as well as various contributions to *Harper's* it is clear that he could express himself in words as well as in pictures. He seems to have formed a particular friendship with the able General Gouverneur K. Warren, who 15 years later called for his help in clearing up the question of Warren's supersession at Five Forks. General Patrick complimented him for having never incorporated in his sketches any information which could be of service to the enemy. After the war Gen. O. O. Howard recommended Waud to the agents of the Freedman's Bureau as a man whom he had found, when he was in command of the Army of the Tennessee, "to be a genial, educated gentleman," and one worthy of all confidence. In 1868 Charles Parsons of Harper's Art Department recommended him to all and sundry as a gentleman competent to execute book or other illustration. In the eighties Alfred Waud contributed his sketches to illustrate the series of articles in the *Century* which became *Battles and Leaders of the Civil War,* but he was given no preëminence among the numerous artists who contributed to that unique work. In 1891, according to the obituary already quoted, he "was making an extended sketching tour of the battlefields in the South" when he died, on April 6, at Marietta, Ga.

Of William Waud we can say even less. We have a letter (October 3, 1864) from him to Alfred, showing that he and his brother were on the most affectionate terms. In the spring of 1862 he went to cover Butler's expedition to New Orleans for *Frank Leslie's Illustrated Newspaper,* which printed a picture of him, complete with bowler hat, sketching in the fore-

top of one of Farragut's big ships. Had we found it in time, we should have reproduced it here. He returned to sketch for *Leslie's* the Peninsular Campaign which his brother was covering for *Harper's* but was disabled by sunstroke and fever. In 1864, by which time he had joined his brother on the staff of *Harper's,* he lost his clothes, blankets and sketchbook in a Confederate raid, and Alfred sent him fresh drawing materials. Whether after the war he remained in America or returned to England we cannot say.

Louis J. M. Daguerre announced his epoch-making discovery in January 1839, and within a few years it had spread all through the Western world, and was making the fortunes of those sagacious individuals who had early mastered its technique. A few daguerreotypes were made during the Mexican War, probably by a Mexican practitioner. One of these dim but fascinating relics is reproduced on page 225 of Robert Taft's *Photography and the American Scene.* In Europe, there was considerable photography of the Crimean War (1855), but the first American war to be extensively recorded by the camera was the Civil War. That it was so was almost entirely the work of one man, MATHEW B. BRADY (c. 1823–96), "the most prominent name in the whole history of American photography." Brady entered upon his Civil War work in the spirit of a sacred duty; there was no material reason why he should have sought the dust and danger of the battlefield. He was the most fashionable and prosperous photographer in New York City, or in the country, and generals, admirals, and heroes would have come to sit for him either there or at his Washington gallery. But, as he said, "I felt that I had to go. A spirit in my feet said 'go' and I went."

To Bull Run he went in 1861, getting as far as Blackburne's Ford, and there, as the *American Journal of Photography* reported in its August number, with the rest of our Grand Army he was completely routed. He managed to salvage his wagons of equipment, but in a battered condition. Thereafter he organized the business of photographing the war on a large scale; since he could not be everywhere himself he hired a staff of photographers, at times employing as many as 20 men, and made a total investment of well over $100,000. Although at his Washington headquarters he was sufficiently busy in directing his field workers as well as his two galleries, he went to the battlefield when he got wind of important operations: he came under fire at Fredericksburg in 1862 and Petersburg in 1864, and he reached Antietam and Gettysburg before there had been time to bury the dead. He and his staff are thought to have taken more than 3,500 negatives, a tremendous documentation of the utmost variety, every possible kind of scene, in fact, where there was not actual motion—to photograph bodies in motion was a task beyond the slow cameras of Brady's day.

It is sad to have to record that Brady was financially ruined by his creation of what should have been, and now is, regarded as a national heritage. The Government eventually paid him $25,000 for a part of his collection of negatives, too late to break his fall into bankruptcy; the other part had to be disposed of in payment of a debt for photographic supplies. Brady's last years were spent most undeservedly in labor, illness, and poverty. The part of his collection purchased by the Government is now in the National Archives, while the other part,

long in private hands, has very recently been acquired by the Library of Congress. This part also includes the Alexander Gardner Collection of negatives, purchased and incorporated with it at a later date. If we have included relatively few Civil War photographs, it is not because we underrate their documentary value; it is merely that many of them are not precisely art, and that the whole *corpus* has been effectively exploited in such works as the 10-volume *Photographic History of the Civil War,* edited by Francis T. Miller (New York, 1911).

PLATE No. 72. *Negroes mounting Cannon in the works for the attack on Ft. Sumter 1861— Morris Island.* ☆ W. Waud.

Wash drawing. March, 1861. On green tinted paper. 9¼ x 13 inches.

PLATE No. 73. *Interior of Fort Sumter. During the Bombardment, April 12ᵗʰ 1861.* ☆ *Published by Currier & Ives, 152 Nassau Sᵗ New York.*

Lithograph, colored by hand. 8⅜ x 11¾ inches.

1861. The backwoods lawyer took his oath as Chief Executive of the United States. He said in his inaugural address: "The power confided to me will be used to hold, occupy and possess the the property and places belonging to the government . . . but beyond what may be necessary for these objects, there will be . . . no using of force . . ."

On April 12 the irrepressible conflict broke out. Fort Sumter stood in the middle of the entrance to Charleston Harbor. Fort Johnson, opposing her, had been already seized by the authorities of the first secession State, South

Carolina. The surrender of Sumter had been demanded and refused. The Confederate States of America had adopted a constitution. President Lincoln was readying an expedition from New York for the relief of Fort Sumter. On April 11 General Beauregard demanded the evacuation of the fort, and Maj. Robert Anderson, in command of the skeleton garrison of 65 men, refused. At 4:30 the next morning Forts Johnson and Moultrie and the batteries on Morris and Sullivan's Islands opened fire.

According to Capt. (later General) Abner Doubleday, one of Anderson's officers and author of the article, "From Moultrie to Sumter," in *Battles and Leaders of the Civil War,* "We have not been in the habit of regarding the signal shell fired from Fort Johnson as the first gun of the conflict, although it was undoubtedly aimed at Fort Sumter. Edmund Ruffin of Virginia is usually credited with opening the attack by firing the first gun from the iron-clad battery on Morris Island. The ball from that gun struck the wall of the magazine where I was lying, penetrated the masonry, and burst very near my head."

The bombardment lasted through 40 hours, without casualties but with great damage by fire to the inflammable structures within the fort. By evening of the 13th Sumter's ammunition was nearly exhausted. At seven o'clock terms of surrender were agreed upon. Major Anderson's handful of Union troops marched out the ruined walls next day, saluting the Stars and Stripes with a volley of 50 guns.

PLATE No 74. *[General Scott and his Staff: Gen. Winfield Scott, Colonel Van Rensselaer, Lieutenant Colonel Cullom, Lieutenant Colonel Hamilton]*

Pencil and wash drawing by A. R. Waud. Undated. 10 x 14½ inches.

PLATE No. 75. *Washington Navy Yard 1861* ☆ *A. R. Waud.*
Pencil and wash drawing. 5¾ x 9 inches.

"Winfield Scott, General-in-chief of the U. S. Army, infirm in body but robust in mind, advised the President that at least 300,000 men, a general of Wolfe's capacity, and two or three years' time would be required to conquer even the lower South" (Morison & Commager). But that was not the attitude of the man in the street or of the Administration. Lincoln's proclamation of April 15, 1861, called for only 75000 volunteers, for three months, to reinforce a regular army which during the months of secession between December 1860 and March 4, 1861 had shrunk from 16,367 officers and men to 13,024. Most disastrous of all, of the 900-odd West Point officers in the service, 269 had resigned and 26 had been dismissed to join the Confederacy. One hundred and eighty-two officers who held during the war the rank of brigadier general or higher, were furnished to the South from the United States Army.

The Confederacy had at its head a trained soldier, Jefferson Davis. A month before Fort Sumter he had called for 100,000 12-month volunteers. Southerners were horsemen, used to handling weapons, and inspired by what they felt to be the cause of freedom. They did not care for discipline, and their social system provided too many officers, but for leaders they had such men as Beauregard, the two Johnstons, Thomas J. Jackson, the two Hills, and J. E. B. Stuart. Robert E. Lee had refused the offer of supreme field command made him by his former chief, Scott, and had gone with the

State of Virginia to which he felt the higher allegiance.

At Lincoln's call the State militia and the volunteers tumbled over themselves in patriotic enthusiasm and Zouave uniforms. Officers were appointed by the State governors, or elected by the untrained recruits themselves. Able young officers of the regular army, men like Philip Sheridan, were not permitted to leave their own units and provide a stiffening in the regiments of the heterogeneous new masses—farmer boys, factory workers and city clerks, many of whom had never held a gun in their hands. McClellan, Grant, Sheridan, many other former West Pointers, were returning obscurely to the army from civil life. In short, the South had several months' head start, and Gen. Winfield Scott, as Alfred Waud has drawn him behind his council table, was perfectly cognizant of the fact. Shown with the septuagenarian general are three members of his staff, Cols. George Washington Cullum, who later compiled the register of West Point graduates, Schuyler Hamilton, and Henry Van Rensselaer.

Naval affairs, on the other hand, were weighted on the Union side. The Confederacy came into the war with no navy and few important seaports. The resourcefulness of the naval officers who "went South" produced a few ships, but Federal superiority at sea was as nearly absolute throughout the war as at the beginning. The few Confederate raiders raised Northern insurance rates skyhigh, and British sympathy for the South and competition for the carrying trade, while it nearly ruined the U. S. merchant marine, had little military effect.

In mid-March, 1861 the U. S. Navy had a total of 90 ships, of which only 42 were in commission, and of these only 12 in the Home Squadron. Soon after the inauguration orders went to 15 vessels, most of the steam ships of the fleet, to return from the foreign stations where they were scattered—report said by the evil intent of the late Secretary of the Navy, Isaac Toucey—and repairs and new construction began in the shipyards. Waud's charming sketch of the Washington Navy Yard shows this renewed activity—chimneys smoking, small boats going to and fro, a large ship having its mast re-stepped, and a new hull nearing completion in the totally closed way.

PLATE No. 76. *Capture of the Forts at Hatteras inlet—First day, fleet opening fire and troops landing in the surf.* ☆ *[Designation of ships and forts]* ☆ *Alf Waud.*

Pencil and wash drawing on light green paper. Undated. 9 x 13¾ inches.

On the 19th and 27th of April President Lincoln issued two proclamations which declared the coast of the new Confederacy under blockade, from Washington down the Potomac, through the Chesapeake Bay to the sea, south on the Atlantic and West on the Gulf, to that same extreme tip of Texas where Matthew Calbraith Perry's squadron had rested 14 years before. It was time; President Davis had authorized privateering, and the daring sea raiders were soon to be at work. Off the Mississippi river, out of Charleston, out of Hatteras Inlet the *Calhoun,* the *Jefferson Davis,* the North Carolina ships *Winslow, Raleigh,* and *Beaufort* operated with increasing success, and increasing alarm among Northern shipowners.

At Hatteras Inlet on Pamlico Sound there stood two small forts, Clark and Hatteras, which protected the comings and goings of the privateers and blockade runners bearing supplies to the army of Virginia. On August 27, 1861, an expedition appeared before the inlet, five steamers and an army tug, the *Fanny,* led by the 40-gun *Minnesota,* from which flew the pennant of Flag Officer S. H. Stringham. [This title was replaced in 1862 by the rank of Rear Admiral.] Land forces came too, in several transports, 860 men under Benjamin F. Butler of Massachusetts. Part of Butler's troops were landed, as Waud's drawing shows, in the surf, under cover of the lighter vessels. As in most landings, there were difficulties; the heavy iron surfboats stuck on the beach, and two flatboats hit rocks. Three hundred and fifteen troops, some of them marines, reached the shore dripping, their provisions lost, and their ammunition soaked. Their activity was limited to a parade down the beach, where they hoisted the flag over Fort Clark, the smaller Confederate work, which had been abandoned at the first round from the Minnesota's big guns. Fort Hatteras held out till mid-morning of the 29th, then ran up a white flag. The chief Confederate waterway north of Charleston was controlled by the Union, and the success was comforting a month after disastrous Bull Run. Butler, strictly a political general, acquired a reputation considerably in excess of his actual abilities.

PLATE No. 77. *The Great Expedition. The Vessels at Anchor at Hampton Roads, From the Top of the Hygeia Hotel, Old Point Comfort, Va.* ☆ *[Designation:] Fortress Monroe Rip Raps.* ☆ *Lith. by E. Sachse & Cº Baltimore Md. Published by C. Bohn. Washington, D. C.* ☆ *Ent. accord. to an Act of Congress in the year 1861 by C. Bohn in the Clerks Office of the Dist. of Columbia.*

Lithograph, printed in color. 8½ x 16¾ inches.

The Hatteras affair gained for the U. S. Navy control of the northernmost Confederate coast line, but a naval base was needed nearer the main southern ports if an effective blockade was to be maintained. This was acquired by the important and successful Port Royal expedition, which left Hampton Roads on October 29, 1861, under Flag Officer S. F. DuPont, and crossed the bar of Port Royal Sound on November 4. The transports bearing troops had been scattered by a gale, and DuPont attacked with the fleet alone, "wooden ships against heavy land fortifications in narrow waters" (D. W. Knox). In a bold and skilfully conducted bombardment of four and a half hours on November 7, DuPont silenced the guns of Fort Walker, the stronger of the two forts protecting the sound. The Confederates evacuated the position, as well as Fort Beauregard on the opposite point, and Port Royal became an invaluable Union base for the remainder of the war.

Our lithograph shows the assembling of the "Great Expedition" at Hampton Roads. From the "widow's walk" of the stylish health-resort hotel the surface of the sea seems blanketed with sail. They had been begged, borrowed and bought for the purpose; warships, transports and coaling schooners now crowded the Roads. Twenty-five coaling vessels, convoyed by a sloop-of-war, got an advance start on October 28. On the morning of the 29th, 50 vessels steamed out of the harbor, forming a double echelon line outside Cape Henry, and proceeded, under sealed orders, to the south.

The lithograph is from the house of EDWARD SACHSE & Co., Baltimore, which did business from 1857 to 1866. They made many good views, mainly of scenes in the South, Baltimore, and Washington. During the war they specialized in military and naval prints, of which Worrel's "Merrimac and Monitor" is noteworthy. Sachse had already, before the war, drawn "Fort Monroe, Old Point Comfort, and Hygeia Hotel, Va." possibly at the instigation of the proprietors of the hotel, to whom he does the favor of advertising their resort in connection with the great naval display.

PLATE NO. 78. *The Naval Engagement between the Merrimac and the Monitor at Hampton Roads on the 9ᵗʰ of March 1862. [Designation of batteries, shore points, ships, etc.]* ☆ *Drawn on the Spot by Charles Worret, Sergᵗ 20 Rgt N Y. V Lith & Print by E. Sachse & Cᵒ 104 S. Charles sᵗ Balto.* ☆ *Published by C. Bohn 568 Pennsylv. Av. Washington D C. & Old Point Comf. Va.* ☆ *Entered according to an Act of Congress in the year 1862 by C. Bohn in the Clerks Office of the Distr. of Columbia.*

Lithograph, printed in color. 9 x 16⅓ inches.

The beautiful slope-of-war, U. S. S. *Cumberland,* 24 guns, Lt. G. U. Morris acting in command, sank below the waters of Hampton Roads, March 8, 1862, her colors flying and her splendid crew steady and defiant, at their guns to the last. Her sister ship, the *Congress,* greatly damaged and her commander killed, hauled down her flag. The other Union vessels huddled in panic off Fortress Monroe to the eastward, as the Confederate ironclad *Virginia* steamed back into the Elizabeth River and Norfolk Harbor. A shock of alarm ran through the North—was this new weapon invincible? Would our cities be shelled, our commerce destroyed, our coast

blockaded, our defeat insured? "To all these terrible questions the triumphant *Virginia* seemed to answer 'yes,'" and the North was stunned.

But on the next day the answer was "no"! At nine o'clock in the evening of that terrible Saturday, the tug *Seth Low* out of New York steamed into Hampton Roads towing a singular contraption, John Ericsson's new-fangled turret ship, *Monitor,* mounting exactly two 11-inch smoothbores. However unimpressive she may have appeared, there was no choice but to try her out, and when the *Virginia* made her anticipated appearance at eight o'clock on Sunday morning, the little *Monitor* took her on. The two vessels exchanged a furious cannonade without inflicting the least damage on each other, until the *Virginia* gave up and returned to Norfolk. "No transition from an old to a new era of naval combat was ever more clearly marked for public understanding" (D. W. Knox).

The novelty was properly in the clash of the two indestructible bodies, not in the idea of armored vessels. These had been the subject of experiment from antiquity, and of serious effort in Europe and the United States since the forties. The French had launched the iron-clad *Gloire* in 1859 and were building a seagoing armored fleet; the British were following suit. Union and Confederate naval architects since the beginning of the war had been rushing designs for ironclads, and the Confederates had won. Says James Phinney Baxter of the *Cumberland*:

"Of the five great naval revolutions of the nineteenth century—steam, shell guns, the screw propeller, rifled ordnance, and armor—one only had influenced her design or equipment; nothing but her heavy battery of 9-inch smooth-bore shell guns would have seemed wholly unfamiliar

172

to the conquerers of the Spanish Armada. But the crude *Virginia,* whose iron prow had just dealt the graceful *Cumberland* her deathblow, embodied all five of those revolutionary features."

In early 1861 the Norfolk Navy Yard had been destroyed to prevent its falling into Confederate hands, and the former U. S. steam frigate *Merrimack,* with engines already condemned as unseaworthy, had been scuttled and burned to the water's edge. The Confederate engineers raised the hull, cut her down almost to the water, and put on her deck a wooden citadel with sloping sides, plated with two thin layers of iron strips. They rechristened her *Virginia.* From 10 openings protruded huge guns—the smoke is belching from them in two prints. On the 9th of March 1862, she was without her wedge-shaped cast-iron ram, torn away by the shock when she sank the *Cumberland* the day before. Her captain, Flag Officer Buchanan, had been sent back wounded to Norfolk, and she faced the *Monitor* under her second in command, Lt. Catesby ap R. Jones. Had he been able to use the ram, the outcome of this day might conceivably have been different, for the tiny "cheesebox on a raft" bore marks on her side where the mutilated *Virginia* had struck a glancing blow.

The *Monitor,* which gave her name to a class of Federal ironclads, was designed for the United States Government by the Swedish engineer, John Ericsson. His plans were submitted on October 4, 1861, and within four hours the contract was being drawn up and the iron plates started through the rolling mill. She consisted quite simply of a hull nearly awash and a revolving gun turret, to the general adoption of which her success gave wide impetus. She had

been built in 100 days, but was not ready for sea until March 3. Then steering troubles took her back to New York, and on the second attempt she had to be towed part way south. She reached Hampton Roads in the evening of March 8, and learned from the distressed *Minnesota* of the disaster just over and the crisis ahead. The crews of both ships worked all night to put the little David in condition.

The famous fight of March 9 lasted four hours. The first print, lithographed from Worrel's drawing, shows accurately the positions in the Roads. The large *Minnesota* lay grounded at the right; in the center the two ironclads turned and maneuvred in their history-making conflict. Several times the speedier *Monitor* retreated to shallow water to renew the ammunition supply in her turret, and then the *Minnesota* suffered from the Confederate guns.

The artillery duel, much of it at point-blank range, was strangely futile—the poor-quality cast-iron shot of the *Monitor,* and the shells of the *Virginia,* proved equally ineffective against the other's armor. Finally the *Virginia's* gunners struck the *Monitor's* pilot house and the iron splinters blinded her captain, John L. Worden. He directed the pilot to shallow water, and Jones thought it meant flight. The Confederate captain delivered a last blow at the helpless *Minnesota,* then, fearing the ebbing tide of the Elizabeth River, steered for Norfolk. The hope of the Confederacy lay stalemated in the harbor, while the army of the Union gathered against Norfolk.

Sgt. CHARLES WORREL, whose sketch was made into a wood-engraving for *Harper's Weekly* before it was lithographed by Sachse, was probably from New York or the vicinity. In both pictures his name is wrongly given, as

Worret. He was a member of Company G, 20th Regiment of New York Volunteers, the "United Turner Rifles", a two-year regiment recruited in New York in May 1861. Worrel was 42 when he was mustered in, on May 7, and immediately promoted to sergeant. On October 4, 1862, he was commissioned as lieutenant. The service of the regiment was mainly at Fortress Monroe, from which Worrel doubtless watched the engagement of the ironclads. Worrel remained in service at Fort Monroe until December 29, 1863, when he resigned.

PLATE No. 79. *Monitor [at top] Grand March, composed by E. Mack. ☆ Lithograph 4 Plain 2½. [Numbers enclosed in star] ☆ T. Sinclair's Lith, Phil^a ☆ Philadelphia Lee & Walker 722 Chestnut St.*

First page of sheet music: Lithograph, printed in color. 7 x 9⅞ inches.

The colored lithograph of the ironclads in combat on the front page of E. Mack's triumphant musical composition was printed by THOMAS S. SINCLAIR, an established Philadelphia lithographer. The business which he opened in 1839 continued until 1889, eight years after his own death. He was a Scotsman, from the Orkney Isles, and had learned the art in Edinburgh. In 1848 he was awarded a prize by the Franklin Institute, and again for his chromolithography in 1849 and 1851. He specialized in views of buildings and in large fashion plates, doing the color work for S. A. & A. F. Ward of Philadelphia. Although he was not one of the outstanding men in the trade, his work has a certain distinction and variety, with some feeling for timeliness and journalism.

We show three of Sinclair's lithographs, the

present plate, and the two views of Andersonville prison, his most notable Civil War prints (Plates 113 and 114).

PLATE No. 80. *The Second Battle of Bull Run, Fought Augt 29th 1862. Between the "Army of Virginia" under Maj^r Genl John Pope, and the combined forces of the Rebel Army under Lee, Jackson, and others. ☆ This terrific battle was fought on the identical battle field of Bull run, and lasted with great fury from daylight until after dark, when the rebels were driven back, and the Union Army rested in triumph on the the field. ☆ Published by Currier & Ives, 152 Nassau St New York.*

Lithograph, colored by hand. Undated. 7⅞ x 12⅜ inches.

The Second Battle of Bull Run, or Manasses (29–30 August 1862) was not, as the Currier & Ives print boasts, a Union victory. On the contrary, it was a dismal defeat. "It was the neatest, cleanest bit of work that Lee and Jackson ever performed. The irresistible combination of bold strategy and perfect tactics had undone the Union gains of an entire year in the Virginia theatre of war" (Morison and Commager).

On the identical battlefield, as the caption relates, only a year and a month before (July 21, 1861) Thomas Jackson's brigade had stood like a stone wall, and the Federal Army had broken and fled in disorder from the first major engagement of the war. In the intervening year authorities had shifted in the Army of the Potomac. McDowell had been swiftly removed, McClellan placed in command. Snubbing Lincoln, he had chosen to undertake the Peninsular campaign, and in return had been checked and hampered by the amateur strategy of the President and his Secretary of War, Stanton. Finally, after the Seven Days' Battles, when the Union Army in front of Richmond was pounced on by Lee and Jackson, and driven back to its new base on the James, McClellan was put in a subordinate command. The President called Gen. John Pope from the Western theatre, where he had achieved some easy victories with the help of the river flotillas, and it was under his guidance that the second defeat at Bull Run placed the Union in the most acutely dangerous position of the war. Pope, after putting forth high-sounding manifestoes which antagonized his own army, officers and men alike, proceeded to demonstrate to the satisfaction of everyone that he knew nothing of the high art of generalship. Washington was in danger and Lee on the point of invading the North. Lincoln found himself under the embarrassing necessity of asking McClellan to reassume command.

The print is included as an instance of how low the popular lithograph, treated as journalism in the tradition of Nathaniel Currier, could sink. Publication was evidently rushed before the actual result of Second Bull Run could be adequately known. The scene depicted has no individuality whatever; it is any mass of soldiers driving before them any other mass of soldiers, on a characterless field. Fortunately, Currier and Ives could do considerably better than this in representing battle, as Plates 73 and 90 attest.

PLATE No. 81. [*First Virginia Cavalry at a Halt. 1862*]

Pencil and wash drawing by A. R. Waud. On light brown paper. 8¾ x 12½ inches.

Said *Harper's Weekly* on September 27, 1862: "We publish on page 612 a fine picture of the

FIRST VIRGINIA CAVALRY, one of the crack regiments of the rebel service. Mr. Waud writes:

Being detained with the enemy's lines, an opportunity occurred to make a sketch of one of the two crack regiments of the Confederate service. They seemed to be of considerable social standing, that is, most of them F. F. V.'s, so to speak, and not irreverently; for they were not only as a body handsome, athletic men, but generally polite and agreeable in manner. With the exception of the officers, there was little else but homespun among them, light drab-gray or butternut color, the drab predominating; although there were so many varieties of dress, half-citizen, half-military, that they could scarcely be said to have a uniform. Light jackets and trowsers with black facings, and slouched hats, appeared to be (in those cases where the wearer could obtain it) the court costume of the regiment. Their horses were good; in many cases, they told me, they provided their own. Their arms were the United States cavalry sabre, Sharp's carbine, and pistols. Some few of them had old swords of the Revolution, curved, and in broad, heavy scabbards.

"Their carbines, they said, were mostly captured from our own cavalry, for whom they expressed utter contempt—a feeling unfortunately shared by our own army. Finally, they bragged of having their own horses, and, in many cases, of having drawn no pay from the Government, not needing the paltry remuneration of a private. The flag represented in the picture is the battle-flag. White border, red ground, blue cross, and white stars."

The First Virginia Cavalry was part of Gen. Fitzhugh Lee's brigade of five regiments which, with two others, Gen. Wade Hampton's and Gen. B. H. Robertson's brigades, made up the Cavalry Division of Lee's army. The commander of the Division was Maj. Gen. J. E. B. Stuart, *beau sabreur* of the South, who twice, during the peninsular campaign (June 12-15, 1862) and again in October, rode his cavalry around McClellan's entire army. We are told in confirmation of Waud's comment, that during this October raid, when McClellan reported that his cavalry horses were too fatigued to move, Lincoln sarcastically inquired "what the horses of your army have done since the battle of Antietam that fatigues anything?" The command of the regiment itself, according to the *Official Reports,* went through rapid changes. On March 31, 1862, Stuart's report mentions Col. W. E. Jones as leader of the First Virginia Cavalry. On August 6th, he writes to Lee from near Fredericksburg that the enemy had its "cavalry advance guard driven back with loss yesterday by Lt. Col. [James H.] Drake, First Virginia Cavalry." By August 27 the reports mention as leader Lt. Col. L. T. Brien. It may be Drake or Brien whom Waud has drawn here, slouch hat over his eyes, sitting his fine horse under the "bonnie blue" cross-barred flag held beside him.

PLATE NO. 82. *[Charge of Humphreys' Division at the Battle of Fredericksburg, Virginia, December 13, 1862.]*
Pencil and wash drawing by A. R. Waud. On light brown paper. 14½ x 21 inches.

PLATE NO. 83. *Gallant Charge of Humphrey's Division at the Battle of Fredericksburg.* ☆ *Sketched by Mr. A. R. Waud.*
Wood engraving. Harper's Weekly, New York, Jan. 10, 1863, vol. 7, p. 24–25. 13½ x 20 inches.

In Fredericksburg, the pretty little town on the bank of the Rappahannock, where the ladies refer to the "late unpleasantness," but prefer tales of Washington's mother, they show bullet holes in old walls facing the river. The point out Marye's Heights to the West, and show where the "sunken road" at the base of the hill led to the impregnable stone wall. They name Lee's hill, where the general, a master player of the game, stood musing—"It is well that war is so terrible—we should grow too fond of it." Beneath that stone wall on December 13, 1862, six times Burnside's blue-clad infantry charged with bayonets across the open plain, and six times fell back, the dead piled literally three deep. The casualties decimated the Army of the Potomac in the most useless sacrifice of the Civil War.

Alfred R. Waud did a number of sketches of the Fredericksburg disaster for *Harper's Weekly.* The two plates here reproduced give an excellent idea of how untenderly the process of wood-engraving treated the artist's work. Waud's word-picture of the battle tells the story of the "magnificent defensible position, strong as Sebastopol," against which "our troops were hurled all day,"—French's division, Sturgis's division, Hancock's and Howard's divisions, "each charging more eagerly than its predecessors . . . The sun had set behind the rebel fortifications . . . The rebel fire breaks out with more ferocity than ever. For sweeping across the fields come the divisions of Generals Humphreys and Griffin. Onward, a forlorn hope, they advance—the ground encumbered by the countless bodies of the fallen; knapsacks, blankets, guns, haversacks, canteens, cartridge-boxes, etc., strewed over the plain. Shot, shell, canister, shrapnel, and grape is hurled as they approach. By column of regiments, led by their generals, and without firing a shot, that noble band continues on. General Humphreys, dashing ahead to a small rise in the ground, takes off his hat to cheer on his men. With reckless ardor his men, rapidly closing on the double-quick, answer cheers with cheers. Every member of the General's staff has been dismounted. The brave Humphreys himself has two horses shot under him . . .

"Humphreys' division has never been under fire till this battle. But before that awful hurricane of bullets no heroism can avail. The hillside appears to vomit forth fire, its leven glare flashing through the fast-thickening obscurity seems to pour with redoubled power upon our storming columns, till, being unable to stand up against it longer—although within eighty yards of the wall—the brave remnant, singing in the *abandon* of its courage, marches steadily back to the place where it formed for the charge, leaving its comrades in swathes upon the bloody ground, where, 'stormed at by shot and shell,' they had been cut down, whole ranks at a time, by that terrible fire."

The Army of the Potomac, tremendous, eager, fantastically brave, was at the mercy of the worst leadership of the war. After Pope's removal, "Little Mac," the darling of the troops, rode out to meet the beaten army, and was greeted with wild enthusiasm. Lincoln gave him, verbally, command of forces in the field, and within a week he was marching toward Frederick, where Lee had invaded Maryland. At South Mountain and Antietam, September 16 and 17, 1862, he caught Lee in a cramped spot and won a technical victory, but failed to follow up the advantage. The Army of Northern Virginia retreated down the Shenandoah Valley, while McClellan, criticized by the pub-

lic, and reproached by Lincoln, delayed action and clamored for supplies. The Emancipation Proclamation had been issued (September 22), the mid-term elections had begun, and Lincoln needed a victory. On November 7th the President relieved McClellan of command of the Army of the Potomac, and appointed Ambrose E. Burnside in his place. It was one of the most costly mistakes Lincoln ever made. Burnside was a brave and honest man, an admirable corps commander and conductor of subsidiary operations, but, as he himself feared, simply did not have the grasp of grand strategy which would enable him to direct the movements of a great army.

PLATE No. 84. *Winter Campaigning. The Army of the Potomac on the move. Sketched near Falmouth—January 21ˢᵗ* ☆ *Alf. R. Waud.* Pencil and wash drawing. 1863. 13⅞ x 20½ inches.

"With the failure of Fredericksburg the nadir of Northern depression seemed to have been reached. Sorrow caused by the death or mutilation of thousands of brave men turned into rage as the people wondered how so fine a fighting instrument as the Army of the Potomac had been used with such stupid futility" (J. G. Randall). Gold went up to 134, and greenbacks depreciated alarmingly. The situation in the army became so dismal that the distracted Burnside asked Lincoln to dismiss some of the best officers, who, like the ranks, lacked faith in their general. After some hesitation, the President approved Burnside's project of another attack across the Rappahannock. The result was the miserable "mud march" of January 20–21st, when the army floundered through a deluge of rain and a slough of adhesive clay, but came no nearer to a vantage-point for attacking Lee. On January 25, Burnside disappeared to his own as well as general relief, and Gen. "Fighting Joe" Hooker took over the wet, cold, and disheartened army.

Alfred Waud's drawing catches with unsurpassable atmosphere the discouragement of the "mud march." The trees, clouds, cloaks, and grasses are whipped by a cruel wind, a baggage wagon lists heavily in the mire, men wade above ankles through the mud, riderless horses struggle in the stream—and still the muffled figures plod forward along the bank and down the farther hill. The banners which waved so bravely against the rebel guns are furled and dejected, and the regiment's dog splashes behind his master, his pessimistic eye on the muddy boot before him, his tail between his legs.

PLATE No. 85. *Embarkation of Ninth Army Corps at Aquia Creek Landing, February 1863.* Photograph by Mathew B. Brady. Negative enlarged from original, 6¼ x 8 inches.

Until the weather should improve Hooker and the Army of the Potomac marked time along the Rappahannock River. Headquarters were at Falmouth, and the Potomac Flotilla was moored in Aquia Creek, the deep tidal channel which runs into the Potomac about 18 miles north of Fredericksburg. The old river-port was still of some importance and its boat landings still sturdy, although the Union encampment and the cavalry regiment which picketed its horses behind the old seventeenth-century church left it forlorn. Meanwhile, parts of Hooker's command had to be detached to other theaters. Thus on February 4 the Ninth Army

Corps, 15,000 strong under Maj. Gen. William F. Smith, received orders to embark for Fort Monroe, "without delay." Maj. Gen. John A. Dix, who commanded the forces holding the Norfolk area, and his second, Gen. John A. Peck at Newport News, were getting nervous about the menacing feints of Gen. Roger A. Pryor and his Confederate troops on the Blackwater. The embarkation which began on February 6 and lasted four days is shown in fairly advanced stage in Brady's photograph.

It is interesting, from the present perfection of photographic technique, to examine the frozen stillness of this picture, and to contrast it with the superb motion in the preceding drawing. Brady had perforce to choose a moment of least action—the sidewheelers cabled, the soldiers sitting, lying, or—if no other position were possible—standing still, the baggage motionless in its heaps, and the rifles stacked about kit bags. The small boy in the foreground—perhaps a young rebel from Aquia, for he does not seem to be in uniform—is fascinated by the tripod and the black cloth beneath which Brady has dived to "catch" this shot.

PLATE No. 86. *Appearance of Cemetery hill previous to Pick[ett's] charge.* ☆ *[References:] Ground over which Louisiana Tigers charged Entrenched Guns Stevens Battery Gettysburg on left*

PLATE No. 87, 88. *[The Battle of Gettysburg: Third Day] [Signed] E F July 3rd 10 A. M. [Indications in pencil and numbers in ink evidently added later]* Pencil drawing by Edwin Forbes, July 3, 1863. 9¼ x 26¼ inches.

Pencil and wash drawing by Alfred R. Waud. On green tinted paper. 8 x 12¾ inches.

"Public Resolution No. 9.

Resolved by the Senate and House of Representatives of the United States of America, in Congress assembled, That the gratitude of the American people, and the thanks of their Representatives in Congress, are due, and are hereby tendered . . . to Maj. Gen. George G. Meade, Maj. Gen. Oliver O. Howard, and the officers and soldiers of [the Army of the Potomac], for the skill and heroic valor which, at Gettysburg, repulsed, defeated, and drove back, broken and dispirited, beyond the Rappahannock, the veteran army of the rebellion.

Approved January 28, 1864."

Edwin Forbes' panoramic drawing shows the great battlefield on that third day, July 3, 1863, which decided that the Nation might live. The artist's pencilled notations indicate that the pictures were made at 10 in the morning, while the Union armies held their positions on Round Top, Little Round Top, Cemetery Ridge, and Culp's Hill, facing the gray force on Seminary Ridge.   The fateful grand charge whose failure broke the Confederacy was still over three hours away, but the guns were entrenched and ready. Gen. Henry J. Hunt, chief of the artillery, crossed at about this hour from Culp's Hill to Cemetery Ridge. "Here a magnificent display greeted my eyes. Our whole front for two miles was covered by batteries already in line or going into position. They stretched—apparently in one unbroken mass—from opposite the town to the Peach Orchard, which bounded the view to the left, the ridges of which were planted thick with cannon. Never before had such a sight been witnessed on this continent."

When, about one o'clock, the Confederate batteries opened, the Union Artillery answered

Forty-seven regiments waited on Seminary Ridge, 15,000 men, the flower of the South.   It seemed madness to send infantry into that fire, but it was the only hope. "General," said George Pickett to Longstreet, "Shall I advance?" Longstreet, unable to speak, nodded. Pickett saluted.

'I shall go forward, sir,' he said and turned to his men.
The commands went down the line. The gray ranks started to move.
Slowly at first, then faster, in order, stepping like deer,
The Virginians, the fifteen thousand, the seventh wave of the tide.

There was a death-torn mile of broken ground to cross,
And a low stone wall at the end, and behind it the Second Corps,
And behind that force another, fresh men who had not yet fought.
They started to cross that ground. The guns began to tear them.

From the hill they say that it seemed more like a sea than a wave,
A sea continually torn by stones flung out of the sky,
And yet, as it came, still closing, closing and rolling on,
As the moving sea closes over the flaws and rips of the tide.
You could mark the path that they took by the dead that they left behind,
Spilled from that deadly march as a cart spills meal on a road,
And yet they came on unceasing, the fifteen thousand no more,

179

And the blue Virginia flag did not fall, did not fall, did not fall.

Armstead leapt the wall and laid his hand on the gun,
The last of the three brigadiers who ordered Pickett's brigades,
He waved his hat on his sword and 'Gave 'em the steel!' he cried,
A few men followed him over. The rest were beaten or dead.

A few men followed him over. There had been fifteen thousand
When that sea began its march toward the fish-hook ridge and the wall.
So they came on in strength, light-footed, stepping like deer,
So they died or were taken. So the iron entered their flesh.

(S. V. Benét, *John Brown's Body.*)

PLATE No. 89. *Artist of Harper's Weekly sketching at Gettysburg.*

Photograph by Mathew B. Brady. Negative from print, 8 x 10 inches.

Alfred Waud's drawing was evidently made as the "furious thunderstorm" of the Union cannonade answered the Confederate guns. The photographer Brady—presumably, as in the latest war, the correspondents banded together in emulous friendship—caught him sitting with pad and pencil, slightly protected by a boulder and tree from the line of fire. Alfred R. Waud was not only a fine artist, but a bold man, with a surpassingly splendid beard. A tribute in *Harper's Weekly* at the close of the war eulogizes him and his fellow-artists:

"[They] have not been less busy, and scarcely less imperiled than the soldiers. They have made the weary marches and dangerous voyages. They have shared the soldier's fare: they have ridden and waded, and climbed and floundered, always trusting in lead-pencils and keeping their paper dry. When the battle began, they were there. They drew the enemy's fire as well as our own. The fierce shock, the heaving tumult, the smoky sway of battle from side to side, the line, the assault, the victory—they were a part of all, and their faithful fingers, depicting the scene, have made us a part also."

PLATE No. 90. *The Pontoon Bridge at Cincinnati. Sketched by A. E. Mathews, 31st Reg't, O. V. ☆ Middleton Strobridge, & Cº Lith. Cin. O.*

Tinted lithograph. Undated. 15 x 21 inches.

PLATE No. 91. *The Battle of Stone River or Murfreesboro'. Representing Gen. Sam Beatty's Brigade on the 31st of December, 1862. ☆ Sketched by A. E. Mathews, 31st Reg., O.V.I. ☆ Middleton Strobridge, & Cº Lith. Cin. O. ☆ [Four lines of small print, quoting from "W. D. B. Correspondent Cincinnati Commercial."] [Five references]*

Tinted lithograph. Undated. 14 x 20¾ inches.

The Thirty-first Ohio Volunteer Infantry was organized at Camp Chase, Columbus, between August 4 and September 7, 1861. Its colonel was Moses R. Walker. The musician of Company E was named Alfred Edward Mathews. He was 30 years old, strong, adventurous, and could make pictures as well as music. He took his sketchbook to war in his knapsack.

On the 27th of September the new regiment

received its orders. As it marched to Cincinnati, an untrained, eager throng, it sang, "We are coming, Father Abraham, five hundred thousand strong." In the city—the largest most of the boys had ever seen—it "received many favors from the citizens." On the 31st it started South. The broad Ohio had been spanned with a pontoon bridge, and the side-wheel river steamers, *Sunny Side* and *Silver Moon* lay by the shore. Colonel Walker on his horse rode before, the long proud line followed over the bridge, and the admiring citizens waved good-bye. The regiment tramped for three days and reached Camp Dick Robinson, near Danville, Ky. Brig. Gen. George H. Thomas reported their arrival in an official report of October 3, and spoke of their embarrassing lack of transportation—"Our supply as yet is very limited, and all the mules have to be broken." On November 4 Brig. Gen. W. T. Sherman, commanding the Department of the Cumberland, wrote of "the raw levies of Ohio and Indiana, who arrive in detachments perfectly fresh from the country and loaded down with baggage, . . . composed of good material, but devoid of company officers of experience," and of the "thorough drill" through which he was putting them.

On December 31, 1862, when Rosecrans' army met Braxton Bragg at Stone River, or Murfreesboro—one of those fierce but indecisive battles typical of the campaign in the West before Grant moved on Vicksburg—the 31st Ohio were still in the main untried. Veterans of long marches through the debatable ground, victims of raids and victors of skirmishes with the rebels, they had not yet been under fire in a pitched field. At Stone River "they acquitted themselves nobly." Artist-musician Mathews probably had time only for mental notes, but he later sketched the charging and firing in exactest detail. Beneath the drawing is quoted a correspondent's account:

"Gen. Rosecrans sent word pressing Gen. McCook to hold the front and he would help him. It would all work right. He now galloped [there he goes, in the exact center of the picture, on a black horse, or maybe farther to the left on a white horse] to the front of Crittenden's left, with his staff, to order the line of battle, when the enemy opened a full battery and emptied two saddles of the escort. Van Cleeves' division was sent to the right, Col. Beatty's Brigade in front. The fire continued to approach on the front with alarming rapidity, extending to the centre, and it was clear that the right was doubling upon the left. The enemy had compelled us to make a complete change of front on that wing and was pressing the centre. Gen. Rosecrans, with splendid daring, dashed into the fire and sent his staff along the lines, starting Beatty's Brigade forward—some six batteries opened and sustained a magnificent fire—directly a tremendous shout was raised along the whole line. The enemy began to fall back rapidly. The general himself urged the troops forward. The rebels thoroughly punished were driven back fully a mile. The same splendid bravery was displayed in the centre, and the whole line advanced."

Alfred Edward Mathews remained in the 31st Ohio till the end of his three-year term, September 22, 1864, still a private, and "reduced from musician, transferred to Company A, April 24, 1864." He had found time for sketches, which were elaborated into lithographs. Those of the Siege of Vicksburg, Grant pronounced "the most accurate and true to life I have ever seen. They reflect great credit upon you as a delineator of landscape views." After the war Mathews went on tour in the Middle West with an exhibition of large canvases—Vicksburg, Stone Ridge, Chickamauga, Sherman's March, Lookout Mountain—a "Topogramical Panorama of the War." Then he went West, and for a time had great success with landscapes and panoramic views of the mighty peaks of the Rockies, the canyons, frontier towns and mining camps. He drew accurately and minutely, correctly placing houses, and buildings, lettering names in, putting pigs and chickens in the streets of Denver, and every spoke in place in the wheels of mining machinery. His first set of western lithographs, *Pencil Sketches of Colorado,* was published in 1866, and he followed it in 1868 with *Pencil Sketches of Montana,* and in 1869 with *Gems of Rocky Mountain Scenery.* The faint blue and tan sketches strike modern eyes as odd and bad, but are of the greatest historical value because of their extraordinary, trivial detail. But the vogue of the brilliant Currier & Ives prints quite overshadowed Mathews, and he soon dropped from public sight. His death was recorded in the briefest of notices in a Boulder, Colo., paper of 1872.

MIDDLETON, STROBRIDGE & Co., originally Middleton, Wallace & Co., were a Cincinnati firm of lithographers who were active from 1855 through the sixties, and produced "a long series of small Civil War views." Mathews also sketched lithographs for the Cincinnati house of Donaldson and Elmes, including some considerably larger views of the fighting around Chattanooga in 1863.

PLATE No. 92. *Admiral Porter's Fleet Running the Rebel Blockade of the Mississippi at Vicksburg, April 16th 1863. [Three lines of type describing action. ☆ Designation of vessels] ☆ Published by Currier & Ives, 152 Nassau St New York. ☆ Entered according to act of Congress, in the year 1863, by Currier & Ives, in the Clerk's Office, of the District Court of the United States, for the Southern District of New York.*

Lithograph. 8 x 12⅜ inches.

The high bluff on which stands the city of Vicksburg, the greatest Confederate stronghold on the Mississippi, dominates the hairpin bend of the great river. There were concentrated the Confederate batteries, making a direct assault from the west inconceivable, while to the north stretched the Yazoo swamps and bayous, impassable to an army. Grant worked out the only approach, a major campaign from the south and east. His Army transferred to the western bank, marched far south, was ferried back across the great water barrier, and now marched through enemy country, without supply bases, over difficult ground, northeastward to Jackson and then doubled back due westward to the siege of Vicksburg. But the lower crossing was dependent on the fleet, and for the fleet there was no choice but to run the gauntlet of the emplanted guns at Vicksburg.

The Currier & Ives, almost as lurid in black and white as in color, figures forth a bombardment quite as furious as Admiral David D. Porter and his ships had to endure. The seven ironclads, each with a coal barge lashed to her side, the captured Confederate ram *General Price* secured to the *Lafayette,* and the three army transports are all named in the print. The ships (not as the designations run, but in order of line) are: Flagship *Benton, Lafayette* and *General Price, Louisville, Mound City, Pittsburg, Carondelet, Silver Wave, Forest Queen, Henry Clay, Tuscumbia.* The caption reads:

"At half past ten P. M. the boats left their moorings & steamed down the river, the *Benton,* Admiral Porter, taking the lead—as they approached the point opposite the town, a terrible concentrated fire of the centre, upper and lower batteries, both water and bluff, was directed upon the channel, which here ran within one hundred yards of the shore. At the same moment innumerable floats of turpentine and other combustible materials were set ablaze. In the face of all this fire, the boats made their way with but little loss except the transport *Henry Clay,* which was set fire & sunk."

PLATE No. 93. *The Army of the Potomac—A Sharp-Shooter on Picket Duty.—[From a Painting by W. Homer, Esq.]*

Wood engraving. Harper's Weekly, Nov. 15, 1862. Vol. 6, p. 724. 10¾ x 15½ inches.

WINSLOW HOMER (1836–1910) was just trying his way in the art career which was to make him one of the greatest among American painters, when the war came. His boyhood in Cambridge had ended with two years as apprentice to the Boston lithographer, John H. Bufford, and from 1858 he had had his own studio, first in Boston, then after *Harper's Weekly* accepted a drawing, in New York. There he had taken evening classes at the National Academy of Design and worked under a French painter, Rondel. In 1861 Harper's sent him to Washington to make pictures of the inauguration, and afterward to the seat of war in Virginia. He was attached to the staff of the youthful Col. Francis

C. Barlow, 61st N. Y. Volunteers, and covered with him the Peninsular campaign, Fair Oaks, Seven Pines, the Wilderness, Malvern Hill. Then he returned to his New York studio and began painting the big war pictures which brought his first real fame. A set of card-size lithographs, "Campaign Sketches," was issued by Prang in 1863, and in the same year he exhibited the "Sharpshooter on Picket Duty," from which this print was made, with several other paintings, at the National Academy. In 1865 he became an Academician. The greatest of his war pictures is generally conceded to be *Prisoners from the Front,* now the property of the Metropolitan Museum of Art, New York, which shows Barlow, "the boy general," inspecting a most heterogeneous batch of four Southerners. *A Sharp-Shooter,* however, will do very well, particularly since it is one instance in which the weeklies' commercial wood engraving did not denature its original, but even provided a quality and an attractiveness all its own.

Wood engraving differs from the woodcut in that the surface of the wood is treated, not with a knife, but with a graver, and to make this possible, the end, across the grain, of a closely-grained piece of wood such as boxwood has to be used. In the hands of its English inventor, the great Thomas Bewick, who made his first attempt in 1779 and had perfected the process before the end of the century, wood engraving was an art. Until about 1832, printing from the blocks had to be done by hand, but by that year technological progress made possible the rapid printing by machine presses, along with type on the same page. As a result commercial wood engravers abandoned the complete transposition of the original which Bewick had achieved, and went in for a humdrum kind of facsimile work. In the case of the *Sharp-Shooter,* however, Homer's painting evidently put the craftsman on his mettle, and the result is handsome and strong.

PLATE No. 94. *The Press on the Field. [Panels:] Contraband News. In Action. Reliable Information. On Staff. Newspapers at Home. The Newspapers in Camp. [Other views:] Our Artist. Taking Notes. Sketching. A Correspondent. Names of the Wounded & Dead. After the Battle. The Sketch Book. [In plate:] Th: Nast.*

Wood engraving. Harper's Weekly, Apr. 30, 1864. Vol. 8, pp. 280–281. 15¾ x 21½ inches.

PLATE No. 95. *The Drummer Boy of Our Regiment—Eight War Scenes. [Panels:] His Toilet. The Favorite in Camp. His Daily Bread. Off to the War. Home Again. Writing Home. In Action. News from Home. [In plate:] Th: Nast.*

Wood engraving. Harper's Weekly, December 19, 1863. Vol. 7, p. 805. 15¾ x 10½ inches.

Of the cartoonist Thomas Nast, Lincoln remarked, "He has been our best recruiting sergeant." Few issues of the great national magazine, *Harper's Weekly,* from 1862 through the war—and after into the eighties, for that matter—were without a cartoon or other drawing from his spirited and able pen. His political caricature was without question one of the greatest influences in American journalism of the period.

THOMAS NAST (1840–1902) was the son of a German regimental musician, born in the barracks of the 9th Bavarian Regiment at Landau, Germany. He was brought to New York in 1846, and as a schoolboy began his drawings

and went to art classes. Frank Leslie, publisher of *Leslie's Illustrated Newspaper,* discovered him when he was 15, and engaged him at $4 a week. In 1859 his first important political cartoon appeared in *Harper's Weekly.* He left Leslie's for the *New York Illustrated News,* and for them covered John Brown's funeral and other important assignments. In 1860 he went to England to sketch a big prize fight, but was attracted by the more serious business of Garibaldi's campaign to Italy. He came back to America just before the war, and quickly found himself a correspondent in the field. In the summer of 1862, Fletcher Harper engaged him as a staff artist, urging him to make pictures with ideas rather than battle reports.

Nast's greatest work, of course, is to be found in his cartoons and propaganda pieces, but these do not fall into the scheme of our Album. His reportorial battle pieces are inchoate and inferior. We have, therefore, compromised by reproducing from *Harper's* two characteristic picture groups on representative Civil War themes, which are in part fact and in part idea, sentimentally treated. One, *The Press in the Field,* has a special relationship to the subject-matter of this book.

PLATE No. 96. *[Slaves Concealing Their Master from a Search Party] From Adalbert John Volck, [Confederate War Etchings (portfolio) Baltimore (?) 18—,] No. 12.*

Etching. 4⅞ x 6⅞ inches.

PLATE No. 97. *[Prayer in Stonewall Jackson's Camp] From Adalbert John Volck, [Confederate War Etchings (portfolio) Baltimore (?) 18—,] No. 24.*

Etching. 4⅞ x 7⅛ inches.

184

On the Southern side, the Baltimore artist John Adalbert Volck endeavored to counteract Nast's influence by his own series of caricatures, published under the pseudonym of V. Blada, [*Adalb*ert backward]. Lincoln and Benjamin F. Butler were the chief targets of his attack—Butler had imprisoned him in 1861—and later reproductions of his savage cartoons served materially in the political general's defeat for the governorship of Massachusetts in 1871. Notable among the "Blada" series is the drawing of Lincoln and Butler as "Don Quixote and Sancho Panza." The book of *Confederate War Etchings* from which the two prints are taken contains 29 plates, divided between political caricature and typical military scenes, and is his most important collection.

Volck, like Nast, was a Bavarian, born at Augsburg in 1828. A student of dentistry at the Polytechnic Institute of Nürnberg, he became involved in the Revolution of 1848 and fled to America. He went first to St. Louis, then tried his fortune in the gold rush. More solid results were attained in his profession; in 1851 he became an instructor in the Baltimore College of Dental Surgery. He was a prominent dentist, a pioneer in the use of porcelain fillings, and a founder of the Association of Dental Surgeons.

Unlike most of the German refugees of 1848, and in an unexplained manner, Volck became an ardent Southern sympathizer, and besides the caricature series did illustrations for a number of Confederate books, during and after the war. In 1870 he painted a portrait in oils of General Lee, which is now in the Valentine Museum in Richmond. The head of Jefferson Davis on the 10-cent stamp of the Confederacy is often attributed to him, but was more prob-

ably done by his brother, Frederick, a sculptor. Later, he worked in bronze and silver—a shield in memory of the Confederate women is in the Confederate Museum in Richmond. One of the founders of the famous Wednesday Club, he was a well-known and popular figure in Baltimore until his death in 1912.

It is difficult to say why Volck resorted to the technique of *etching* for reproducing these simple line drawings; his plates are certainly very unremarkable specimens of that noble art. The best of them, from a purely aesthetic standpoint, is indubitably *Vicksburg Canal,* but since the original drawing for this has been reproduced in the *American Battle Painting* catalogue, and differs only very slightly from the etching, we have chosen instead two pieces in which, at this early date, Volck seizes upon two themes long characteristic of Southern sentiment.

A noticeable feature of Volck's etchings of Southern scenes is that he had the least possible comprehension of Negro physiognomy. This is conspicuous in the frightened child on the floor of the slave cabin in *Slaves Concealing Their Master.* The mammy, mainly because of the traditional headdress, is somewhat more convincing.

Prayer in Stonewall Jackson's Camp is no masterpiece, but it does summarize a whole phase of the Civil War. Through the efforts of the Bible Societies, the Tract Societies, and church publishing houses, the Confederate armies in 1861 and 1862 were flooded with religious literature. In 1863 began the great religious revivals in camps. Bell Irvin Wiley tells us in his *Life of Johnny Reb* that the revivals in Jackson's corps started early in March, and quotes a private's letter of April 12:

"Gen Jackson (God Bless him) has given us

the privileg to be exempt from Morning's Drill in order that we may attend preaching . . . we have two sermons each day & although we have no church to worship in we all sit around on the ground and listen to the sweet sound of the Gospel."

Gen. Thomas J. Jackson, Lee's right-hand man—"I know not how to replace him," wrote Lee after the fatal accident in the twilight on the victorious field of Chancellorsville—was himself a devoted Presbyterian. After Bull Run he was hero and legend to the South and to his adoring soldiers, who cheered wildly whenever "Old Jack" came in sight. The piety of this figure out of the Old Testament was well known in the Army of Virginia. "On the eve of battle, he would rise several times during the night for prayer, and he was so strict in his observance of the Sabbath that he would not even write a letter to his wife when he thought it would travel in the mails on Sunday. His favorite company was that of Presbyterian divines; his chosen topic of conversation was theology" (*Dictionary of American Biography*). He stands at the left in Volck's drawing, his hands folded in prayer, the eyes that flashed with intense excitement in action now stern and raised to a stern God of Battles.

PLATE No. 98. *Plate 21, Going into Camp at Night. [Below plate:] Copy-righted 1876 by E. Forbes. [Signed in pencil:] Mrs. Edwin Forbes.*

Etching, printed in sepia. 11 x 15⅞ inches. From Edwin Forbes, Life Studies of the Great Army: A Historical Work of Art, in Copper-plate Etching, Containing Forty Plates, Illustrating the

186

Life of the Union Armies during the Years 1862–'3–'4–'5.

PLATE No. 99. *[Infantry Soldier on Guard], William J. Jackson Serg^t Maj 12th N. Y. Vol. Sketched at Stoneman's Switch near Fredricksburg, V^a Jan. 27th/63.*
Pencil drawing by Edwin Forbes. 12½ x 9¼ inches.

EDWIN FORBES, staff illustrator for *Frank Leslie's Illustrated Newspaper* from 1861 to 1865, is known entirely through his war drawings. The best of them were collected in the volume of copper-plate etchings, *Life Studies of the Great Army,* in which *Going into Camp* is the twenty-first plate. The set received an award at the Centennial Exposition in Philadelphia in the year of its publication. Forbes, a New Yorker, was born in 1839 and lived till 1895, when he died in Flatbush. After the war he continued to trade on his sketches of camp and battle life, illustrating in the same hasty manner a number of children's stories. In 1891 he wrote his reminiscences, *Thirty Years After, An Artist's Story of the Great War,* an entertainingly chatty text to accompany his remaining sketches. For several years before his death he was paralyzed on one side, and painted and wrote with his left hand. This may possibly account for the curious circumstance of his wife's signature on Plate 21.

The list of titles for the plates in *Life Studies of the Great Army* bears explanatory legends. *Going into Camp at Night* is glossed: "The fields on all sides are covered with troops who are engaged in cooking supper, the column in the road marching on and disappearing over the hill in the distance."

Forbes had begun his art study in 1857 by specializing in animal painting, and then had turned to *genre* and landscape. Few of his sketches are portraits, and of those few, most are stiff and wooden; but the sketch of Sgt. William J. Jackson, a solemn lad with his arm resting on his rifle, has a direct emotional appeal considerably beyond that of Forbes' crowded scenes. Sergeant Jackson is young but toughened by campaigning; the sorry fortunes of the ill-generalled Army of the Potomac have led him to expect little, but it is not likely that rebel raiders will knock out Stoneman's Switch without paying a stiff price for it.

PLATE NO. 100. *Fort Albany, at Arlington Heights Erected 1861 by the 25th Regiment, N. Y. S. M. Colonel: M. K. Bryan. Lieut. Colonel: J. Swift. — . — Major: D. Friedlander. [16 references]. ☆ Published by E. F. Ruhl, No 114 Broad St Albany, N. Y. ☆ Entered according to Act of Congress in the Year 1862 by E. F. Ruhl, in the Clerks Office of the United States District Court, for the Northern District of N. York.*

Lithograph, printed in color. 12¾ x 19½ inches.

Fort Albany, just below the turn from Arlington Ridge Road into the old Columbia Turnpike on Arlington Heights, was the fourth of the fortifications erected on the Virginia side for the defense of Washington. On May 23, 1861, three columns of the volunteer army crossed the Potomac—one by the Georgetown Aqueduct, one by water to Alexandria, the third across the Long Bridge, at the foot of Fourteenth Street. This last was under Maj. Gen. Samuel P. Heintzelman, commanding the New York Volunteers. He reported:

"We advanced with the 25th N. Y. on the Columbia turnpike and took post between Roach's and Dr. Antisell . . . The 25th N. Y. S. M. was posted at the toll-gate and Vose's Hill on the Columbia turnpike."

By dawn of next day ground was broken for Fort Corcoran below the Aqueduct and Fort Runyon just across the Long Bridge—on about the site where in a later struggle the largest war office in the world has placed its Pentagon Building—but it was a week more before Fort Albany was laid out and its construction commenced. The buildings and works were put up by the 25th N. Y. Regiment on the spot where they had encamped, and there a part of the Army of the Potomac wheeled and turned practising the formations which prepared them to break the charge at Malvern Hill and face the fire of Fredericksburg. The fort is described in the report of a commission of Engineers to the Secretary of War late in 1862:

"Fort Albany is a work partly bastioned, well built and in admirable condition; the parapets being turfed and the scarps revetted with boards. It is well defiladed and in a very advantageous position to cover the Long Bridge and look into the gorges of Forts Richardson and Craig. It sees the high ground in front of Fort Tillinghast and commands the valley between Forts Richardson and Scott. It is well provided with magazines, embrasures, and bomb-proofs. Some heavy rifled pieces are required."

It will be noted that there is no lithographic artist or printer named on this view, but only the Albany publisher, E. F. Ruhl. It may be guessed that Ruhl had commissioned one of the larger houses to produce a print which could be most widely marketed in Albany; or that one of these houses had selected him as their Albany agent in the local marketing of a series of such views.

PLATE No. 101. *Commissary Department. Encampment of the Mass. 6ᵗʰ. Regiment of Volunteers at the Relay House near Baltimore Md. 1861. Published by J. H. Bufford, Boston. ☆ From a sketch by Alfred Ordway. J. H. Bufford's Lith. 313 Wash. St. Boston. ☆ Entered according to Act of Congress in the year 1861 by J. H. Bufford in the Clerk's Office of the District Court of Mass.*

Tinted lithograph. 9 x 13⅝ inches.

The proud Sixth Massachusetts Regiment of Volunteer Militia, "first to offer its services; first to reach its State's capital; first to reach the nation's capital; first to inflict suffering on traitors; first to attest its sincerity with its blood" (*Historical Sketch of the Old Sixth Regiment,* by John W. Hanson, Chaplain, 1866), was also the first regiment of the war to see its commissary tent set up on the march, complete with market building and supply tent, signs from home on the trees, and sides of beef beneath the butcher's knife. The encampment at the Relay House, near Baltimore, here sketched by Alfred Ordway, lasted only two hours on April 19—4 days after Lincoln's call for volunteers—but the boys, risen in the Concord and Lexington tradition from Middlesex, Essex, Suffolk, and Worcester Counties, were already veterans. Within two days they had mustered at Lowell, Boston, and Worcester, and entrained for the South. At New York, Jersey

City, and Philadelphia, huge ovations awaited them, thousands of people lining the tracks, and making "all possible demonstrations of applause."

In the early morning of April 19 they crossed the Mason and Dixon line—the first Yanks to invade the Southland. And at Baltimore there waited another crowd, this time a mob with stones and pistols. Four Massachusetts soldiers lay dead and 36 bore wounds for the Union when that shed, the "Washington Market," was taken over by the commissary, the sign of "Bay State House" tacked up, and dinner cooked. By suppertime they were in Washington.

An interesting touch in Ordway's sketch is the white headdress, the "havelock," worn by the soldier on the right, a phenomenon of 1861. The "name came from the designer, the British General, Sir Henry Havelock, whose troops suffered from exposure in India." Made of heavy white drilling, they hung in long flaps over the soldiers' necks. "As havelocks were declared to be a perfect protection from sunstroke, they were made in enormous quantities by ladies who longed to be of service. All over the Union, bales of white drilling piled up in church sewing circles, and soon the volunteers, wearing a faintly Bedouin air, were enduring the heat of the havelocks, as well as the rays of the sun" (Margaret Leech).

The lithographer JOHN H. BUFFORD worked in this profession from at least 1835 until after 1871. He had begun as an apprentice under William S. Pendleton in Boston, but about 1835 went to New York, where he worked for Endicott and Nathaniel Currier. In 1841 he went back to set up his own lithographing firm in Boston, where he became one of the principal

American lithographers, publishing a great number of prints and issuing catalogs. He is most often recalled in connection with his apprentice, Winslow Homer, who got his professional start in Bufford's shop.

ALFRED ORDWAY (1819–97), the Boston landscape artist who sketched the scene at the Relay House, may also have exerted an influence on the young Homer whose reputation was so far to outshine his own. Ordway in 1854 had been founder of the Boston Art Club, and his canvases of spots around Boston, such as *On the Charles River,* and *Newton Lower Falls,* were well known to Boston art lovers. As an older man and already an established artist, it is not improbable that he was with the 6th Massachusetts in a reporting capacity.

PLATE No. 102. *Funeral of Col. Vosburgh— The hearse approaching the R. R. Depot.*

Pencil and wash drawing by A. R. Waud. Undated. 10½ x 14¾ inches.

On May 22, 1861, in Richmond a Confederate correspondent noted, "Flags halfmast yesterday [presumably in Washington] for the death of Col. Vosburgh, 71st N. Y. Regt." The funeral procession which Alfred Waud sketched as it passed from the navy yard toward the railway depot on the Mall below the capitol, must have been the first of many such cortèges to take its sad and stately way through the Washington streets during the war, and was probably much more elaborate than those in its later stages. Interesting points in this impressive drawing are the dome of the Capitol, still under construction, the riderless horse led behind the hearse, and the Zouave uniforms of the military escort.

Abram S. Vosburgh had been since 1852 colonel of the "American Rifles," of the old New York State Militia, the predecessor of the 71st Regiment. This regiment, known as "Second Excelsior Brigade," had signed at once in 1861 as three-month volunteers. With 950 men, Vosburgh sailed on April 21 in the vanguard from New York for the defense of Washington. But the gallant charge at Fair Oaks, the chief glory of the 71st N. Y., was ordered by another leader; Vosburgh died of a hemorrhage of the lungs in his bed at the Navy Yard on May 20. In fact he had no business to take the field at all.

Both as first officer casualty of the New York volunteers, and as a leading citizen, Colonel Vosburgh received distinguished honors. *Harper's Weekly* of June 8, 1861, carries an illustration of a magnificent funeral parade in New York City, where he was buried on May 23. It was led by two regiments of cavalry and detachments of at least five regiments, and followed by an escort of the 71st, the Home Guard, and "Tammany Society of which the deceased was a member."

A few days later in Washington came the funeral procession of the young and vastly popular Col. Elmer E. Ellsworth of the New York Fire Zouaves, shot down by a secessionist innkeeper as he removed the Confederate flag from the Marshall House in Alexandria, which town his regiment had been sent to occupy. Washington, not yet inured to daily violent death, was plunged in mourning.

PLATE No. 103. *Skedaddler's Hall, Harrison's Landing ☆ Sketch in Sutler's store Excelsior Brigade July 3ʳᵈ [1862]*

Pencil and wash drawing by Alfred R. Waud. On brown tinted paper. 10 x 14¼ inches.

189

Harrison's Landing on the James River was the base to which McClellan transferred his army before winning the victory of Malvern Hill during the Peninsular Campaign. In that battle of July 1, 1862, the "brilliant conduct" of the "Excelsior Brigade" (72d N. Y.) was especially noticed by General Hooker. So it is a false impression that is given by the soldiers' appellation, "Skedaddler's Hall" where on July 3d the valiant warriors are sketched taking their ease.

"To skedaddle," meaning "to retire hastily, to decamp," or in plainer words, to run away, was a bit of Civil War soldiers' argot that replaced an earlier favorite verb, "to absquatulate." The *New York Tribune* on the 10th of August 1861, regarded it as confined to enemy behavior: "No sooner did the traitors discover their approach than they 'skidaddled' (a phrase the Union boys up here apply to the good use the secesher make of their legs in time of danger)." Apparently "Skedaddler's Hall" was the nickname for the 1862 version of a U. S. O. center, where the first to retire from action may have found the softest seats. Like much other Civil War slang, the word has found a lasting, though now somewhat archaic, place in the American language.

PLATE NO. 104. *A Sutler's Tent, Aug 1862.*

Pencil and wash drawing by Alfred R. Waud. On gray paper. 7⅞ x 9¼ inches.

In his exhaustive study, *The Organization and Administration of the Union Army, 1861–65,* Fred Albert Shannon speaks of the various camp followers, "grafters, pay-discount sharks, gamblers and sutlers . . . ever ready to relieve the soldier of any inconvenient burden

of money." Others came and went, but "sutlers were an ever-present evil." Their tents or booths were set up in each encampment, and there only could the soldier go for any relief from the monotonous army fare. The rations were one pound of "hardtack," one and one-quarter pounds of fresh or salt beef or three-quarters of a pound of bacon, beans, rice or hominy, and coffee. Such delicacies as fruit, cheese, butter, jam, and above all tobacco, could be had only by recourse to the sutlers. Beer and whiskey they sold publicly or in private. They were protected in their trade by the government, no other salesmen peddling their commodities being permitted in the camps. Concessions to sutlers were usually secured in their states through political influence, and they enjoyed a semiofficial connection with the regiments. Their charges were what the traffic would bear—60 cents for a pound of cheese, a dollar a plug for tobacco, $1.00 or $1.25 for a can of fruit, 15 cents for cigars. They very soon took all a soldier's money in hand, and established a lien on his pay for his purchases on the cuff.

By the autumn of 1861 congressional legislation was needed to straighten out the difficulties of soldiers and sutlers. The camp merchants fought against its enactment. An act of December 24, 1861, repealed the earlier legislation that had allowed the sutlers to attach monthly pay; but in March 1862 this was changed to permit a slight lien. The final provision was that "no sutler could sell to any soldier on credit to the extent of more than a quarter of his month's pay each month and his legal claim was to be only one-sixth." Sale of intoxicants was forbidden. A board of officers in each regiment was appointed to fix prices, which they did with infinite diversity and frequent cases of split profits.

The soldiers naturally rejoiced when the En-rollment Act of 1863 specifically stated that sutlers were not to be exempt from the draft.

Alfred Waud's drawing was made five months after passage of the act of March 1862, but apparently this sutler was doing as he pleased about the limitation on whiskey. Were the double-X bottles opened for privates as well as for officers? Beside the partly-cut cheese on the shelf hang the scales, for which the artist may have felt as much distrust as does the soldier turning resignedly away with his bundle.

PLATE No. 105. *Confederate Camp, during the late American War.*

Chromolithograph, after the painting by C. W. Chapman, Ordnance Sergeant, 59th Virginia Regiment, Wise's Brigade, by M. & N. Hanhart, London, 1871. Louis Zimmer, Publisher, No. 83, Charlotte Street, Fitzroy Square, London, England. 10⅛ x 15¼ inches.

CONRAD WISE CHAPMAN, of whose work the *Confederate Camp* is one of the finest and most polished examples, was by profession an artist and the son of an artist. His father, John Gadsby Chapman of Virginia, was an Academician, a distinguished portrait, historical and landscape painter, illustrator, etcher and wood engraver. The father's textbook on drawing, *Chapman's Drawing Book,* was familiar to all art students of the time, and his panel of the "Baptism of Pocahontas" is in the rotunda of the Capitol at Washington. He went to live in Rome in 1848, when his son Conrad was six years old. The 19-year-old, romantic boy was beginning to paint under his father's tutelage in Italy when the war broke out. He at once rushed home to America, worked his way West from New York, and joined a Kentucky regiment. A violent partisan, he was conspicuous for courage. At Shiloh he received a bad head wound, from which he never fully recovered. Through his father's influence he was transferred to General Wise's brigade, where he held the nominal rank of ordnance sergeant.

Wise's brigade was sent to Charleston, S. C., and there Chapman was detailed to make paintings of the fortifications of Charleston Harbor. The 31 paintings that resulted are among the treasures of the Confederate Museum in Richmond. It was perhaps at this time that he also painted the picture of camp life from which this elegant colored lithograph, produced in England, was made. The live oaks and pine trees dripping with grey moss suggest a locale in the deep South. Chapman made other pictures of camp life, microscopically fine and delicate in detail, as well as portrait sketches of Confederate soldiers and officers.

In December 1864, he was given leave to go to Rome with Bishop Lynch of Charleston, and ran the blockade. In the spring of 1865 he started to return, but on the way back learned of the fall of the Confederacy. He drifted down to Mexico and there did more painting as well as taking part in the troubles of Maximilian's day. The old wound in his head bothered him, and the fear of being considered a deserter preyed on his romantic temperament. When he went back to Rome and to art he lost his mind. He eventually recovered, lived in Mexico, and came back to Richmond hoping to enlist in the Spanish-American War, but was rejected as too old. He tried Mexico again, then New York, and finally came home, very poor and proud, to die in Virginia. A few years before his death (1910) he gave his remaining pictures and those of his father to the State of Virginia. They are now in the Virginia State Library.

PLATE NO. 104. *[Mustered Out] A. R. W.*

Pencil and wash drawing by Alfred R. Waud. On green tinted paper. 9¾ x 14¼ inches.

No note can be found as to where Waud sketched this proud and happy homecoming scene. From the numbers of wives, sweethearts, and offspring, it may be assumed to be one of the Southern or border States. Free Negroes had from the first tried to enlist, both in Confederate and Union armies. After the Emancipation Proclamation (September 22, 1862), Lincoln authorized four Negro regiments, and the total enrollment of Negroes in the Federal forces during the war approximated 200,000. The larger part were recruited in Confederate territory. They were used mainly for garrison duty, guarding lines of communication and the like, but at the Petersburg Crater, Fort Pillow and other battlefields, they fought bravely. *A History of the Negro Troops in the War of the Rebellion,* by Col. George W. Williams (1888), expresses the metamorphosis of the Negro in glowing language:

"The part enacted by the Negro soldier in the war of the Rebellion is the romance of North American history. It was midnight and noonday without a space between; from the Egyptian darkness of bondage to the lurid glare of civil war; from clanking chains to clashing arms; from passive submission to the cruel curse of slavery to the brilliant aggressiveness of a free soldier; from a chattel to a person; from the shame of degradation to the glory of military exaltation; and from deep obscurity to fame and martial immortality."

It is pleasing to have evidence in Waud's sketch that the reward of the Negro soldiers was not limited to glory and military exaltation. The mustering-out process here includes a file into the building auspiciously marked "Banking Office." Alfred Waud, an Englishman by birth, appears from this and other sketches to have found in the negro countenance a source of innocent merriment.

PLATE NO. 107. *Interior View of the Cooper Shop Volunteer Refreshment Saloon, the first opened for Union Volunteers in the United States. 1009 Otsego St. Philadelphia. [Names of the committee, including that of Wm. M. Cooper].* ☆ *[Above:] Exterior View.* ☆ *Chromo-Lithography of M. H. Traubel 409 Chestnut St. Phil^a.* ☆ *[Copyright notice by Wm. M. Cooper and C. V. Fort, 1862.]*

Chromolithograph. 32¼ x 19¾ inches.

At Philadelphia the troops from the Northern States changed trains. The railroad brought them to Camden and ferries took them across the river to the foot of Washington Avenue, where the Philadelphia, Wilmington and Baltimore Railroad had its station near the Navy Yard. The soldiers arrived hungry. On May 26 and May 27, 1861, two "refreshment saloons— free" were opened by the patriotic Philadelphians. Both were volunteer organizations, supported by private contributions, and both kept up their work throughout the war. The larger of the two, the Union Volunteer Refreshment Saloon, was the better known, feeding nearly 900,000 soldiers through the four years of war, but the Cooper Shop Volunteer Refreshment Saloon beat its competitor by one day in its official opening. Mr. William M. Cooper and Mr. Henry W. Pearce, partners in an "oak-cooper's" (barrel manufacturer's) firm, were the leading spirits, provided one of their buildings on Otsego Street, just southwest of Washington Avenue, and stand in the forefront of the Philadelphia lithograph, not averse to the free advertising afforded by public philanthropy and patriotism.

The gentlemen of the committee stood for their portraits in front, but the ladies, who blushed at showing their faces in a public scene—note in the "Exterior View" above how many of his ladies the artist has drawn in hoop-skirted and shawled rear views—contributed unceasingly of their time and skill. As a troop train left Jersey City, day or night, a telegram was sent to the Union, and a small cannon fired. Like the O. C. D. volunteers of 1942–43 at the "blue" siren signal, the ladies poured out and hurried to the rival sheds, where they began cooking. Small boys watched the river bank and rushed up to call for the second gun when the boats came in sight.

A soldier's letter home, dated June 1, 1863, describes what followed:

"Dear Parents:—I will endeavor to give you a faint description of our reception in Philadelphia, but I know that my pen cannot half do justice to the subject, but I do know that the remembrance of it will live in the hearts of our brave artillery boys as long as they are able to train a gun or draw a sword in the defence of their country. As soon as we reached the city we marched to the dining saloon, about ten or fifteen rods from the ferry. As soon as we got there we entered the washroom, a room large enough to accommodate sixty or seventy men to wash at a time. Then we marched into a splendid hall, with room enough to feed five hundred men at a time. There were gentlemen to wait on us, and they would come around and ask if we had plenty and urge us to eat more. We had nice white bread, beautiful butter, cold boiled ham, cheese, coffee, with plenty of milk and sugar . . . After we had eaten our fill, which was considerable, for we had eaten nothing since morning, we returned to the streets. Our knapsacks on the sidewalk were left without a guard, but they were almost covered with little children who were watching to see that no one disturbed them . . . It seemed that the people could not do us enough honor . . ."

The two Volunteer Refreshment Saloons did not limit their USO service to food, but each maintained a small hospital as well. Letter paper, stamps, "Soldiers' Guides," Bibles, prayer books and tracts, and even daily newspapers were given to any boy who asked, and there were occasional entertainments, and religious services on Sundays.

To see that their good works were not hidden under a bushel, Messrs. Cooper and Fort commissioned a large chromolithograph from Morris H. Traubel & Co. Like many of the Philadelphia and Cincinnati lithographers, Traubel (1820–97) was of German birth, and had learned lithography in his native city of Frankfurt am Main. In business in Philadelphia from his thirtieth year, and by himself from 1854 to 1869, Traubel successfully applied the new methods of color or chromolithography.

Plate No. 108. *Soldiers Rest, Alexandria, V.ª*

193

Commanded by Capt. John J. Hoff. ☆ Entered according to Act of Congress A. D. 1864 by Chas. Magnus in the Clerks Office of the S. District of N. Y.

Lithograph, colored by hand. 10¾ x 16¾ inches.

PLATE No. 109. *U. S. A. Gen Hospital Patterson Park, Baltimore M.ᵈ ☆ [Names of officers in charge.] ☆ Lith & Print by E. Sachse & Co. 104 S. Charles St. Balto. ☆ Entered according to Act of Congress in the year 1863 by E. Sachse & Co. in the Clerks Office of the Dist. Court of Md. ☆ [Above: View of Baltimore, with two references.]*

Lithograph, printed in color. 11 x 17 inches.

The first wounded of the war, streaming back from Bull Run, met an appalling lack of preparation. The antiquated Army Medical Bureau had no hospitals, few nurses, and pitifully small supplies of food, clothing and medicines. Churches, halls, and warehouses were turned into hurried substitutes for hospital wards, while charitable ladies gathered in relief societies. To meet an acute need the United States Sanitary Commission was formed in June 1861. This most important of all organizations for war relief, which absorbed most of the local Aid Societies, was supported by private contributions, church offerings, and "Sanitary Fairs" throughout the North. Its work, directed by its able secretary, Frederick Law Olmsted, and carried on before the end of the war by 500 agents, covered all forms of aid—in field, camp, and hospital, transportation, nursing, inspection, relief to the disabled, and care of dependent families.

Large on the list of the Sanitary Commission's charges bulked the convalescent soldiers. The trains and troop ships after every battle unloaded in Washington and the other cities crowds of disabled men, too exhausted and weak to go on with their regiments, yet not so desperately wounded as to be allowed hospitalization. Streets were filled with stragglers and walking wounded. Convalescents were discharged from the overcrowded hospitals still weak and ill, far from home and penniless. The Sanitary Commission established soldiers' lodges to care for these victims of war.

In Washington and in nearby Alexandria, where the first tide of retreat from the battle front in Virginia rolled in its flood, the lodges were placed near the depots. There hot meals were served, first aid given, and the soldiers sorted out, housed, and cared for till ready to return to their regiments, or provided with money to make their painful way home. In the picture of the Alexandria Soldiers' Rest, the receiving lodge is right beside the station, a long shed, with the name of the Sanitary Commission above it. Soldiers pile into it from the train. Farther on, in a big enclosure dominated by a huge flagpole, stand the rows of barracks which the poor convalescents called "Camp Misery."

By 1863 the Army Medical Service had undergone reorganization and with the aid of the Sanitary Commission was establishing general military hospitals. Miss Dorothea Dix, appointed Superintendent of Female Nurses by the Surgeon General in June 1861, had organized her staffs of devoted women. Typical of the buildings erected was the Patterson Park General Hospital in Baltimore, which is pictured in the second print—long barracklike rows around a court, with fairly adequate windows and balconies. For the interior scene in such hospitals, Walt Whitman has left his testimony:

"There is a long building appropriated to each ward. Let us go into ward 6. It contains to-day, I should judge, eighty or a hundred patients, half sick, half wounded. The edifice is nothing but boards, well whitewash'd inside, and the usual slender-framed iron bedsteads, narrow and plain. You walk down the central passages, with a row on either side, their feet towards you, and their heads to the wall. There are fires in large stoves, and the prevailing white of the walls is reliev'd by some ornaments, stars, circles, etc., made of evergreens. The view of the whole edifice and occupants can be taken at once, for there is no partition. You may hear groans or other sounds of unendurable suffering from two or three of the cots, but in the main there is quiet—almost a painful absence of demonstration; but the pallid face, the dul'd eye, and the moisture on the lip, are demonstration enough" (*Specimen Days in America*).

And in *Drum Taps,* "The Wound Dresser":

Bearing the bandages, water and sponge,
Straight and swift to my wounded I go . . .
To the long rows of cots up and down each
  side I return,
To each and all one after another I draw
  near, not one do I miss,
An attendant follows holding a tray, he car-
  ries a refuse pail,
Soon to be fill'd with clotted rags and blood,
  emptied, and fill'd again.
I onward go, I stop,
With hinged knees and steady hand to dress
  wounds,

I am firm with each, the pangs are sharp yet
  unavoidable,
One turns to me his appealing eyes—poor
  boy! I never knew you,
Yet I think I could not refuse this moment to
  die for you, if that would save you.

On, on I go, (open doors of time! open hos-
  pital doors!)
The crush'd head I dress, (poor crazed hand
  tear not the bandage away,)
The neck of the cavalry-man with the bullet
  through and through I examine,
Hard the breathing rattles, quite glazed al-
  ready the eye, yet life struggles hard,
(Come sweet death! be persuaded O beauti-
  ful death!
In mercy come quickly.)

Soldiers Rest was turned out by CHARLES MAGNUS & Co., a New York lithographic house with a Washington branch at 520 Seventh Street. They specialized in letterheads and views, but during the Civil War brought out a great body of war scenes. The firm lasted from 1858 through the 1870's, and aimed at time-liness rather than any more enduring quality in their output.

PLATE NO. 110. *Union Prisoners at Salisbury, N. C. ☆ Lith of Sarony, Major & Knapp, 449 Broadway, N. York. ☆ Drawn from Nature by Act. Major Otto Boetticher. ☆ New York, Published by Goupil & Co., [Su]ccessor, 772 Broadway Paris, Goupil & Cº London, Goupil & Cº [Copyright notice to Otto Boetticher, 1863.]*

Lithograph, printed in color. 20¾ x 37¼ inches.

The tragic condition of prisoners, Union and Confederate, is remembered as perhaps the most cruel aspect of the long civil strife. Out of the vituperation and recriminations on both sides, and from close study of official reports, the historians have sifted a few facts. "Professor Channing concludes that 'each government cared for its enemy prisoners about as well as . . . for its own soldiers'; while Dr. Hesseltine pointed out that each side displayed mismanagement, congestion and unfitness of officer personnel, and that in the North as well as the South one finds disease, filth, depression, disorder, vermin, poor food, lack of elementary sanitation, and as a result, intolerable misery and death on an appalling scale" (J. G. Randall). The difficulties of exchange and release were such that no enduring plan could be worked out. A cartel arranged on July 22, 1862, for the exchange of prisoners soon broke down because of many such complications as those of parole and the Confederate refusal to exchange Negro soldiers. From 1863 on enormous numbers of prisoners were taken and held by both sides. Official reports show that, without reckoning captured men released on the field, the Confederates took nearly 195,000 Union prisoners and the Federals about 215,000 Confederates. "The embarrassment of the South, especially in the later part of the war, in attempting to care for these hordes of captives at a time when its own transportation and supply system was broken down . . . must be remembered in judging the admittedly frightful conditions which existed at Andersonville, Belle Isle, and Salisbury."

In January 1862, the Confederate prison at Salisbury, N. C., was opened. Prisoners taken at Bull Run and succeeding battles of 1861, who had been crowded at Richmond, were sent to

the site, an abandoned cotton factory, with neighboring buildings, formerly boarding houses, shaded by a grove of oaks, the whole surrounded by a board fence. Food in 1862 was fairly plentiful, though the prisoners pronounced the beef to be horse or mule. By the time of Jackson's victories in the Shenandoah Valley early that year, the prison was too crowded to receive more occupants. The Union soldiers were released under the cartel of exchange in the late summer, and the prison was continued for political prisoners and deserters. There were 800 of these when in early October 1864, 7,500 Yankee captives from the horribly overcrowded Richmond prison, Belle Isle, were transferred there.

"Salisbury on a smaller scale reproduced all the defects of Andersonville," comments Dr. Hesseltine. There was a scarcity of water, unbearable stench, only 11 acres of red clay mud; the rations, like those of the Confederacy itself in that bleak year, were all too meagre; the local wheat crop failed. Disease was prevalent; "from October 1864 to February 1865, 3,479 prisoners died out of a total of 10,321 confined there."

OTTO BOETTICHER's picture has nothing to do with the horrors of the Salisbury prison camp. There is a fence, it is true, but the men strolling, sitting, lying, smoking and sporting in the enclosure all seem sufficiently clad, sturdy and cheerful. The new national game is going spiritedly forward in the center of an apparently contented ring. Captain Boetticher was at the camp only for a few months in 1862, at a time when conditions were not yet out of hand. The Muster Rolls show that he was captured on March 29 and exchanged for a Confederate of equal rank, Capt. F. Culbertson, 7th Vir-

196

ginia, at Aiken's Landing on September 30.

The 68th New York Volunteer Regiment of Infantry, a largely German organization of which Boetticher was a member, was raised at the call for three-year volunteers in July 1861. On July 22d, Col. R. J. Belge, of New York City, received authority from the War Department to recruit a regiment. The New York Muster Rolls show that Otto Boetticher, age 45 years, was enrolled on July 22, and mustered in as Captain, Co. G, on August 14, 1861. The 68th N. Y. was with the Army of the Potomac, and if the date of March 29 given for Captain Boetticher's capture is accurate, he must have been caught in reconnoitering or skirmishing at the very opening of the Peninsular Campaign, as no regular fight is recorded for the regiment on that day. Captain Boetticher was "dismissed" from the regiment on April 18, 1862—perhaps as missing. His exchange in September has already been noted. He spent a few months at home, and was mustered in again as Captain, Co. B, on February 28, 1863. His discharge came on June 9, 1864, and with it a brevet as lieutenant-colonel for gallant and meritorious conduct.

Boetticher's drawing from nature has been turned into a magnificent color lithograph by our old friends Sarony and Major, now with an additional partner, Joseph F. Knapp. The firm was now increasingly immersed in commercial commission work, and it is therefore not surprising that this print was published by GOUPIL & CO., a New York branch of the Paris house which has always been renowned for superb illustration.

PLATE No. 111. *Libby Prison, Richmond, V*ª ☆
*Published by J. L. Baldwin C*ᵒ*B, 58*ᵗʰ *Reg*ᵗ *Ind*ª

*Vet. Vol*ˢ*. Sketched by W. C. Schwartzburg C*ᵒ *A, 24*ᵗʰ *Wis. Vol*ˢ ☆ *Entered according to Act of Congress in the year 1864 by J. L. Baldwin in the Clerks Office of the District Court of Md.*

Lithograph, printed in color. 8½ x 11⅜ inches.

PLATE No. 112. *Libby Prison, Richmond, Va.*

Photograph by Alexander Gardner, April 1865. Original negative. 9 x 11 inches.

The evil name of Libby Prison is second only to that of Andersonville. It had been a tobacco warehouse in Richmond, belonging to the firm of Libby & Son, whose advertisement, obvious in the sketch, says, "Ship chandlers and groceries." Here, in a constant storm of indignation, the commissioned Union officers were held. Conditions were certainly equally bad if not much worse, on hopelessly overcrowded Belle Isle, the island in the James which was the Richmond prison camp for enlisted men, where New York "bounty-jumper" toughs ran wild, but the rank of the inmates of Libby Prison gave greater publicity to their protests. The prison contained eight rooms, 103 by 42 feet each, with unplastered walls, a water-closet—the officers called it a foul privy—on each floor, and a stove to each room. The officers cooked their own food, supplementing the prison fare with purchases of vegetables and fruit; there were bitter and frequent complaints of the rations, which produced official investigations. An acute shortage of supplies, especially meat, in the winter of 1863–64, sent Richmond prices skyhigh, and for a time Libby prisoners received no meat at all. In February 1864 the famous "tunnel escape" was accomplished by 109 officers. Almost half were recaptured, but those who reached Union lines did not understate their sufferings in the prison.

In the fall of 1863 General Lee had protested against holding prisoners in Richmond, and the crowded conditions, lack of guards, and shortage of supplies there had decided General J. H. Winder, inspector-general of prison camps, to remove the prisons farther south. Andersonville, near Macon, Ga., was selected for the new location. Transfer had already begun when, at the end of February came rumors of a Federal cavalry raid under way against Richmond, specifically aiming to free the prisoners. The city was thrown into panic, and the warders placed a charge of powder under Libby Prison, warning that if any attempt were made at escape the warehouse would be blown up. As the raid failed, it could not be proved that the authorities had seriously contemplated such action. However, the prisoners were moved rapidly thereafter to the South, officers to Macon, soldiers to Andersonville, and Libby Prison became only an overnight stop on the trip to a still more fatal place.

By rights, neither WILLIAM C. SCHWARTZ-BURG of the 24th Wisconsin Volunteers, who drew the sketch, nor John L. Baldwin, 58th Regiment, Indiana Veteran Volunteers, who published it, should have been acquainted with the interior of Libby Prison, which was supposedly reserved for officer guests. Schwartzburg was a private from Milwaukee, mustered in on August 1, 1862, who had been wounded and taken prisoner at Chickamauga. He was eventually mustered out, probably after exchange. He might, being wounded, have been at one of the Richmond hospitals rather than at Belle Isle. John L. Baldwin was from Princeton, Ind., and

had been mustered into the 58th Regiment on November 12, 1861. There is no record of his being a prisoner. He served his three years and was mustered out on November 11, 1864.

The photograph of Libby Prison, taken after the surrender of Richmond, shows a curious crowd gathered about the blackly famous building. No doubt some of them are former inmates. The stars and bars, which Schwartzburg saw flying from the roof, are gone, replaced by the victorious Union flag. Miss Josephine Cobb of the National Archives informs us that the photograph was taken from Castle Thunder, in April 1865, by ALEXANDER GARDNER. This Scotchman was brought to America in 1856 by Mathew B. Brady, who valued his experience in the collodion process—the "wet" process which was the first great improvement in photographic technique and supplanted the daguerreotype in the course of the later fifties—and his (then rare) ability to make enlargements. After two years in the New York Studio he was sent, in 1858, to take charge of the new gallery which Brady was opening in Washington. After four years he seceded and opened his own gallery in the capital, but was soon thereafter employed in making maps at the headquarters of the Army of the Potomac. This position on the inside gave Gardner and his son Jim an admirable opportunity for war photography, which was seized, and the result practically incorporated in a two-volume *Sketch Book of the War,* with 50 actual photographs in each volume, published in 1866. This invaluable collection gives the names of many of the Brady and Gardner staff photographers, the men who actually made the negatives. Gardner declared, in his first advertisement of May 26, 1863, that he had "a corps of artists constantly in the field, who are adding to the collection every day." Some 20 years after the war, the Gardner negatives were secured and added to one of the portions of the Brady Collection by its then owners, and it is difficult today to distinguish what is Brady from what is Gardner.

PLATE No. 113. *Andersonville Prison, Georgia. Representing the imprisonment of 33,000 Union Soldiers during the months of June, July and August, 1864.* ☆ *[At top:] N⁰ 1. North View.* ☆ *Sketched by John Burns Walker Co G 141ˢᵗ Regᵗ P V I* ☆ *[8 References.] [In plate:] Hohenstein* ☆ *T. Sinclairs lith, 311 Chestnut St. Philada.* ☆ *Entered according to an Act of Congress in the year 1865 by John B. Walker in the Clerks Office of the District Court of the U States for the Eastern District of Pennsylvania.*

Tinted lithograph. 14⅜ x 20⅛ inches.

PLATE No. 114. *Andersonville Prison Georgia. Numbers 1 and 2 comprise Andersonville Prison an area of 26 acres, nearly 5 acres of which was an uninhabitable swamp. In June, July and August, 1864, 33,000 Union Prisoners were crowded on the remaining 21 acres. [8 references.] Sketched by John Burns Walker, Co G 141ˢᵗ Reg P V I* ☆ *T. Sinclair's lith 311 Chestnut St. Philadelphia.* ☆ *Entered according to an Act of Congress in the year 1864 by John B. Walker in the Clerks Office of the District Court of the U. States for the Eastern District of Pennsylvania.*

Tinted lithograph. 14½ x 20⅛ inches.

In December 1863 Capt. Richard B. Winder, a cousin of the harassed commander of Richmond prisons, was sent to the "miserable little hamlet" of Andersonville, near Macon, Ga., to prepare a place for 10,000 prisoners. He encountered considerable opposition in the neighborhood and had to impress labor; supplies were not forthcoming and the prison was in no way ready when the first prisoners arrived on February 27. The 16½ acres (later enlarged to 26) had been enclosed by a stockade of 20-foot pine logs with roofed sentry boxes at intervals. The two gates on the west were protected by a double stockade (shown in the North View, Plate 113). A stream ran through the middle of the yard, and the ground sloping toward it on either side was soon turned into a muddy swamp by thousands of Union feet.

The first comers found no shelter and no bake house. All trees had been cut down and there was no protection from the Georgia sun, welcome enough in February, but soon to become hideously cruel. Lumber needed for barracks was not to be had; the cook house was put by the stream just outside the stockade, where the refuse polluted the water; rations, as more and more prisoners were brought in, grew smaller and smaller—"corn bread and beans," rarely meat. Many arrived sick from the camps to the northward and hospital facilities were hopelessly inadequate. By early May there were 12,000 prisoners in the stockade, and 1,026 had already died.

On March 27, Capt. Henry Wirz, the Swiss-American disciplinarian who had begun as sergeant in charge of prisoners at Tuscaloosa and had been General Winder's assistant in Richmond, came to command the interior of the prison. The only man convicted after the close of the Civil War as a "war criminal," he was tried and hanged in November 1865; and his name has since been synonymous with vindictive cruelty. Reference No. 7 in the "North

199

View" shows "Capt. Wirz taking a prisoner to the stocks." He was accused of the wanton murder of prisoners, of pursuing escaped Yankees with bloodhounds, of personal responsibility for the horrible suffering. Later investigation has shown him to have been an efficient and reasonably well-meaning man, faced with hopeless conditions.

By the end of July there were 31,678 prisoners in the stockade; during the six months from March 1 to August 31, 42,686 cases of disease and wounds were reported. There are 12,912 graves in the National Cemetery—John Burns Walker has printed on the side of the death wagon in his picture, "Dead, 12,877."

John Burns Walker was a Pennsylvanian, private in the 141st Regiment, which was recruited in Bradford, Wayne, and Susquehanna Counties in 1862, and mustered in on August 26. The regiment went first to the defenses of Washington, and then fought at Fredericksburg, Chancellorsville, Gettysburg, and Petersburg. Walker was not with it at the Siege of Petersburg; he had been taken prisoner on May 28, 1864, probably in some of the manoeuvering between Spotsylvania and Cold Harbor, as Grant side-slipped his forces toward Richmond. A strong lad he must have been, well-fortified by Allegheny mountain air, to have stayed alive through those horrible summer months at Andersonville. His release came only at the end of the war, with the General Order of May 26 emptying the Confederate prisons.

Walker had his sketches turned into lithographs by the well-known Philadelphia firm of Sinclair, and we have here a rather late instance of the craftsman who drew the sketch on stone, inserting his name in the plate, a practice which waned with the commercialization of lithog-

raphy. "Hohenstein," who signed the "North View" and was doubtless also responsible for the "South View" since the style is identical, is in all likelihood the Anton Hohenstein who drew a handsome portrait of General Lee for Spoliny of Philadelphia in 1867; it is reproduced as Plate 141 in *America on Stone*.

Plate No. 115. *Council of War at Massaponax Church; General Grant, General Meade, Assistant Secretary of War Dana, etc., May 21, 1864.*

Photograph by Mathew B. Brady. Negative enlarged from original. 6 x 8 inches.

At last President Lincoln had found his general. The valiant Army of the Potomac, welded through three years of discipline and drill and up-and-down warfare under changing leadership into a massive and superb fighting instrument, was handed over on March 9, 1864, to Ulysses S. Grant, along with the President's commission as lieutenant general in general command of the Union armies.

Grant lost no time and spared no strength. Since Gettysburg the Union armies in the east had manoeuvred bloodlessly in Northern Virginia, just above the Rappahannock, which had been the southernmost boundary of Federal progress. Richmond, the rebel capital, was still nearly a hundred miles away. On May 4, Grant launched his army across the Rapidan and into the Wilderness. For two days the tangled woods glowed with forest fires, set by the bitter fighting. The result was indecisive, both armies shattered and exhausted. McClellan, Hooker, Pope or Meade would have withdrawn to recuperate: Grant thrust forward to Spotsylvania. Wrote the Confederate, George Cary Eggleston:

"Here was a new Federal general, fresh from the West, and so ill-informed as to the military customs in our part of the country that when the battle of the Wilderness was over, instead of retiring to the north bank of the river and awaiting the development of Lee's plans, he had the temerity to move by his left flank to a new position, there to try conclusions with us again. We were greatly disappointed with General Grant . . ."

Around Spotsylvania the battle raged from May 8 until May 21. Grant wrote to the Chief of Staff, Halleck, on May 11: "We have now ended the sixth day of very hard fighting . . . I propose to fight it out on this line if it takes all summer." Headquarters moved rapidly. Grant's own *Memoirs* describe the stream-filled land:

"The Mattapony River is formed by the junction of the Mat, the Ta, the Po and the Ny rivers, the last being the northernmost of the four. It takes its rise about a mile south and a little east of the Wilderness tavern. The Po rises south-west of the same place, but farther away. Spotsylvania is on the ridge dividing these two streams, and where they are but a few miles apart."

The Telegraph Road, Stanard's Mill, Guiney's Bridge, the Mud Tavern, unknown little local names, figure in the despatches and reports that flew between the field commanders. On May 21, 1864, at 8:25 A. M., Grant sent word to Major General Burnside, Ninth Army Corps, that at 10 his headquarters would be moved to Massaponax Church. By 8:30 the next morning his date line was Guiney's Sta-

tion, whence he wrote to Halleck, "We now occupy Milford Station and south of the Mattapony on that line." By June 3 he had pushed far south to Cold Harbor, where Lee's army squarely blocked the way on the Richmond road. There three army corps were hurled into the enfilading Confederate fire, and in eight minutes Grant lost most of his 12,000 casualties. The month's campaign, from the Wilderness to Cold Harbor, cost the Union 55,000 soldiers, almost as many as Lee's whole army. But the advance had begun, the smaller Confederate loss could less easily be replaced, and the final grand strategy of the war was being unfolded.

The photographer has caught a moment in the design of this strategy, as Grant and his staff sit studying their maps during the few hours at Massaponax Church. It was perhaps around noon, when the light would be good for a picture. Benches have been brought out of the church for the officers to pose on. The saddled horses are ready—in a few minutes the despatches will be flying. The officer standing at the lower right is not used to being photographed—he moved, and his head is a double blur. Grant himself is lost in thought and does not glance at the camera. Is there a cigar in the side of his mouth?

We have attributed this photograph to Brady, because the negative is in the Brady Collection of the Library of Congress, but there is strong evidence that it was actually taken by Alexander Gardner, or under his auspices. *America in Stone* reproduces as Plate 77 a lithograph drawn and published by C. Inger of Philadelphia which is almost certainly derived from this photograph, and which states that it is "From Small Photograph by Gardner." If this one is representative, the practice of deriving lithographic prints from photographs was aesthetically dismal. In spite of a number of alterations by Inger—most of them decidedly for the worse—the scene is cluttered and inferior in composition. However, Inger was satisfied that Grant did have, or should have had, a cigar in his mouth. The lithograph claims that Sherman, Grant, Hancock, Meade, Garfield, Thomas, Heintzelman, Sickles, and Warren were all present. This was complete nonsense: Sherman and Thomas were fighting the Atlanta campaign; Sickles had not yet returned to active duty after losing a leg at Gettysburg; Heintzelman was in command of one of the northern departments, etc.—another instance of the journalistic abuse of the lithograph.

PLATE No. 116. *Ponton Bridge on the Appomattox, before Petersburg. Point of Rocks. Butlers Headquarters. A R Waud.*

Pencil and wash drawing, on gray-tinted paper. Undated. 8¾ x 13½ inches.

PLATE No. 117. *Dutch Gap.*

Pencil and wash drawing by Alfred R. Waud, on green-tinted paper. Undated. 6½ x 9 inches.

The bloody check at Cold Harbor caused Grant to change his "fight it out on this line" strategy. He abandoned the frontal attack on Richmond, and transferred his whole army south of the James, a notable feat of logistics and engineering. By the 17th of June his armies were in front of Petersburg.

A subsidiary campaign had been planned in that region; the "Army of the James," which had been placed under the command of Gen. Benjamin F. Butler, was to move from its head-

quarters at Fort Monroe up the James River against Richmond and Petersburg. On May 4 Grant directed Butler to advance. The Army of the James embarked on steamers and sailed toward almost undefended Petersburg. By May 6th Butler was far up the James, and had seized City Point and Bermuda Hundred. In the next week he advanced slowly to Drewry's Bluff. Beauregard, called hurriedly from Charleston to command the Department of North Carolina, which was extended to include Petersburg, resisted Butler with scratch troops, and the political general drew into a strong natural position on a point between the James and the Appomattox Rivers. There he sat, unable to move, while Beauregard gathered together an army from North and South Carolina. Said Grant in his official report: "His [Butler's] army, therefore, though in a position of great security, was as completely shut off from further operations directly before Richmond as if it had been in a bottle strongly corked."

This hermetically sealed spot of Butler's headquarters, Point of Rocks, forms the subject of Waud's drawing. A print from the sketch—wrongly attributed to William Waud—appeared in *Harper's Weekly* on July 23. In the background is identified the *Greyhound*, General Butler's flagship. The date may be any time in late May, June or early July, judging, that is, from the *Harper's* print. Butler's headquarters remained unchanged until the next spring, when the Union drive finally forced the Confederates to withdraw and "uncork the bottle" Butler himself was replaced in the command by Gen. E. O. C. Ord on January 8, 1865.

Apparently both Waud brothers visited Butler at his well-placed camp, for it was there that William painted the stirring picture of night signalling. Alfred also sketched the excavating and teamster activities at Dutch Gap Canal. This unfortunate project was an inspiration of General Butler's. During Grant's first attack on Petersburg (June 15–18) a communication was sent to the commander of the Army of the James, in which "the importance of holding a position in advance of his present line [was] urged upon him" (Grant's Report). Butler thought it over, called in the Engineer, Gen. P. S. Michie, and conceived "the idea of cutting a canal through the narrow neck of land, known as Dutch Gap, for the passage of the monitors." On August 10, ground was broken, while Grant's army lay recovering from the terrible repulse of the Crater (July 30). The canal was to be only 174 yards long, but it would cut off 4¾ miles of river navigation. Sixty-seven thousand cubic yards of dirt were excavated. The diggers worked under continuous fire; there were great losses in mules, horses, and carts, and occasional human casualties. "The greater part of the excavation was done by colored troops, who displayed the greatest courage and fortitude, and maintained under the most trying circumstances their usual good humor and cheerful disposition." But the need for the canal diminished as changes of strategy moved the main fighting away from Petersburg, and, though Dutch Gap Canal was completed on December 30, 1864, it was never used during the war.

PLATE No. 118. *[Night Signalling.]*

Wash drawing by William Waud. Undated. 5¾ x 10½ inches.

Harper's Weekly of November 12, 1864, published a print of *Signalling by Torches across*

James River from General Butler's Headquarters. An explanation accompanies the picture:

"The messages from the high signal-tower on the other side of the river are read by the sergeant or officer at the telescope, and the reply is signaled by the man with the torch."

It must be seen to be believed, the distressful result of the process which transferred William Waud's fine wash drawing—a high point of his work, as represented in the Library of Congress collection—to the pages of *Harper's*. Every iota of artistic quality has evaporated.

PLATE No. 119. *Before Petersburg—at Sunrise, July [3]0ᵗʰ 1864—A R Waud.*

Pencil and wash drawing. 13½ x 20 inches.

Petersburg, the gateway to Richmond from the South, was confronted by the Union forces in mid-June 1864. General Beauregard, resisting desperately against heavy odds, held off the first attack on June 15–18. Then Lee arrived with the remnants of the Army of Northern Virginia, and Grant and his legions settled down to the siege which was not to be broken till Lee took the final road to Appomattox in the following spring.

The chief event of the long siege was the Battle of the Crater, July 30, 1864. One of Burnside's officers in the Ninth Corps, which held an advanced position in the Union lines, was Lt. Col. Henry Pleasants, a mining engineer from the Pennsylvania coal region. His suggestion that a mine be run under the enemy forts was approved by Burnside, and for a month "the spade took the place of the musket." A 500-foot gallery was run under the lines, with two short lateral galleries. The dirt had to be carried the whole length of the gallery in baskets, and shortage of proper tools slowed the undertaking. But Colonel Pleasants had the mine finished on July 23, and eight magazines of powder were placed in the two side galleries, ready for the explosion. Confederate papers were already carrying accounts of the mining processes going on.

Burnside's original plan was to have the attack following the explosion spearheaded by the Fourth Division of the Ninth Corps, the only division of Negro soldiers in the Army of the Potomac. They had not yet been used in active fighting, they had been thoroughly drilled by their brigadier, Gen. Edward Ferrero, and their enthusiasm was high. In *Battles and Leaders of the Civil War* a colonel of the brigade (later General), Henry Goddard Thomas, gives a moving account of the black troops. When, some time before, they had received the news that they were to lead, they did not fall into excited discussion, as white soldiers would have done; they sat quiet, "studying." Then one began to sing:

"We looks like men a-marchin' on,
    We looks like men-er-war."

For the remaining days before the battle the Negroes sang this song. After the crater it was not heard again.

There has been much speculation as to what might have been the results if the Fourth Division had been sent forward as planned, but late on the night of the 29th, with the explosion of the mine set for 3:45 the following morning, Grant and Burnside changed the orders, at General Meade's very reasonable objection. Grant testified in his evidence before the Committee on the Conduct of the War: "General Meade said that if we put the colored troops in

front . . . and it should prove a failure, it would then be said, and very properly, that we were shoving these people ahead to get killed because we did not care anything about them."

The mine was exploded before dawn on July 30. "It was a magnificent spectacle, and as the mass of earth went up into the air, carrying with it men, guns, carriages, and timbers, and spread out like an immense cloud as it reached its altitude, so close were the Union lines that the mass appeared as if it would descend immediately upon the troops waiting to make the charge" (Maj. William H. Powell in *Battles and Leaders*). A "crater" 30 feet deep and 170 feet long was left, and through it Burnside's men attacked, in a hopeless confusion of débris. The furious Southerners, fighting at the peak of their magnificent courage, flung them back. The whole operation cost almost 4,000 Union men—"a stupendous failure," Grant said.

Powell's "magnificent spectacle" is the subject of Alfred Waud's fine drawing, in which the staff, well back on high breastworks, watches the explosion as it occurs. The mouth of the mine gallery is evident behind a small clump of trees at the right. The towers of Petersburg stand out in the distance.

PLATE No. 120. *Sheridans Wagon Trains in the Valley—Early morning—[A] R Waud.*

Pencil and wash drawing. Undated. On light brown paper. 6¾ x 19¼ inches.

While Grant and the main force of the Army of the Potomac lay facing Lee's worn veterans at Petersburg, diversionary activities raged in western Virginia. The brilliant Confederate cavalry general, "Jeb" Stuart, was dead—killed at Yellow Tavern, six miles north of Richmond, which he had saved from the raid (May 9–24, 1864) of three divisions of Northern cavalry, 10,000 strong, under its new commander, Maj. Gen. Philip Sheridan. But Lee's able infantry general, Jubal A. Early, was moving in the Shenandoah Valley. Lee had detached him from the main force to drive away a small Union division near Lynchburg, and Early turned in a bold and dangerous move northeastward. Washington was again in panic as Lew Wallace with a ragtag force delayed but did not stop Early at the Monocacy (July 9). Lincoln wired to Grant for aid, and, to Baltimore citizens, "Let us be vigilant but keep cool." While inspecting the Washington defenses, the President was sworn at and unceremoniously ordered out of danger by a young lieutenant from Massachusetts, named Oliver Wendell Holmes, Jr. Then Grant sent troops, Early retreated behind the Blue Ridge, and Washington recovered from its "terrible fright."

Sheridan and his cavalry now moved against Early in the Shenandoah Valley. Their orders were to devastate. There were quick movements, skirmishes, battles. On September 19 the armies clashed near Winchester. Sheridan had been in Washington, consulting with the General Staff; on his return he heard the firing "twenty miles away," and rode post-haste to snatch victory out of what looked like disaster. Northern schoolrooms ever since have thrilled to Thomas Buchanan Read's stirring martial verses, "Sheridan's Ride." The Union success was followed on September 22 by another victory at Fisher's Hill, and Early retired, to fight no more till spring.

Then Sheridan turned to his second task. Alfred Waud's picture shows the early morning movement of the procession of wagon trains.

Nothing that could be of use to the army was left behind them.

> *In the Shenandoah Valley, the millwheels*
> *   rot.*
> *(Sheridan has been there.) Where the houses*
> *   stood,*
> *Strong houses, built for weather, lasting it*
> *   out,*
> *The chimneys stand alone. The chimneys are*
> *   blackened.*
> *(Sheridan has been there.) This Valley has*
> *   been*
> *The granary of Lee's army for years and*
> *   years.*
> *Sheridan makes his report on his finished*
> *   work.*
> *"If a crow intends to fly over the Valley now*
> *He'll have to carry his own provisions," says*
> *   Sheridan.*
>
> (S. V. Benét, *John Brown's Body*.)

PLATE NO. 121. *Bombardment of Fort Fisher Jan. 15th 1865. To Commodore G. W. Godon this Print is respectfully dedicated. By his obedient servant T. F. Laycock, U. S. N. ☆ [Names of ships.] ☆ From a drawing by T. F. Laycock. Lith and Published by Endicott & Co 59 Beekman St. N. Y. [Copyright notice, 1865]*

Lithograph, printed in color. 6 x 17½ inches.

The reduction of Fort Fisher was the final large-scale naval action of the war. This strong coastal defense stood at the entrance to the Cape Fear River before Wilmington, N. C., guarding that last remaining harbor of the blockade-runners bringing supplies from overseas. Lee had written from Petersburg in the winter of 1864 that Fort Fisher must be held at all costs. Gens. B. F. Butler and Godfrey Weitzel, in combination with Admiral Porter's 60-ship squadron had tried to take it in December 1864, but the stout North Carolina garrison held out behind their powerful works.

In January 1865 a second expedition was sent out. On the 13th, 8,000 Union troops under Gen. Alfred H. Terry were landed on the beach to the north. Porter's armada (with 600 heavy guns, according to Gen. Braxton Bragg, the commander of the Confederate forces in Wilmington, who failed to support the fort) attacked from the sea. The bombardment went on for three days, the five monitors keeping up a fitful fire all night. The guns of the fort were silenced on the 14th. On that day, relates Col. William Lamb, the Confederate commander, a "stupid" flat-bottomed steam transport, loaded with stores for Lee's army, sailed right into the enemy's fleet and, of course, fell an easy captive.

On January 15th the full bombardment reopened at 9 a. m. At noon a landing detachment of sailors and marines, about 2,000 men from 35 ships, were sent ashore. At the angle of the two faces of the fort they were caught in an intense rifle fire from the ramparts. There were many casualties, and the mixed force retreated in "a disorderly rout" (Lamb). Meanwhile the troops under Terry had approached and gained the highest parapets to the north. The way was cleared before them by renewed heavy fire from the monitors. The iron-clad vessels can be seen to the right behind the line of larger ships in Laycock's print. The fight lasted till 10 p. m., when the hopeless defenders surrendered. The last Confederate stronghold on the Atlantic had fallen.

Of T. F. LAYCOCK, the sailor artist who dedi-

206

cated his picture to his commanding officer, nothing is known beyond his record in Callahan's *List of Officers:*

Laycock, Thomas F. Mate, 26 January, 1863. Acting Ensign, 7 April, 1864. Acting Master, 20 March, 1865. Honorably discharged 2 December, 1865.

The officer honored by his obedient servant was Commodore Sylvanus W. Godon, an officer of the old Navy, who had started his career as a midshipman in 1819. In 1855 he was a commander, in 1862 a captain, commanding the sloop *Mohican.* He was promoted to commodore on January 2, 1863. In 1866 he was named Rear Admiral, and retired with that rank in 1871. The lithograph, from the great house of Endicott, is a handsome piece of work.

PLATE No. 122. *[On verso of drawing:] General Sherman reviewing his Army in Savannah before starting on his new campaign.* ☆ *Among the mounted officers behind Major General Sherman are Gen. Williams Logan, Slocum, Geary, Baird, Woods Smith &c* ☆ *[References:] Bay Street Custom House.*

Pencil and wash drawing by William Waud. 9 x 12¾ inches.

"Savannah, Georgia, December 22, 1864.
To His Excellency President Lincoln,
  Washington, D. C.
I beg to present you as a Christmas gift the city of Savannah, with one hundred and fifty heavy guns and plenty of ammunition, also about twenty-five thousand bales of cotton.
[Signed] W. T. Sherman, *Major-General.*"

The famous march to the sea began on November 16, 1864. General Sherman, commanding the Military Division of the Mississippi, had the day before burned Atlanta, ending the long summer campaign against Joe Johnston and Hood. His army consisted of 55,329 infantry, 5,063 cavalry, 1,812 artillery, an aggregate of 62,204 officers and men. They marched out of the city smouldering in ruins by the Decatur road, singing "John Brown's body lies a-mouldering in the grave, His soul goes marching on."

Their purpose was the destruction of supplies, and the sixty-mile-wide course through Georgia was to the Union soldiers a picnic procession. Field orders specified that the order of march should be as nearly as possible by four parallel roads, that "the army will forage liberally on the country during the march," that foraging parties, "under the command of one or more discreet officers," were to gather and keep in the wagons 10 days' provisions and three days' forage. "To corps commanders alone is intrusted the power to destroy mills, houses, cotton-gins etc.; . . . should the inhabitants . . . manifest local hostility, then army commanders should order and enforce a devastation more or less relentless . . ." Horses, mules and wagons might be appropriated "freely and without limit," though with discrimination in favor of the "poor and industrious, usually neutral or friendly." The troops were ordered to "refrain from abusive or threatening language."

Sherman describes in his Memoirs the exhilaration of the march, the singing and foraging soldiers, the negroes, "simply frantic with joy," trooping after the army. "No doubt," he admits, "many acts of pillage, robbery, and violency, were committed by . . . parties of foragers, usually called 'bummers'; for I have since heard of jewelry taken from women, and the plunder of articles that never reached the commissary; but these acts were exceptional and incidental." However, probably few of Sherman's soldiers returned home without a well-selected store of "souvenirs."

The right wing of the army, under Gen. O. O. Howard, met some slight resistance near Macon, but Sherman and his staff marched unopposed into the State capital, Milledgeville, on the 23d. The State officials had fled, and the officers "(in the spirit of mischief) gathered together in the vacant hall of Representatives, elected a Speaker, and constituted themselves the Legislature of the State of Georgia." Sherman "was not present at these frolics, but heard of them at the time, and enjoyed the joke." Farther on, at the Oconee, there was feeble resistance, soon broken. The march went on, through Waynesboro and Millen, and on December 10 Sherman invested the city of Savannah. On the 13th Fort McAllister, the main defense on the Ogeechee River guarding the approach by sea, was captured. After a 10-day siege the Confederate defenders fled across the Savannah River into South Carolina, and Sherman estimated that damage in Georgia had amounted to $100,000,000—most of it "simple waste and destruction."

The general stayed in Savannah until January 21, 1865, when he started his troops northward for a campaign in South Carolina. It was during these first three weeks of the last year of the war that William Waud sketched Sherman reviewing his troops. The picture was reproduced in *Harper's Weekly* of February 11, with an additional section at the right in which are shown the heads and shoulders of marching infantry, and ranged behind the band a row of civilian

207

spectators. The explanatory text on a later page says: "General Sherman has instituted careful reviews of his entire army previous to its entrance upon a new campaign."

PLATE NO. 121. *The last of Genl. Lees Headquarters, Petersburg—after the battle—A. R. Waud.*

Pencil drawing, on light green paper. Undated. 6½ x 9 inches.

On April 3, 1865, after more than eight months of siege, the Union army marched into abandoned Petersburg, a ruined city of the dead. The desolation of defeat breathes heavily through Waud's tragic drawing, in which the four chimneys of the house rise starkly from shattered walls, and the very débris takes on the shape of hooded mourners.

PLATE NO. 124. *Grand Review of Army, at Washington, May 1865, Scene at Capitol.*

Photograph by Mathew B. Brady. Original negative, 8 x 10 inches.

On the Capitol of the United States the flag flies at half mast, the windows and pillars are bound with crape. The joy of victory, the happiness of welcoming home brave soldiers, is shadowed by the cruel sense of loss. Not only will half a million men who lie in the Southland never again come home; Lincoln, leader and symbol, is barely a month in his grave, and many spectators of the Victory Parade are still dressed in mourning black. The trial of the assassins, Paine, Atzerodt, Herold, Mrs. Surratt and the rest, has been suspended during the grand review of the armies.

On May 23 the spectators gathered. The re-

208

viewing stand for President, Cabinet and General Grant was in front of the White House, but the crowds lined the streets solidly from the Capitol the length of Pennsylvania Avenue. All day the veterans of the Army of the Potomac rode and marched by. The next day too, from early morning to late afternoon, the armies paraded. By nightfall 150,000 veterans had passed the reviewing stand.

Brady's photograph shows a tiny section of the spectators. Congressmen with their wives, daughters and parasols, sit and stand before the Capitol where, as in 1945, the bands, the floats, and the machines of war gather for the formation of the parade. The dome has been finished during these four long years of war, and though she cannot be seen in this picture, the nation knows that helmeted Freedom rests victorious on her sheathed sword.

PLATE NO. 125. *Lee and his Generals [Names under figures:] B. Bragg Pemberton Beauregard Fitz Hugh Lee J. E. B. Stuart Wade Hampton Joe Johnston Jubal Early J. C. Breckinridge A. S. Johnston E. K. Smith R. E. Lee Hardee Longstreet Forrest J. B. Hood A. P. Hill Stonewall Jackson J. H. Morgan R. S. Ewell Polk Mosby. ☆ [In plate:] Tholey. ☆ From an original sketch. Published by John Smith, 804 Market Str., Philadelphia ☆ [Copyright notice, 1867.]*

Tinted lithograph. 20 x 24 inches.

It is 80 years since the meeting in Appomatox Courthouse. All but the last few veterans of the valiant defeated Army of the Confederacy, "Marse Robert's" army, have died. But the names are still household words in the South. Here are the proud names, that have rung through a thousand meetings of the Daughters of the Confederacy, that have formed the subjects of hundreds of romantic novels or controversial volumes. If Jackson had missed that fatal bullet in the Wilderness, if Stuart and his cavalry had moved to Ewell's right flank, if Longstreet had arrived earlier on Seminary Ridge, if Beauregard . . . if Joe Johnston . . . if Bragg—

Here, too, are the faces, stiff photographic portraits attached to bodies sketched in a posed group, assembled in the print as never in fact, with the Virginia landscape, a squadron of Stuart's cavalry, and a line of bayoneted infantry behind them. In the central foreground, a spot which none will deny him, Traveller tosses his proud grey neck. When he died, fine old horse, after his master's end, his flowing mane and tail were thin—thousands of Southerners cherished each a hair. Of the rider let his biographer, Douglas Freeman, speak: "Others survive who shared his battles and his vigils, but none who so completely embodies the glamour, the genius, and the graces with which the South has idealized a hideous war." As man, as general, in defeat as in victory, Robert E. Lee wears the mantle of sure immortality.

Tholey, the signature in the plate, may stand for either or both of the brothers, CHARLES P. and AUGUSTUS THOLEY, Alsace-Lorrainers who came as boys to Philadelphia in 1848. Among the best lithographic craftsmen in Philadelphia, and as fast as they were expert, they specialized in drawing on stone, sending out the finished stones to be printed and published by other hands. A number of famous Civil War pictures were produced by them. John Smith was one of their regular publishers from 1863–69.

PLATE No. 126. *Lincoln and His Generals [Names:] Porter Farragut Lincoln Sherman Thomas Grant Sheridan.* ☆ *[In plate:] P. Kramer.* ☆ *Printed by A. Brett 83 Nassau St. N. Y. [Published by] C A Asp, 129 Washington St., Boston, Mass.* ☆ *Entered According to Act of Congress AD. 1865 by N. P. Beers in the Clerk's office of the district court of the U. S. for the Southern district of N. Y.*

Lithograph. 17¼ x 20⅝ inches.

Like the group photograph of the Southern leaders, the combined portraits of Lincoln and his generals are posed solely for the purpose of giving the hero-worshipping public its great figures *en masse*. Unlike the Confederate assemblage, this group does not include faces of the earlier days of the war—McClellan, Burnside, Buel, Halleck, Rosecrans, Hooker, all those whom the years of failure and frustration have seen superseded, have been dropped from the public eye.

At the left stand the admirals, Porter and Farragut, with behind them a glimpse of water, a frigate and an ironclad. On the right sits Sheridan, the great cavalry chief whose powers Grant brought to full development. Next to him, facing the President, stands Ulysses S. Grant, the general who brought victory. Behind are Sherman, the studious general who thought war was hell but knew how to wage it, and George H. Thomas, the "Rock of Chickamauga."

Lincoln sits on a stage rock, his beloved homely face turned to his general in chief. The long crisis, the fratricidal struggle is over, the mighty scourge of war has passed away. The words of his great address, a month before the end, are left as an enduring heritage:

With malice toward none; with charity for all; with firmness in the right, as God gives us to see the right, let us strive on to finish the work we are in; to bind up the nation's wounds; to care for him who shall have borne the battle, and for his widow, and his orphan—to do all which may achieve and cherish a just and lasting peace among ourselves, and with all nations.

The lithographer, ALPHONSE BRETT, was a veteran who had been active since the latter forties. In the course of the next decade he transferred his operations from Philadelphia to New York City. Although the present print is black and white, he usually preferred color. His business successor, the Brett Lithographing Co., is still active in New York in 1946.

PLATE No. 72. Negroes Mounting Cannon in the Works for the Attack on Fort Sumter, March 1861. Drawing by William Waud.

211

INTERIOR OF FORT SUMTER.

DURING THE BOMBARDMENT, APRIL 12TH 1861

PLATE No. 73. *Interior of Fort Sumter during
the Bombardment, April 12, 1861. Lithograph
by Currier & Ives.*

212

PLATE No. 75. *Washington Navy Yard, 1861.*
Drawing by Alfred R. Waud.

214

Minnesota Cumberland Wabash Susquehannah Fort Clark Ft Hatteras

Harriet Lane

Capture of the Forts at Hatteras inlet. First day, fleet opening fire and troops landing in the surf.

PLATE No. 76. *Capture of the Forts at Hatteras Inlet—First Day, August 27, 1861. Drawing by Alfred R. Waud.*

FORTRESS MONROE   RIP RAPS.

THE GREAT EXPEDITION...THE VESSELS AT ANCHOR AT HAMPTON ROADS,
FROM THE TOP OF THE HYGEIA HOTEL, OLD POINT COMFORT, VA.

PLATE NO. 77. *The Great Expedition—The Vessels at Anchor at Hampton Roads, c. October 28, 1861. Lithograph by Edward Sachse & Co., 1861.*

216

1.Sewall's Point Battery 30 Guns_ 2.Craney Island Battery 42 Guns_3.Yorktown_ 4.Jamestown_ 5.Monitor_ 6.Merrimac_7. Norfolk_8.Portsmouth_9.Suffolk_10.Minnesota_11.Pig Point Battery_12.Barre Point Battery_
13.Burning of the Congress_14.The Cumberland sunk_15.Newport News Point & Camp_16.St.Lawrence_17. Rip Raps_18.French Man-of War_

THE NAVAL ENGAGEMENT BETWEEN THE MERRIMAC AND THE MONITOR AT HAMPTON ROADS
ON THE 9TH OF MARCH 1862.

PLATE No. 78. *The Naval Engagement between the Merrimac and the Monitor at Hampton Roads, November 9, 1862. Lithograph by Edward Sachse & Co., 1862.*

217

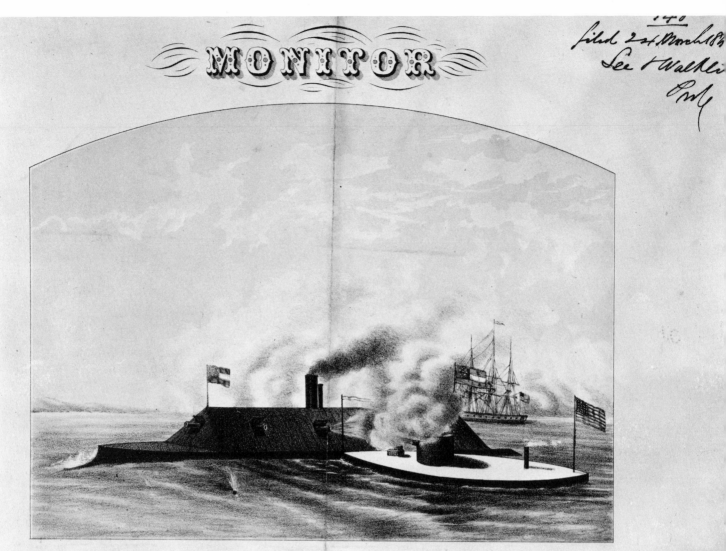

PLATE No. 79. *Monitor and Merrimac: Grand March, composed by E. Mack. Sheet music with lithograph by Thomas S. Sinclair, 1862.*

HED BY CURRIER & IVE'S.   152 NASSAU S! NEW

THE SECOND BATTLE OF BULL RUN, FOUGHT AUGT 29TH 1862.

Between the "Army of Virginia" under Maj. Gen. John Pope, and the combined forces of the Rebel Army under Lee, Jackson and others.__ This terrific battle was fought
e identical battle field of Bull run, and lasted with great fury from daylight until after dark, when the rebels were driven back, and the Union Army rested in triumph on the fie

PLATE No. 80. *The Second Battle of Bull Run,
Fought August 29, 1862. Lithograph by Currier
& Ives, 1862.*

219

PLATE No. 81. *The First Virginia Cavalry at a
Halt, Antietam Campaign, c. September 1862.
Drawing by Alfred R. Waud.*

220

PLATE No. 82. *Gallant Charge of Humphreys'*
Division at the Battle of Fredericksburg, Decem-
ber 13, 1862. Drawing by Alfred R. Waud.

221

PLATE No. 83. *Gallant Charge of Humphreys'
Division at the Battle of Fredericksburg, Decem-
ber 13, 1862. Wood engraving from "Harper's
Weekly," 1863.*

222

PLATE No. 84. *Winter Campaigning: The Army
of the Potomac on the Move, January 21, 1863.
Drawing by Alfred R. Waud.*

223

PLATE No. 85. *Embarkation of Ninth Army
Corps at Aquia Creek Landing, February 1863.
Photograph by Mathew B. Brady.*

224

PLATE No. 86. *Cemetery Hill previous to Pick-ett's Charge, July 3, 1863. Drawing by Alfred R. Waud.*

PLATE NOS. 87, 88. *The Battle of Gettysburg,
Third Day, July 3, 1863. Drawing by Edwin
Forbes.*

226

Plate No. 89. *Artist of "Harper's Weekly"*
(A. R. Waud) Sketching at Gettysburg. Photo-
graph by Mathew B. Brady.

228

PLATE No. 90. *The Pontoon Bridge at Cincinnati, 1862. Lithograph by Middleton, Strobridge & Co.*

229

The Battle of Stone River or Murfreesboro'.

Representing Gen. SAM. BEATTY'S Brigade on the 31st of December, 1862.

SKETCHED BY A. E. MATHEWS, 31st REG, O. V. I.

PLATE NO. 91. *The Battle of Stone River or Murfreesboro, December 31, 1862. Lithograph by Middleton, Strobridge & Co.*

TUSCUMBIA.   HENRY CLAY. FOREST QUEEN. SILVER WAVE. CARANDELET. PITTSBURG. MOUND CITY.   LOUISVILLE.   LAFAYETTE & GEN¥ PRICE.   FLAG SHIP BENTON.

ADMIRAL PORTER'S FLEET RUNNING THE REBEL BLOCKADE OF THE MISSISSIPPI AT VICKSBURG, APRIL 16TH 1863.

...all past ten P.M the boats left their moorings & steamed down the river, the Benton, Admiral Porter, taking the lead ___ as they approached the point opposite the town, a terrible con__ __rated fire of the centre, upper and lower batteries, both water and bluff, was directed upon the channel, which here ran within one hundred yards of the shore. At the same moment innume__ floats of turpentine and other combustible materials were set ablaze. In the face of all this fire, the boats made their way with but little loss except the transport Henry Clay which was set on fire & sunk.

PLATE NO. 92. *Admiral Porter's Fleet Running the Rebel Blockade of the Mississippi at Vicksburg, April 16, 1863. Lithograph by Currier & Ives, 1863.*

231

THE ARMY OF THE POTOMAC—A SHARP-SHOOTER ON PICKET DUTY.—[FROM A PAINTING BY W. HOMER, ESQ.]

PLATE No. 93. *A Sharp-Shooter on Picket Duty.*
Wood engraving after Winslow Homer, from
"Harper's Weekly," 1862.

232

PLATE No. 94. *The Press on the Field. Wood engraving after Thomas Nast, from "Harper's Weekly," 1864.*

233

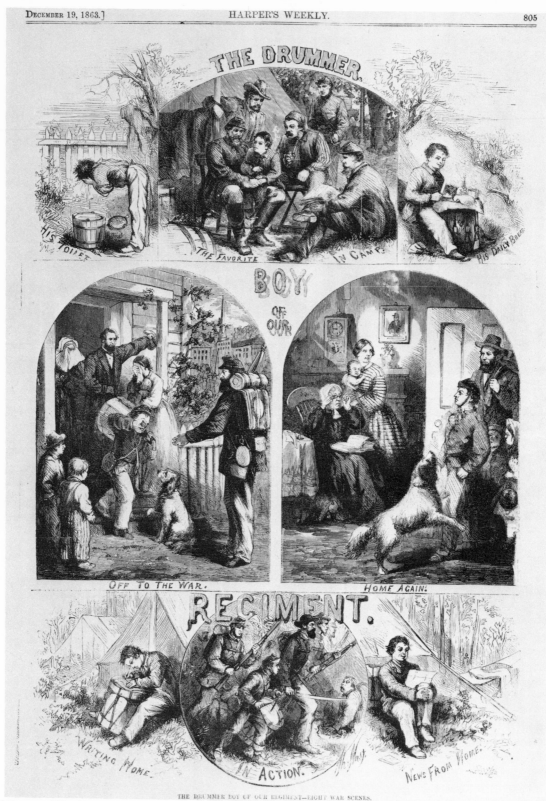

PLATE No. 95. *The Drummer Boy of our Regiment—Eight War Scenes. Wood engraving after Thomas Nast, from "Harper's Weekly," 1863.*

PLATE No. 96. *Slaves Concealing their Master from a Search Party. Etching by Adalbert J. Volck, 1862.*

235

PLATE No. 97. *Prayer in Stonewall Jackson's Camp. Etching by Adalbert J. Volck, 1862.*

236

PLATE No. 98. *Going into Camp at Night.*
Etching by Edwin Forbes, 1876.

237

PLATE No. 99. *Infantry Soldier on Guard: Sergeant William J. Jackson, January 27, 1863. Pencil drawing by Edwin Forbes.*

238

1. Rifle Comp?, Cap! F. Newdorf.
2. Light Infantry, Cap! J.J. Huber.
3. Emmet Guard, Cap! H. Mulholland.
4. Montgomery Guard, Lieut. T. M? Dermott.

5. Toll Gate.
6. Blacksmith Shop.
7. Roche's Farm.
8. Doctor's House.

FORT ALBANY,
AT ARLINGTON HEIGHTS
ERECTED 1861 BY THE 25TH REGIMENT, N.Y.S.M.
Colonel: M.K.BRYAN.
Lieut. Colonel: J.SWIFT. ———— Major: D.FRIEDLANDER.

9. Well.
10. Artillery, Cap! J. Fredendall.
11. Field & Staff Officers.
12. Musicians.

13. Lafayette Guard, Lieut. G. Godefroy.
14. City Volunteers, Cap! Frank Marshall.
15. Worth Guard, Cap! J. Gray.
16. Burgesses Corps, Cap! H. Kingsley.

PLATE No. 100. *Fort Albany, at Arlington Heights, Erected 1861 by the 25th Regiment, New York State Militia. Lithograph published by E. F. Ruhl, Albany.*

239

WASHINGTON MARKET

BAY STATE HOUSE

PLATE NO. 101. *Commissary Department, Encampment of the Massachusetts 6th Regiment of Volunteers near Baltimore, 1861. Lithograph by John H. Bufford.*

240

PLATE NO. 102. *Funeral of Colonel Vosburgh— the Hearse Approaching the Railroad Depot, May 1861. Drawing by Alfred R. Waud.*

PLATE NO. 103. *Skedaddler's Hall, Harrison's Landing, July 3, 1862. Drawing by Alfred R. Waud.*

PLATE NO. 104. *A Sutler's Tent, August 1862.*
Drawing by Alfred R. Waud.

PLATE No. 105. *Conféderate Camp, during the late American War. Chromolithograph by M. & N. Hanhart, London, 1871.*

244

PLATE No. 106. *Negro Soldiers Mustered Out.*
Drawing by Alfred R. Waud.

245

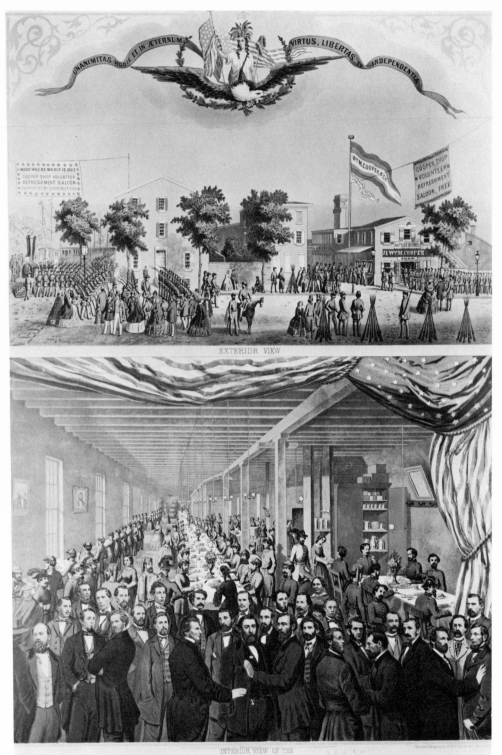

EXTERIOR VIEW

INTERIOR VIEW OF THE

COOPER SHOP VOLUNTEER REFRESHMENT SALOON,
THE FIRST OPENED FOR UNION VOLUNTEERS IN THE UNITED STATES.
1009 Otsego St. PHILADELPHIA.

PLATE No. 107. *Cooper Shop Volunteer Re-*
freshment Saloon, Philadelphia. Chromolitho-
graph by Morris H. Traubel, 1862.

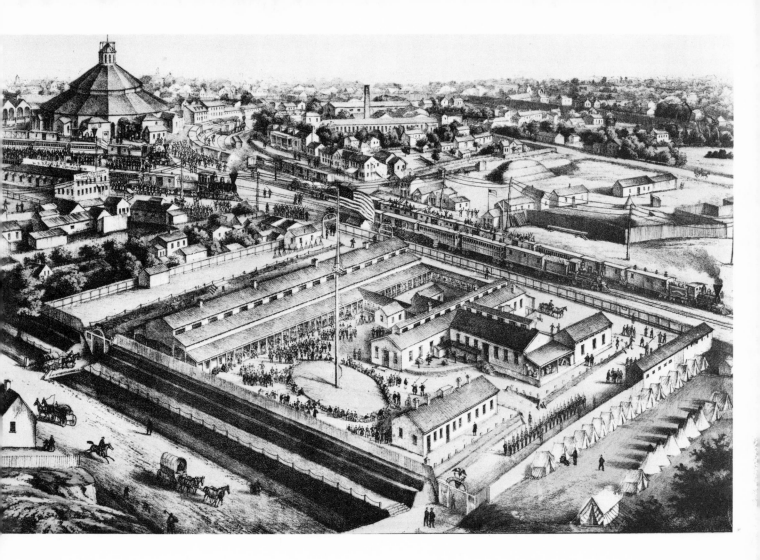

PLATE No. 108. *Soldiers' Rest, Alexandria, Va.*
Lithograph by Charles Magnus, 1864.

247

PLATE No. 109. *U. S. A. General Hospital, Patterson Park, Baltimore, Maryland. Lithograph by Edward Sachse & Co., 1863.*

248

PLATE No. 110. *Union Prisoners at Salisbury,
North Carolina, Lithograph by Sarony, Major &
Knapp, 1863.*

LIBBY PRISON, RICHMOND, VA.

PLATE No. III. *Libby Prison, Richmond, Va.*
Lithograph after W. C. Schwartzburg, 1864.

250

PLATE No. 112. *Libby Prison, Richmond, Va.*
Photograph by Alexander Gardner, 1865.

251

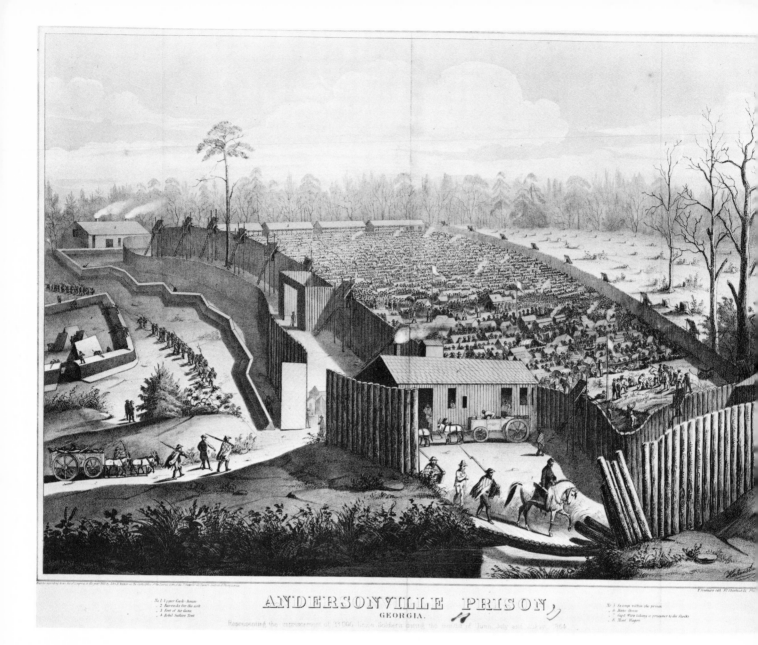

ANDERSONVILLE PRISON,
GEORGIA.

PLATE No. 113. *Andersonville Prison, Georgia:*
North View. Lithograph by Anton Hohenstein,
1865.

252

ANDERSONVILLE PRISON
GEORGIA.

PLATE No. 114. *Andersonville Prison, Georgia: South View. Lithograph by Anton Hohenstein, 1864.*

253

PLATE NO. 115. *Council of War at Massaponax Church, Virginia, May 21, 1864. Photograph by Mathew B. Brady.*

254

PLATE No. 116. *Pontoon Bridge on the Appomattox, below Petersburg, c. July 1864. Drawing by Alfred R. Waud.*

255

Dutch Gap

PLATE No. 117. *Dutch Gap Canal, c. October 1864. Drawing by Alfred R. Waud.*

256

PLATE No. 118. *Signalling by Torches across James River, c. October 1864. Drawing by William Waud.*

PLATE NO. 119. *Before Petersburg—Explosion
of the Mine at Sunrise, July 30, 1864. Drawing
by Alfred R. Waud.*

258

PLATE No. 120. *Sheridan's Wagon Trains in the Valley—Early Morning, c. October, 1864. Drawing by Alfred R. Waud.*

PLATE NO. 121. *Bombardment of Fort Fisher,*
January 15, 1865. Lithograph by Endicott & Co.,
1865.

260

PLATE No. 122. *General Sherman Reviewing his Army in Savannah, January 1865. Pencil drawing by William Waud.*

261

the last of Genl Lees Headquarters. Petersburg - after the battle

PLATE No. 123. *The Last of General Lee's Head-quarters, Petersburg, after the Battle, c. April 3, 1865. Drawing by Alfred R. Waud.*

262

PLATE No. 124. *Grand Review of the Army at Washington—Scene at Capitol, May 1865. Photograph by Mathew B. Brady.*

263

PLATE No. 125. *Lee and his Generals. Lithograph by Charles P. & Augustus Tholey, 1867.*

264

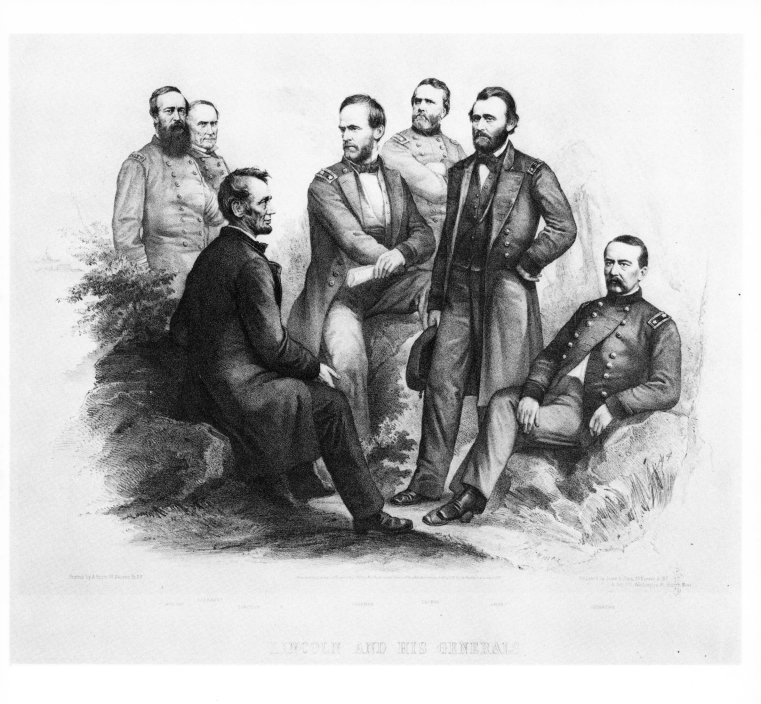

PLATE No. 126. *Lincoln and his Generals. Lithograph by P. Kramer, 1865.*

VIII

The Plains Indians
1862-1890

SIOUX, Cheyenne, Ute, Pawnee, Comanche, Kiowa, Arapaho: the names of the Plains Indians ring an echo of terror across the pages of our western history. As the new trans-Mississippi states filled the settlers, as the buffalo hunting grounds were stamped out by the oncoming railroads, and the nomadic tribes were pushed back, robbed, cheated and starved, the braves trained to the game of war turned it to deadly earnest, and resisted with unsurpassed ferocity. For thirty years, from the early days of the Civil War, when the outraged Sioux rose in Minnesota, until the remnants of Sitting Bull's bands—warriors, women and children—surrendered at Wounded Knee, December 28, 1890, and were brutally massacred on the next day by the vengeful Seventh Cavalry, the Indian wars are a tale of teachery, murder and rapine on one side and the other. But also of heroism—the great Indian leaders, Sitting Bull, Crazy Horse, Roman Nose, Red Cloud, Satanta, Chief Joseph of the Nez Percés, Little Wolf, bringing all the resources of primitive cunning to bear against the white men who threatened their people with extinction. No less stalwart were the American generals, who by patient and unremitting watchfulness, skill and courage overcame them—General Sheridan, Crook, Custer, Howard, Miles, and many more, with their tiny commands spread over a huge territory through which roamed hundreds of thousands of hostile Indians, their life devoid of comfort under the hardest frontier conditions, subject to uncomprehending reproach from public and government in the East, for over-severity as well as for lack of it. Little by little they reduced the savage bands, brought peace to the land, and—if they lived—put in their memoirs extenuation if not praise of their enemies and victims.

PLATE No. 127. [*A Sioux Chief.*] ☆ *Frederic Remington 1901.* ☆ *Copyright, 1901, by Robert Howard Russell.*

Color reproduction of a pastel. From Frederic Remington, A Bunch of Buckskins: Eight Drawings in Pastel, New York, R. H. Russell, 1901. [5th plate.] 20 x 15 inches.

The Plains Indians, says Catlin in his *North American Indians,* were "a bold and desperate set of horsemen." The whole character of Indian life west of the Mississippi was very different from the semiagricultural, foot- or canoe-traveling village culture of the East, in large part because of the wild horses, which, originating in strays from Spanish Mexico, multiplied into herds, and ran wild over the plains, the fleetest animals on the prairie. The Indians of the region, always nomadic, caught and broke the horses, and, says W. P. Webb, "the Plains Indians became the horse Indians." The buffalo of the prairies, which they hunted on their swift ponies, provided their chief means of existence. Their mode of warfare was not the stealthy

267

woodland rush of the Eastern Indians, but the charge of a natural cavalry. The Indian east and west fought with wariness and treachery, boldness and cruelty in advantage, or flight in necessity. "The horse fitted into this complex, made the Indian bolder in advance, faster in pursuit, and fleet as the wind in retreat" (Webb). Their savagery did not change—with them, said Col. Richard Dodge, "cruelty is both an amusement and a study."

Catlin's description of the buffalo hunter might have been written for the Sioux brave whom Remington painted, motionless on his buckskin pony, scanning the far horizon for the great beast who was to give him food, clothing and shelter, or for the white enemy:

"In the chase of the buffalo, or other animal, the Indian generally 'strips' himself and his horse, by throwing off his shield and quiver, and every part of his dress, which might be an encumbrance to him in running; grasping his bow in his left hand, with five or six arrows drawn from his quiver, and ready for instant use. In his right hand (or attached to his wrist) is a heavy whip, which he uses without mercy, and forces his horse alongside of his game at the swiftest speed . . . No bridle whatever was used in this country, by the Indians, as they have no knowledge of a bit. A short halter, however, which answers in place of a bridle, is in general use; of which they usually form a noose around the under jaw of the horse, by which they get great power over the animal; and which they use generally to *stop* rather than *guide* the horse."

To the American public the name of Frederic Remington (1861–1909) is synonymous with the Wild West: the Indian, the cowboy

and the broncho. His bronze sculpture group, "Broncho Buster," was perhaps the most popular American drawing-room piece for a generation after its exhibition at the Pan-American Exposition in Buffalo in 1901. Coming into vogue in the era of Teddy Roosevelt and the Rough Riders, and picturing the heyday of the western range, in his illustrations he set a style for the presentation of frontiersmen and horses. Himself a cowboy, he made his greatest contributions in the character interpretation of his *vaqueros,* ranchers and prospectors. However, all his figures are alive; his Indians are not just red men, but Sioux or Apache.

Remington was born at Canton, N. Y., of New England colonial stock. After the Civil War his father became editor of the *Ogdensburg Journal* and an influence in upstate New York politics. Remington went to a Vermont prep school and had two years at the Yale School of Fine Arts, where he played football on the eleven with Walter Camp. On the death of his father in 1880 he left Yale and went West, where he became a cowboy, scout and rancher. He came back, broke, with a bundle of drawings in 1883, got married and went to New York to study at the Art Student's League and to become an illustrator. He was over six feet tall, blonde, and was described as "very much like some Greek god in modern clothes." The rest of his life was spent in his chosen career, traveling wherever adventure or a life close to nature was to be found—Germany, Russia, North Africa, Cuba as a war correspondent in 1898, and above all, the American West. He produced an enormous stock of illustrations, paintings and sculpture, and wrote fresh, journalistic books as vehicles for his art. In later life he painted more in oil and illustrated less. His collection of his own work, with the Indian and cowboy trappings and equipment from which he achieved his accurate detail, is now in the Remington Art Memorial at Ogdensburg, and another large collection of his pictures is in the New York Public Library. He died in a new home at Ridgefield, Conn. in 1909. "Though there were delineators of the West and frontier before Frederic Remington . . . and there have been many since, none have surpassed him. He remains the outstanding artist in his field" (*Dictionary of American Biography*).

A Bunch of Buckskins, color reproductions of eight large pastels, number 5 of which is the *Sioux Chief,* was published, unaccompanied by text or even captions, in 1901. The other drawings are of cowboys, miners and horses.

PLATE No. 128. *Hostile Indian Camp.* ☆ *Photo and copyright by Grabill, '91. Deadwood, S. D.* ☆ *J. C. H. Grabill, Official Photographer of the Black Hills & F. P. R. R., and Home State Mining Co., Studios: Deadwood and Lead City, South Dakota.*

Photograph. Negative from print. 8 x 10 inches.

By 1891, when the frontier photographer, Grabill of Deadwood, S. Dak., took this picture, the warlike Sioux were beaten, scattered and dispirited. From 1877, when Gen. Nelson A. Miles had defeated Crazy Horse and ended the Sitting Bull war, they had been comparatively quiet on their reservations. Their great buffalo hunts were over, and they were sullen wards of a faraway Great White Father, whose agents were not always virtuous.

In 1889–91 the Sioux made one final, hopeless, warlike gesture. A religious excitement, the ceremonial Ghost Dance, originated by the Paiute Wovoka who preached a messianic doc-

trine, had swept through the plains. In the encampments the warriers painted their faces, sounded their war drums, and beat the earth in the long rhythm of the dance. Neighboring settlers were in panic, and the agent at Pine Ridge, S. Dak., wired for troops. When the soldiers came, led by Miles, the Indians fled to the Badlands. There were a few skirmishes, and the tragic and disgraceful Battle of Wounded Knee, when, after Chief Big Foot's surrender, the U. S. 7th Cavalry mercilessly cut down his band. Complete capitulation of the Sioux took place at Pine Ridge Agency early in January 1891.

The chief impression given by this panorama, "Hostile Indian Camp," with its tents spread over the plain as far as the distant foothills, is one of utter dejection. Only one human soul, a squaw, is in plain sight; a few others hover by the tepees. The wild swift ponies of the early days are now a sad *remuda,* their heads hanging as they cluster near the shafts of the high-wheeled wagons, which are symbols of the white man and of the red man's degradation.

PLATE No. 129. *Execution of the Thirty-Eight Sioux Indians. At Mankato, Minnesota, December 26, 1862.* ☆ *The Milwaukee Litho. & Engr. Co.* ☆ *Entered According to Act of Congress, in the Year 1883 by John C. Wise in the Office of Librarian of Congress at Washington.*

Lithograph. 11⅞ x 17½ inches.

The first serious outbreak of the Plains Indians took place in Minnesota in 1862. The Sioux, who had ceded their lands and found themselves starving when agents and traders failed to deliver the promised stores, rose under the semicivilized leader, Little Crow. Nearly 500 settlers were massacred in a month of

269

terror. At last Minnesota troops, under Col. Henry H. Sibley, subdued the bands, released the captives they had carried off, and rounded up about 1,500 Indians who were placed in prisons at Fort Snelling and Mankato. "The rest scattered far and wide over the plains, carrying the seeds of their grievance to the other tribes" (Paul I. Wellman). Three hundred and ninety-two prisoners, accused of extreme cruelty, were tried at one great court-martial, and nearly all were sentenced to death. This wholesale retribution was too much for the American conscience, and President Lincoln commuted the death sentences of all but 38. The mass hanging upon one scaffold took place at Mankato on February 26, 1863. The scene depicted by the lithograph was described by Gen. Oliver O. Howard in his memoirs:

"The Indians' . . . ages ranged from 16 to 70 years, although the majority were young men. All but three half-breeds were dressed in breech-clout, leggings, and blankets.

Early on Friday morning the irons were knocked off the condemned and their arms tied behind with cords at the elbows and at the wrists. At ten o'clock began the march to the scaffold. As they ascended the steps the death song was started, and when they had got upon the platform the noise of their deep, swelling voices was truly hideous. The ropes were adjusted about their necks, the white caps pulled down, and at a signal followed three slow but distinct taps on a drum. The rope holding the scaffold was cut by a man named Duly, whose family had been murdered."

The MILWAUKEE LITHOGRAPHIC & ENGRAVING Co. functioned in Chicago at least as early as

1876, some seven years before the *Execution of the Thirty-Eight Sioux Indians* was produced. It is an obvious derivative from a print of the same title published by Wise & Clark of Mankato, Minn., in 1865, which is reproduced in *America on Stone* (Plate 39). As John C. Wise took out the 1883 copyright, it may be that the Milwaukee Lithographic Co. was the successor of Wise & Clark. But in the 18 years between the two plates, technique had declined; the later *Execution* is a pallid and inferior copy.

The same firm produced in 1876 the chromo of *Custer's Last Charge,* our Plate 130. There was also a Milwaukee Lithographing Co. in Milwaukee, which in that year issued a memorable chromo, *Custer's Last Fight,* taken from O. Becker's original painting presented to the Seventh Regiment, U. S. Cavalry, by the Anheuser-Busch Brewing Association, St. Louis. Mr. Peters calls it a "prime buckeye," and recalls it as a "piece of bar-room and barber-shop art," the endless and lurid detail of which could never be forgotten by one who had observed it in impressionable youth. A few years ago the Anheuser-Busch Company resurrected their old favorite and distributed a good-sized reproduction of it among the nation's beer joints.

PLATE No. 130. *Custer's Last Charge.* ☆ *Custer's Todes-Ritt.* ☆ *Designed by Feodor Fuchs. Published by the Milwaukee Litho & Engr. Co.* ☆ *Entered According to Act of Congress in the Year 1876 by Seifert Gugler & Co. with the Librarian of Congress at Washington, D. C.*

Lithograph, printed in color. 21 x 26 inches.

High on the list of romantic American warrior heroes stands George Armstrong Custer, the yellow-haired, handsome, dashing cavalry-man, who in 1864 became the youngest Major General after Lafayette. Returned after the Civil War to his regular army rank of lieutenant colonel, Custer was detailed to western patrol and Indian fighting. In 1876 he and his regiment, the Seventh Cavalry, were given the job of capturing or dispersing the bands of Indians who had come out of their Dakota reservations for the annual buffalo hunt toward the upper Yellowstone. The Indians were encamped on the south bank of the Little Big Horn River, and Custer divided his command of 12 companies, sending Major Reno to attack on one side, Captain Benteen on the other. He himself led five companies down for an attack on the lower camp. Reno and Benteen retreated across the river—they were exonerated of defection by a later court martial, but the controversy rages to this day—so that the whole force of the Indian attack was concentrated upon Custer. His troopers fought back furiously, but were forced to fall back, were surrounded, and then annihilated. The next day Bradley, General Terry's chief of scouts, found on the battlefield of the Little Big Horn the stripped and mutilated bodies of 206 men. The leader alone still bore his long yellow hair.

Paintings and prints of this spectacular event long competed with luscious nudes in the decoration of barrooms, and for 15 years the Seventh Cavalry lost no occasion to avenge the death of Custer.

FEODOR FUCHS, who designed the lithograph for the Milwaukee company was probably the same Feodor or Theodore Fuchs who had been operating at 17 Minor Street, Philadelphia in 1856, and did frontispieces for the *Horticulturalist and Journal of Rural Art and Rural Taste*. He was responsible also for Civil War portraits, notably one of General Sigel. His *Custer's Last Charge* is less well known than the famous Anheuser-Busch offering painted by O. Becker, but is not dissimilar in technique and violent detail.

PLATE NO. 131. *Capture & Death of Sitting Bull. Dec. 15, 1890. Ind. Police K^d: Little Eagle, Afraid of Soldiers, Hawk Man, Broken Arm, W^d: Bull Head, Shave Head, Alex. Middle. Hostiles K^d: Sitting Bull, Crow-Foot S[itting] B[ull's] Son, Brave Thunder and Son, Catch-the-Bear, Black Bear, Assinaboine & Spotted Horn Bull. ☆ Copyrighted 1891 by Kurz & Allison, Art Publishers, 76 & 78 Wabash Ave, Chicago, U. S. A.*

Lithograph. 17⅜ x 25½ inches.

The Chicago "art publishers", Kurz and Allison, were apparently not personally familiar with the appearance of the fighting Sioux, and in their print the buckskin-clad Indians lying or falling dead bear more resemblance to the Mohicans of Cooper's tradition than to the naked warriors of the plains. They have done well, however, in giving to Sitting Bull, who is to be seen falling from his white, feather-bedecked charger in the center of the plate, a noble aspect. Stanley Vestal has written a stirring biography of this foremost champion of the Sioux, leader in the wars from 1876 to 1890, in which due honor is given to the famous chief. In Mr. Vestal's view, America was formed by the Frontier, and the Frontier was formed by the Indian. "Sitting Bull, leader of the largest Indian nation on the continent, the strongest, boldest, most stubborn opponent of European influence, was the very heart and soul of that Frontier. Sitting

271

Bull was one of the Makers of America."

The print gives a totally erroneous impression of the end of Sitting Bull, with its depiction of a battlefield, cannon, and troops facing Indian tepees. The old Hunkpapa Sioux leader in 1890 was living on the Standing Rock reservation, where he had been placed after his surrender at Fort Buford in 1881. The Ghost Dance excitement and the Messiah craze which spread among the Plains Indians in 1890 led to agitation for an uprising in which the irreconcilable chief participated. On December 15, Indian police—whose names Kurz and Allison have listed with accuracy—were sent to arrest him. They found him in bed in his cabin, forced him up, made him dress—in an issue shirt and blue leggings—and started him out. His mount was an old grey circus horse, which had been given to him by Buffalo Bill. Sitting Bull's own band crowded about and their attempt at rescue led to a general melee. Mr. Vestal tells us that as the shots rang out, the grey horse sat down, and held up his front hoof in his old circus trick. Sitting Bull fell, shot through the breast, and around him were piled the corpses of braves and Indian police which Kurz and Allison have so painstakingly enumerated.

KURZ & ALLISON, of Chicago, had by the 1890's degenerated badly from their earlier standards, excellent of their kind. EMIL KURZ, the senior partner, was an Austrian, born in 1834, who came to the United States as a boy of 14 and fought in the Civil War. He became well known as a mural painter and was one of the founders of the Chicago Art Institute. In 1864 he was publishing lithographs of his own design at Madison, Wis., and in 1865, at Chicago, he issued a fine print of Lincoln (reproduced in *America on Stone*, Plate 91) whom he is said to have known. Kurz issued a long series of Civil War views during the next two decades, and at some time in this period took Allison as his partner. Like most lithographers, they specialized in reportorial matter; their *Great Conemaugh Valley Disaster* (the Johnstown Flood), published in 1890, is also reproduced by Mr. Peters, who calls it a triumph of "pure, wild, unadulterated American lithography running wild."

Considerable wildness and the disappearance of any feeling for the general design is evident in the plate of *The Capture and Death of Sitting Bull,* but it may be considered restrained in comparison with the absolute badness of our final Kurz & Allison offerings, Plates 132 and 135. With those and the Muller, Luchsinger & Co. atrocity (Plate 133) we take our farewell of the popular lithograph. It had a great past, but after 75 years all virtue, all charm, and all taste had gone out of it, and it was time for it to die.

PLATE No. 127. *A Sioux Chief. Drawing by Frederic Remington, 1901.*

273

PLATE No. 128. *Hostile Indian Camp, 1891.*
Photograph by J. C. H. Grabill.

274

EXECUTION OF THE THIRTY-EIGHT SIOUX INDIANS

AT MANKATO, MINNESOTA DECEMBER, 26.1862.

PLATE No. 129. *Execution of the Thirty-eight Sioux Indians at Mankato, Minn., December 26, 1862. Lithograph by Milwaukee Lithographing Co., 1883.*

275

CUSTER'S LAST CHARGE
Custer's Todes-Ritt.

PLATE NO. 130. *Custer's Last Charge, June 25,*
1876. Lithograph by Milwaukee Lithographing
Co., 1876.

276

CAPTURE & DEATH OF SITTING BULL.

PLATE No. 131. *Capture and Death of Sitting Bull, December 15, 1890. Lithograph by Kurz & Allison, 1891.*

IX

The Spanish-American War, and Philippine Insurrection   1898-1899

AFTER the first quarter of the Nineteenth Century all that was left of the once mighty empire of Spain in the New World was the island of Cuba with her lesser satellite of Puerto Rico. The Spanish government obtained some psychological compensation for its losses by ruling these remainders with all the old absolutism, and left arbitrary powers in the hands of the Captain-General at Havana. The exclusion of natives of whatever race from all political participation, combined with the example of self-government on every side, brought the Cubans to revolt in 1868, and to wage a savage and exhausting war of 10 years against Spanish power. American patience was considerably tried by a succession of incidents at our doorstep, but intervention was carefully avoided. The rebellion was put down at last, but within 18 years (1895) the Cubans rose again, and this time, after three years, the United States took a hand. A diplomatic historian explains the difference: "The insurrection of 1895–98 took place in a different generation, when the American people had become fed up with stay-at-home activities, when shrewd young expansionists were demanding a larger national policy, when the energies and imagination of the nation conscious of its strength were expectant for new and adventurous activities, emotions, and experiences, when the people had come to turn their faces outward from the continent" (S. F. Bemis). Into this inflammable situation the destruction of the *Maine* in Havana harbor—more likely than not a complete accident—introduced the necessary spark. In spite of the customary American unpreparedness, what followed was a short and easy war, for Spanish armaments and efficiency did not match Spanish inflexibility and pride. The United States destined Cuba for early independence, but retained Puerto Rico in the West Indies and the Philippines in the Far East. And here, as the latest imperialist power, we found ourselves with a revolt of the native population on our hands—an uncomfortable situation for a nation which considered that it had gone to war to free the Cubans.

PLATE NO. 132. *Destruction of the U. S. Battleship Maine in Havana Harbor Feb'y 15th 1898. ☆ Launched 1890, Blown up in Havana Harbor at 9.40 P.M. Dimensions—: . . . Officers and Crew 450, Killed & Drowned 258. ☆ [Insets at top:] Location of the Maine—Havana Harbor. Recovering the Dead Bodies. Admiral Sicard. Captain Sigsbee. ☆ Copyrighted 1898 by Kurz & Allison, 267–269 Wabash Ave., Chicago.*

Lithograph. 17¾ x 24¾ inches.

The American people's vague sympathy, persisting over many years, with the Cubans whose insurgent leaders worked from New York headquarters, had been raised to a high pitch by the inflammatory headlines and novel journalistic practices of William Randolph Hearst and Joseph Pulitzer. This sympathy, rather than the imperialist leanings of the "Manifest Destiny" statesmen of the Republican Party, was expressed in President McKinley's message to Congress of April 11, 1898, calling for war against Spain; "In the name of humanity, in the name of civilization, in behalf of endangered American interests which give us the right and the duty to speak and to act, the war in Cuba must stop." The immediate cause, however, was what has been termed, not very precisely, "the complete irrelevance of a boiler explosion." The U. S. second-class battleship *Maine,* Capt. Charles D. Sigsbee, was paying a "friendly" visit—not altogether welcomed perhaps, but most politely received by her cautious Spanish hosts—to Havana, and lay at anchor in the harbor, 500 yards off the arsenal. At 9:40 p. m. on February 15, 1898, two explosions, one dull, the second tremendous, shook the *Maine,* throwing parts of the ship 200 feet in the air in a burst of flame that illuminated the entire harbor. Her forward part a shapeless mass of wreckage, the *Maine* slowly sank. Two officers and 258 of the crew were lost.

In spite of American and Spanish investigations at the time, and the studies of a board of experts in 1911–12, when the wreck was raised, it has never been conclusively settled whether the explosion came from external or internal causes. The Spanish had every reason to avoid such an incident, and later disasters of a similar nature in other navies indicated that warships could be blown up as a result of the deterioration of the explosives in their own magazines. But a new slogan swept the country, and volunteers flocked to the colors with the cry, "Remember the *Maine!*"

PLATE No. 133. *Battle of Manila.* ☆ [*At bottom:*] *Fought by Admiral Dewey, May 1st, 1898, Spanish Loss: 11 ships destroyed, 150 men killed, 250 wounded. American Loss: None.* ☆ [*Portrait, lower left:*] *Rear Admiral Dewey* ☆ *N°. 1110 copyrighted 1898 by Muller, Luchsinger & Co., New York.*

Chromolithograph. 15 x 19⅜ inches.

Facing the headlines of the morning papers on Monday, May 2, 1898, the whole war-minded United States joined in a paroxysm of rejoicing. Commodore Dewey, sailing with six warships from Hong Kong, had the day before entered Manila Bay and destroyed the Spanish Fleet. Every Spanish ship was "sunk, burned or destroyed," and the Spanish sources, from which alone the news had come, knew of no American losses. They were, in fact, nine men slightly wounded.

Ironquill (Eugene F. Ware) had some jubilant doggerel ready for the next day's issue of the *Topeka Capital:*

> *"Oh, dewy was the morning*
> *Upon the first of May,*
> *And Dewey was the Admiral*
> *Down in Manila Bay;*
> *And dewy were the Regent's eyes,*
> *'Them' orbs of royal blue!*
> *And Dewey feel discouraged?*
> *We Dew not think we Dew!"*

Ironquill's Regent was, of course, the Queen Regent of Spain, Maria Christina, ruling on behalf of her minor son, Alfonso XIII, who might well have shed a few tears over the fate of her Philippine squadron. An additional reason for grief could have been the fact that the Spanish flagship, which Dewey had sent to the bottom of Manila Bay, was the *Reina Cristina.*

280

No one will deny that the New York chromo-lithographers, Muller, Luchsinger & Co., have here achieved a superlative blend of the horrors of war with the horrors of art.

PLATE No. 134. [*Admiral Dewey on the Bridge of His Flagship at the Battle of Manila Bay, May 1, 1898*]

Anonymous, untitled etching. Received by the Library of Congress 1899. 27¾ x 21¾ inches.

Rear Admiral Dewey returned from the Philippines in September 1899, to meet the greatest ovation yet offered by the American nation to a conquering hero. A grateful people accompanied their cheers with the more solid testimonial of a house in Washington. The next year, in an interview concerning his willingness to accept the presidential nomination, the Admiral said: "Since studying the subject I am convinced that the office of President is not such a very difficult one to fill."

He was not given the opportunity to discover whether holding the office would be, like his celebrated victory, a comparatively easy matter. The Battle of Manila Bay, for the Americans almost bloodless, presented the United States with an empire. It came at the very outset of the short war. On April 25, the day that the cables carried the declaration of war, the neutral British at Hong Kong ordered Commodore Dewey to leave port with his squadron. General Aguinaldo, leader of the Filipino insurgents, had confered at Singapore with Consul E. Spencer Pratt, and had issued a proclamation to his people:

"Compatriots! Divine Providence is about to place independence within our reach, and in a way the most free and independent nation could hardly wish for. The Americans, not from mercenary motives, but for the sake of humanity and the lamentations of so many persecuted people, have considered it opportune to extend their protecting mantle to our beloved country."

Dewey sailed from Hong Kong and anchored opposite in Chinese territory, where he waited for orders. They came on April 27th, and in the afternoon the squadron, "with a smooth sea and favoring sky . . . set [its] course for the entrance to Manila Bay, six hundred miles away." There were seven men of war: four "protected cruisers," including Dewey's flagship *Olympia,* two gunboats and a revenue cutter. They carried 1,743 officers and men and three war correspondents. In the harbor toward which they were steering waited the Spanish Admiral Montojo, with two small protected cruisers and five miscellaneous vessels, in greater or lesser states of worthlessness. The land batteries were mainly museum pieces and the mines, with which the Ministry of Marine in Madrid had ordered Montojo to close the ports, were nonexistent.

In the darkness of evening on April 30 the American squadron steamed into Manila Bay, with the *Olympia* in the lead, and Dewey with his spyglass on her navigating bridge. They passed safely the batteries of El Fraile, missing three shots; Corregidor opposite did not open fire. The ships reduced speed in order to arrive off Manila at daybreak. Montojo, sparing the city from exposure to fire, had retired to the Navy Yard before Cavite and was there awaiting battle. A few minutes after five he gave the signal to fire on the Americans.

For two hours the opposing lines fired at each other, the Spaniards in a stationary position, the American ships cruising back and forth before their line. Then came the startling word on the *Olympia* that the ammunition was almost exhausted. The thick powder smoke obscured the Spanish fleet and Dewey, fearing disgrace if not defeat, turned his ships northward for time to deliberate. Looking back, however, he gradually perceived that the victory was already won; most of the enemy ships were on fire, the flagship was being abandoned, the others retreating. Spanish naval resistance was over. Dewey signaled for his captains and ordered breakfast served. It was discovered that there was a reserve of ammunition, that two officers and six men were wounded "very slightly," and that one engineer had died of heat stroke. It had all been very simple, and it was not until the newspapermen got to work that the American sailors discovered they had won "one of the most important battles that had ever been fought in any country or in any age."

Before Monday, May 2, had passed in Washington, Dewey was a rear admiral, appointed to a vacancy "created and confirmed" for him by Congressional action.

Our plate is something of a curiosity: a huge etching deposited in the Library of Congress in 1899; since the process of copyright was never completed, the artist's name cannot be ascertained. He did not get too much individuality into Admiral Dewey's face, and put rather better work into the folds of the jacket; but he correctly represents Dewey in the hunting cap which was sent for at the beginning of the action. The background, it is to be feared, he derived from a chromolithograph!

282

PLATE No. 135. *The Battle of Quasimas near Santiago June 24th. 1898. The 9th and 10th Colored Cavalry in Support of Rough Riders.* ☆ *Copyrighted 1899 by Kurz & Allison, 267–269 Wabash Ave., Chicago.*

Chromolithograph. 19½ x 25½ inches.

The main Spanish force in Cuba was entrenched in the city of Santiago, protected by the fortified hills of San Juan and by Cervera's fleet in the harbor. The invading American army, the Fifth Corps, commanded by Gen. William R. Shafter, came in transports from their fever-ridden Florida camps to the little harbor of Daiquiri, 18 miles east of Santiago. There on June 22 the first men went ashore. A few regiments, under Gen. Henry W. Lawton, pushed on eight miles west of Siboney, and almost without opposition took the tiny settlement. Landing operations were in part transferred to the Siboney beach, and in the two harbors for five days the 16,000 men and their equipment were slowly and clumsily deposited on Cuban soil.

In the meantime the second ranking officer, the former Confederate general, "Fighting Joe" Wheeler, with the Tenth (Negro) and First Cavalry Regiments, now dismounted, and accompanied by the problem children of the campaign, former Assistant Secretary of the Navy Lt. Col. Theodore Roosevelt's volunteer Rough Riders, commanded by Col. Leonard Wood, reached Siboney. Shafter remained on board overseeing landing operations, his plan being to rest and reorganize his force before attacking on the city. But "Fighting Joe," eager for honors, on June 24 ordered an advance along the Santiago road.

Through thick jungle he sent on two columns, the First and Tenth Cavalry on the left, and the Rough Riders on the right. All were on foot, and cutting their way with machetes through the vines and Spanish bayonets, when suddenly they found themselves under the hot fire of Spanish Mausers, from behind stone breastworks on the hill of Las Guásimas ahead. Since men were falling fast, Wheeler sent back for reinforcements; but before they could arrive, the Spanish broke and fled. General Wheeler, "laboring under a pardonable confusion in the excitement," was heard by war correspondents to shout, "We've got the damn Yankees on the run!" (Walter Millis.) The regulars, white and colored, and the Rough Riders, advancing from two sides, "gained the breastworks, victory, and the headlines," in the first real engagement of the campaign.

The lithograph is in error in asserting the support of the colored Ninth Cavalry during the action. According to the reports of Gen. Young and Col. Wood, portions of the Ninth arrived after firing had ceased. The First Cavalry, which fought with the colored Tenth and the Rough Riders at Las Guásimas, was a White regiment.

PLATE NO. 136. [*Roosevelt and the Rough Riders at San Juan Hill*]. *W. G. Read. ☆ Copyright, 1898, by W. F. McLaughlin & Co., Chicago, Ill. Geo. S. Harris & Sons, N. Y.*

Chromolithograph. 13½ x 19½ inches.

W. G. Read's depiction of Colonel Roosevelt and his Rough Riders in their cavalry charge up San Juan Hill, with bugles blowing, banners and Stetsons flying and warsteeds plunging, makes an inspiring scene and was just what the public at home came to believe as it read the colorful accounts of the "more than an army"

of war correspondents who accompanied the invading forces and reported the campaign. According to more sober narratives, this much publicized regiment had left its horses behind, as unsuited to the terrain, and struggled afoot up the hill along with the regular troopers of the First and Ninth (colored) Cavalry, likewise dismounted. As a historian of the army says, "the Rough Riders really became dogged walkers" (W. A. Ganoe). But the picture does not exaggerate the spirit of this regiment of men picked from cattle ranges, mining camps, and college gymnasiums: "If they can be criticized at all, it is that their eagerness sometimes exceeded their technic." Concerning their fire-eating leader, Walter Millis says, "The reputation so brilliantly begun at Las Guásimas was enormously enhanced; and as the newspaper despatches went off describing the heroism of the Rough Riders and their lieutenant colonel, another military genius had been given to American history."

It is so unusual to find a moderately tasteful and competently executed lithograph from the era of the Spanish-American War that we regret our inability to tell our readers anything about W. G. Read and his printers and publishers.

PLATE NO. 137. *Sixteenth Infantry in San Juan Creek bottom, under Spanish fire from San Juan Hill, July 1st. [Photographed] By William Dinwiddie. 1898.*

Photograph. Negative from print. 8 x 10 inches.

The road into Santiago ran over the San Juan Hills into the city. In the village of El Caney, two miles to the northward, Spanish artillery flanked any possible encircling movement against the fortified ridge. The only way to San Juan lay straight down the Santiago road, through close jungle to the point where it forded the San Juan river and came to an open meadow directly under enfilading fire.

After Las Guásimas the American troops were eager for glory and scornful of Spanish marksmanship. They started enthusiastically from Siboney on the afternoon of June 30th and spent a happy night on the road. At daybreak Lawton's division was started to take El Caney, the rest waiting for the guns to be silenced before they advanced. At 7 o'clock the Spanish fire began, and after two hours it still continued. The two other divisions were waiting impatiently for the assault, and finally Colonel McClernand, directing operations in General Shafter's place, ordered them forward. 10 or 12,000 men plunged almost simultaneously into the narrow jungle trail, and a terrific traffic jam ensued. As it unscrambled itself at the mouth, the Sixth and Sixteenth Infantry, regulars, were toward the front, but ahead of them a regiment of raw volunteers, the 71st New York, had been pushed into the lead. The dismounted cavalry, coming behind, had turned off to the right, where they were slightly protected by the cover at the edge of the stream bed. More regiments crowded the road behind.

As the 71st New York moved out into the open at the ford, they were caught in a heavy fire, and "recoiled in disorder on the troops in the rear." Gen. J. F. Kent, commanding the division, with "splendid poise" ordered them to "lie down in the thicket and clear the way." They did, abjectly, and the Sixth and Sixteenth Infantry stepped forward. " 'Tell the brigade', said Kent to their officers, pointing at the unhappy National Guardsmen, 'to pay no atten-

tion to this sort of thing, it is highly irregular' " (Walter Millis).

The Sixth and Sixteenth deployed along the thicket at the ford, the target of the Spanish volley 600 yards away across the meadow. It is probably at this "bloody angle" that the correspondent-photographer, William Dinwiddie, took his photograph, showing the soldiers waiting in what concealing brush they can find, the five horses standing motionless and unconcerned by the noise of the guns. There was a long wait during which fairly heavy losses were suffered. Other regiments had followed into the ford. At last a battery of Gatling guns came up, and though at first it drew the heaviest Spanish fire, it finally made its way past the crowded corner and opened up on the ridge. The Spanish were seen to waver, and some to flee, and the order was at last given for the charge. From one side the infantry, from the other the cavalry, burst into the meadow and struggled up the hill—considerably hampered by fire from their own artillery in the rear—and a final rush carried the trenches. The Spaniards were already down the other side, in the valley beyond. San Juan Hill was ours.

PLATE NO. 138. *Wagon Train in the Philippine Islands at a Halt in the Road, 1899-1900.*

Photograph by U. S. Army. Negative copied from original.

ORIGINAL IN THE NATIONAL ARCHIVES, WASHINGTON, D. C.

Not unnaturally the Filipino insurgents, already in arms against Spain, and misled by American disclaimers of imperialist intentions, had expected that peace would bring them independence. The cession of the Islands to the

United States, announced in the Treaty of Paris which was signed on December 10, 1898, came as a shock to Emilio Aguinaldo and his followers. Friction naturally ensued, and within two months, on February 4, 1899, guns were fired. Some 40,000 Tagalogs attacked the small American army of occupation on Manila. After hard fighting they were thrown back and retreated to northern Luzon. The Americans followed, and on March 31 took the native capital, Malólos. Their commanding officer bore a name that foreshadows Bataan and VJ Day, Lt. Gen. Arthur MacArthur. Aguinaldo withdrew northward, was again defeated at Tarlac, and fled to the inaccessible northeastern mountains. His insurgent armies disintegrated into guerrilla bands which kept up a strenuous resistance until 1902, when the last important chief surrendered. Aguinaldo himself had been captured by a ruse of General Funston's in the previous year.

Most of the Filipino population at first was in sympathy with the insurrectionists. The two native lads resting beside the two-wheeled supply cart in the photograph would seem to have taken the other side. The young soldier on top of the baggage load has the average footslogger's instinct for a soft berth.

This is the earliest official photograph of the United States Army which we reproduce. The Army has increasingly recognized and assumed the responsibility of keeping a photographic record of our wars, an activity now concentrated in and most competently performed by the Signal Corps.

PLATE No. 139. *China Relief Expedition: General Chaffee.* ☆ *[On negative:] U. S. Engineer Office, China Relief Expedition. Photo by Capt. C. F. O'Keefe 36ᵗʰ Inf. U. S. V.* Photograph by C. F. O'Keefe, 1900. Negative copied from original. 4 x 5 inches.

In the year 1900 there came the inevitable and violent reaction of the Chinese against the steady penetration of their country by western influences and the European powers. British, Russian, French, German, and Japanese "spheres of interest," treaty ports, extraterritoriality, and the American "open door policy" had intensified the traditional Chinese hatred of the "foreign devils." Following the Empress Dowager's conservative *coup d'état* of 1898, an extremist movement to oust the foreigners arose—the train-bands of the old village militia organized with rowdy secret societies into groups known as the *I Ho Ch'uan,* "Righteous Harmony Fists," which phrase was rendered in English as "Boxers." Their program was "Protect the country, destroy the foreigner," and they set about executing it with vigor. After a number of murders and attacks on Christians had taken place, the Powers intervened. On June 17 European naval forces in China seized the Taku forts on the way to Tientsin and Peking and the infuriated old Empress ordered that all foreigners be killed. The German minister was murdered while he was on his way to demand an interview with the Chinese Foreign Office, and the Western diplomatic staffs isolated in Peking remained under a state of siege in the legation compound from June 20 until August 14, a period of 56 days. Outside the capital Western missionaries and several thousands of their Chinese converts were massacred in the Northeastern provinces.

The Powers got together an expeditionary force of some 18,000 men, 8,000 of whom were contributed by Japan, while the American contingent consisted of 2,500, hastily rushed north from the Philippines. The first to arrive was the Ninth Infantry, whose commander, Col. Emerson H. Liscum, lost his life in the capture of Tientsin on July 13. The American contingent consisted of the Fourteenth Infantry in addition to the Ninth, two troops of cavalry and one battery of artillery, and the commander designated for it was a hard-bitten old campaigner who had served under Sheridan in the Valley and with Crook on the Southwestern frontier, Gen. Adna R. Chaffee. Selected on June 26, 1900, Chaffee made the long trip from Washington across the continent and the Pacific and arrived in China on July 29. A campaign of two weeks brought the leaderless international army before the walls of Peking, which were speedily breached, and the legation finally relieved. Major General Chaffee, as he had now been promoted in reward for his services in China, spent the winter of 1900–01 in Peking, viewing with a disapproving eye the harsh policy of reprisals which was now being carried out by the new German commander of the international forces, Count von Waldersee. Disagreements among the powers prevented a final settlement until September 7, 1901, when a protocol was signed which imposed various penalties upon China, including a total reparations bill of $332,000,000, of which the comparatively modest share of $24,500,000 went to the United States. Even this was found to be nearly twice as much as our actual claims and expenses, and some $17,000,000 was eventually remitted by the United States Government.

The official photograph which is here reproduced is labelled by Chaffee's biographer, "General Chaffee entering Peking with Artillery." Chaffee and his men are passing a group on the left who are certainly not a part of his American contingent.

PLATE No. 132. *Destruction of the U. S. Battle-ship Maine in Havana Harbor, February 15, 1898. Chromolithograph by Kurz and Allison, 1898.*

287

BATTLE OF MANILA

PLATE No. 133. *Battle of Manila, May 1, 1898.*
Chromolithograph by Muller, Luchsinger & Co.

PLATE No. 134. *Admiral Dewey on the Bridge
of his Flagship, May 1, 1898. Etching, 1899.*

289

PLATE No. 135. *The Battle of Quasimas near Santiago, June 24, 1898: The 9th and 10th Colored Cavalry in Support of Rough Riders. Chromolithograph by Kurz & Allison, 1899.*

290

PLATE No. 136. *Roosevelt and the Rough Riders at San Juan Hill, July 1, 1898. Chromolithograph by George S. Harris & Sons, 1898.*

291

PLATE No. 137. *Sixteenth Infantry under Fire in San Juan Creek Bottom, July 1, 1898. Photograph by William Dinwiddie.*

PLATE No. 138. *Wagon Train in the Philippine Islands at a Halt in the Road, 1899-1900.* U. S. Army Photograph.

PLATE No. 139. *Major General Chaffee on the Chinese Relief Expedition, 1900. Photograph by Captain C. F. O'Keefe.*

294

X

The First World War
1917-18

THE great European War of 1792–1815, arising out of the French Revolution and its Napoleonic sequel, let the United States off lightly; as we have seen, we were drawn in for only two brief periods, and one of those was a limited war. For a century there was no general war in Europe, and such wars as broke out between the major powers were brief if bloody. America's wars from 1815–1917 were generated in our own continent. But in the fall of 1914 the tense diplomatic atmosphere of Europe was finally precipitated in a great war between the great powers: France, Russia, and Britain against Germany and Austria. The only neutral great power, Italy, came in with the first-named in 1915. The apparent disparity in resources was more than balanced by the terrible efficiency of the German war machine and the superiority of German generalship, and the war at no time took a course too favorable for the Allies until its final months.

American opinion favored the Allies from the beginning, but it seemed inconceivable in September 1914 and for long thereafter that we should take any active part in the conflict. It was the ruthlessness of German methods of war making, and the disregard of the German government for international law and neutral opinion that brought about a change. Unrestricted submarine warfare, typified in the sinking of the *Lusitania*, was a new and horrible form of attack upon that Freedom of the Seas which the United States had insisted upon since it became a nation. Germany made concessions under diplomatic pressure for a while, but notified her intention once more to sink without warning after February 1, 1917. By April 6 President Wilson had called for and the Congress had declared war.

The United States, in a state of almost complete unpreparedness for modern war, drafted four million men in addition to the regular army and the National Guard, and sent two million to Europe. As things went, our intervention turned out to be most timely; in the course of 1917 Imperial Russia collapsed in chaos and revolution, and Italy suffered crushing defeat and had to be propped up by France and Britain. The liquidation of her Eastern Front enabled Germany to send vast reinforcements to the Western, and in the spring of 1918 Ludendorff's offensives punched great dents in the Franco-British line. But it did not break, and by the end of May American troops were ready to join in the counteroffensive. From then on the effects of the blockade and the exhaustion of German manpower became increasingly apparent; the Allies seized and held the initiative and were about to drive the Germans back through Belgium when, on November 11, 1918, Germany accepted the fact of defeat and begged for an armistice.

This time the War Department saw to it that there would be a first-hand graphic record of

American soldiers at war, and most of our plates are made up of drawings by staff artists of the A. E. F. and staff photographers of the Signal Corps.

PLATE No. 140. *Expeditionary Forces in Mexico: Brigadier General John J. Pershing and Lieutenant James Collins, A. D. C., near El Valle, crossing Santa Maria River.*

Photographed by Underwood and Underwood. Negative copied from original. 4 x 5 inches.

ORIGINAL IN THE NATIONAL ARCHIVES, WASHINGTON, D. C.

In 1910 the dissatisfaction of the Mexican people with the long "benevolent" dictatorship of President Diaz culminated in revolution, and for the next decade our southern neighbor republic suffered the pangs of a great social and political upheaval. For five years or more conditions remained chaotic. The constitutional president Madera was overthrown and shot by the counterrevolutionary Huerta, whom the United States refused to recognize. The masses, led by Carranza, Villa, and Zapata, overthrew Huerta. Then these leaders fought among themselves. Carranza in 1915 brought about some semblance of order and reform and won United States recognition. Since 1911 the border had been in a state of unrest, with refugees tearing across and bullets occasionally flying, and a sizable part of the United States army was set to border patrol, from the mouth of the Rio Grande to San Diego, Calif.

In 1916 occurred the only genuine warlike action between the two countries. The bandit leader Pancho Villa, in revolt against his former ally Carranza, crossed the border on the night of March 8–9, and attacked the town of Columbus,

N. Mex., killing nine soldiers and eleven citizens and destroying property. It was apparently a deliberate attempt on Villa's part to provoke an international incident which would involve Carranza's government. Gen. John J. Pershing was at once directed to pursue and capture Villa, and the Punitive Expedition into Mexico began. On March 15 Pershing crossed the border with a rapidly assembled force of all arms, including, for the first time in our history, an airplane squadron. There were a few small skirmishes, some with groups of Villa's guerrillas, and some with Mexican government troops who chose to look on the chastising army as invaders. Pershing penetrated 400 miles into Mexico and succeeded in breaking up Villa's bands among the mountains, although Villa himself was not to be caught. On February 5, 1917, the punitive force was ordered back to the United States, leaving the Mexicans themselves to control their side of the border, while strong units of National Guard and regular army stood ready to prevent further incursions on our soil. The hardening and discipline afforded our troops in this, the first real campaign in 15 years, was, in the light of approaching events, of the greatest value.

The camera of a news photographer has caught "Black Jack" Pershing and his aide fording their horses across a Mexican stream. This West Pointer of the class of 1886 had made his reputation by a four-year job of conquering and pacifying the Moros, fierce Mohammedan tribes of the Southern Philippines whose subjection to the Spanish regime had been only nominal. He had received special commendation in a message to Congress from President Roosevelt, and in 1906 had been promoted to brigadier general over the heads of 862 senior officers. In 1905 he had watched the campaign in Manchuria as an official American observer with the Japanese armies. Black Jack Pershing was known in the army as a man who spared neither himself, his men, nor the enemy. Three months after returning from Mexico, he was chosen to command the American Expeditionary Force in Europe.

PLATE NO. 141. [*American Troops disembarking at Brest*]. ☆ *W. J. Duncan, Brest, July 22/18.* Crayon and wash drawing. 12½ x 16½ inches.
ORIGINAL IN THE U. S. NATIONAL MUSEUM, SMITHSONIAN INSTITUTION, WASHINGTON, D. C.

The first AEF division to land in Europe reached the port of St. Nazaire in July 1917. They were a token force, regulars fresh from the Mexican border. The great army which was to turn the tide of the World War only began to arrive many months later. Rear Admiral Henry B. Wilson set up the headquarters of his huge naval establishment at Brest, on the northwestern tip of the Breton peninsula, and this excellent harbor was the chief point of debarkation for the big transports which, under convoy and without loss, brought over two million American soldiers to France. In the month of July 1918, when Duncan's picture was drawn, 297,000 men were transported overseas. His drawing shows a troopship, a smaller vessel than the huge liners such as the *Leviathan* or the *George Washington* with their swarming human cargoes, drawn up to the dock while the men carrying their heavy equipment file down the gangway from the crowded decks.

WALTER J. DUNCAN, an illustrator for *Century Magazine, Scribner's, McClure's,* and *Harper's,* was one of the group of eight official artists commissioned as captains in the Engineer Reserve Corps to sketch the visible forms of the war. He went to France in 1918 and sent back many drawings, now included with the entire collection at the National Museum. Captain Duncan was born at Indianapolis in 1881, and had been a pupil of John Twachtmann at the Art Students' League of New York. He died in 1941. The drawing which we reproduce displays to advantage the rapid and sure touch and the abundant detail of the professional illustrator.

PLATE NO. 142. [*In Belleau Woods.*] *W. Morgan—1918.*
Charcoal drawing by Wallace Morgan. 22¼ x 18½ inches.
ORIGINAL IN THE U. S. NATIONAL MUSEUM, SMITHSONIAN INSTITUTION, WASHINGTON, D. C.

When the last German offensive began in March 1918, four American divisions, about 112,000 troops, were ready for combat. On March 28, General Pershing visited Marshal Foch, who had just been named head of the Allied armies. "The American people", he said, "would hold it a great honor for our troops were they engaged in the present battle. I ask it of you in my name and in that of the American people." On May 20 the First American Division took Cantigny; on May 30 the Second and Third Divisions checked the German drive at Château-Thierry; and on June 4 a brigade of the United States marines began an attack on Belleau Woods. Adequate artillery support was lacking, but for six days they held on, "a test of courage well met." Finally guns were assembled to rake the woods, and the marines could go forward and take the position. There was no further question among the British and French Allies or the German enemy as to whether Americans could fight.

Capt. WALLACE MORGAN, another of the A. E. F.'s official artists, was a well-known New York newspaper and book illustrator. Born in New York in 1873, he had studied at the National Academy of Design, and afterwards taught classes in illustration there. Since the war he has continued his career as illustrator, with his studio in New York, and from 1929–36 served as president of the Society of Illustrators. His drawing depicts a lone marine making his cautious way through a thick growth of young trees, with barbed wire strung between them; two of his fellows are obscurely visible in the background, but the effect is one of isolation and dim light.

PLATE No. 143. *Shadows. Kerr Eby imp.*

Etching. 10¼ x 15 inches.

KERR EBY, who made the fine etching *Shadows,* told Dorothy Keppel, his biographer in the *Print Collector's Quarterly* for 1939, that "the scenes of the Great War, though long past, still march on with no flagging vitality in his visual memory, and will march . . . right up to the Pearly Gates." It may be that now they have been supplanted—or perhaps only mingled in one long panorama of tragic beauty—with scenes of the exotic South Seas where boys like the Eby of 1918 go through the same seemingly aimless motions, to use his own words again, "the endless piling up of the minutiae of the human side of war." Only he himself is older, and in the South Pacific he was not a sergeant of engineers, but an artist war correspondent with the marines.

Mr. Eby was born in Tokio in 1890, where his Canadian father was a Methodist missionary. In 1907 the family came to the United States, and Kerr grew up knowing what he was going to do. He had to take jobs first, for Methodist mis-

sionaries' sons cannot ordinarily afford expensive art educations, but at last he reached New York and Pratt Institute, followed by another job in a printing office and night classes at the Art Students' League. But he was drawing and etching, fairly embarked on his career, when the war came. He enlisted in 1917 and was put in the Camouflage Corps, which like "anything that was queer or out of the way was put on to the Engineers." He went to France with the 40th Engineer Regiment, and was steadily at the front seeing action with various regiments of artillery. Eby made sketches and brought them back in 1919 when he returned to the career which has established him firmly as one of America's foremost etchers. In 1936 a collection of his etchings made from these notes and memories was published in book form by the Yale University Press, under the simple title, *War.*

Shadows employs the same effects of masses of undifferentiated faceless human figures and sombre *chiaroscuro* as the huge drawing, *September 13, 1918: St. Mihiel,* which is reproduced in the *American Battle Painting* catalog. The original drawing for *Shadows,* 16 by 22 inches in size, was included in the Battle Painting Exhibition.

PLATE No. 144. *Capturing St. Mihiel Salient: An American ammunition wagon Northeast of St. Mihiel stuck in a bad place in the road, holds up the advance of a whole column. 1st Division, St. Baussant, France, September 13, 1918.*

Photographed by Sergeant J. A. Marshall, U. S. Signal Corps. Original glass negative. 4 x 5 inches.

ORIGINAL IN THE NATIONAL ARCHIVES, WASHINGTON, D. C.

PLATE No. 145. *Capturing St. Mihiel Salient: Columns of German prisoners taken in the first day of the assault, marching in the rain toward the prison pens prepared for them back of the American lines.*

Photograph by Corporal R. H. Ingleston. Negative copied from original. 6½ x 8½ inches.

In July 1918 the fourth and last German offensive was stopped, and Foch drove back the enemy from the Marne salient. Our troops were with the French in the pursuit, but by September 1 Pershing had achieved a cherished objective: his divisions were withdrawn and formed into the First American Army which was to undertake a strictly American show—the reduction of the St. Mihiel salient, cutting across the Meuse southeast of the massive forts of Verdun, where through 1916 the French had worn out 44 German divisions. The Germans had held the St. Mihiel salient since September 1914; it was still a nuisance and had the advantage of constituting a relatively limited objective. At dawn on September 12, 1918, the American infantry went over the top against the enemy trenches and by afternoon of the next day all objectives had been taken, with nearly 16,000 prisoners. Our army strength in the battle was 500,000 Americans, supported by 100,000 French. "We suffered less than 7,000 casualties during the actual period of attack" (Pershing's Final Report). An opportunity to break through to Metz was not seized, and eventually the American heavy artillery and divisions were moved through Verdun, now safe from German shells, to the edge of the Argonne Forest.

The two photographs from the St. Mihiel operation are dated on the second day. The first exhibits in a vivid manner the difficulties of supplying an infantry advance: an ammunition wagon has become stuck, and tugging from in front and exhortation from the rear are neither having much effect upon the mules who draw it; meanwhile the whole column stretching back to the horizon must wait. The second, the march of German prisoners to the rear, is doubtless not to be compared to the mass captures of the spring of 1945, but such losses were steadily undermining the power of the German nation to make war.

PLATE No. 146. *Verdun Offensive.* ☆ *Geo. Harding AEF. Montfaucon Sept. 1918.*
Wash and charcoal drawing. 20½ x 29½ inches.
ORIGINAL IN THE U. S. NATIONAL MUSEUM, SMITHSONIAN INSTITUTION, WASHINGTON, D. C.

"With the organization of the first American Army on August 10th, under the personal command of General Pershing, the history of the A. E. F. entered upon a new stage. The last two offensives—St. Mihiel (September 12th–14th) and the Meuse-Argonne (September 26th–November 11th)—were major operations planned and executed by the Americans" (G. L. McEntee). And of the two, the latter was vastly the greater and more difficult undertaking, and was still in progress when the armistice was signed. It was, and remained until 1943, in General Pershing's phrase, the greatest and the most prolonged battle in American history. "Through forty-seven days we were engaged in a persistent struggle with the enemy to smash through his defenses. The attack started on a front of twenty-four miles, which gradually extended until the enemy was being assailed from the Argonne Forest to the Moselle River, a distance of ninety miles." The terrain was certainly the worst which confronted any section of the allied armies during the final offensives of 1918—a series of heavily wooded ridges between the tangled and almost impenetrable Argonne Forest on the west and the Heights of the Meuse on the east. In the center on high ground was the strong point of Montfaucon, to attack which Pershing's men had to advance through a double defile subject to artillery attack from three sides. It was from this eminence that the German Crown Prince had watched the siege of Verdun in the dark days of 1916. Nevertheless on the second day of the offensive, September 27, the Yanks pushed doggedly forward and took Montfaucon. George Harding, whose drawing is somewhat confusingly titled "Verdun offensive" because Verdun lay to the south of the extreme right of the American sector, pictures the doughboys plunging with bayonets into a German trench.

GEORGE HARDING, like Morgan and Duncan, held the rank of captain in the Engineers as one of the official artists of the A. E. F. Born in 1882 in Philadelphia, he had received his art training at the Pennsylvania Academy of Fine Arts and under the master of illustration, Howard Pyle. From 1908 to 1913 he had acted as special travel artist for *Harper's Magazine,* going first to Newfoundland, Greenland and the West Indies, and sending back pictures and articles. In 1912–13 he had been sent on a journey round the world, to Australia, the East Indies, China and Arabia. During the war he covered with his pastel and charcoal sketches the Château-Thierry defense, the Marne offensive, the St. Mihiel offensive, the Argonne-Meuse offensive and all American sectors from Amiens to Baccarat, and he afterwards accompanied the Army of Occupation into Ger-

many. After the war he joined the faculty of the Pennsylvania Academy, in the department of mural decoration. His studio is at Wynnewood, Pa. Two of his panels are in the Post Office Building in Washington, and he has done murals for the Philadelphia Post Office, the U. S. Government Building in New York, the World's Fair of 1939, and many other public buildings. In June 1942 he received a commission as captain in the U. S. Marine Corps, to repeat his World War activities in the Pacific theatre.

PLATE No. 147. *In Rebeuville J. André Smith 1918.*

Crayon and wash drawing. 10¾ x 13¼ inches.

ORIGINAL IN THE U. S. NATIONAL MUSEUM, SMITHSONIAN INSTITUTION, WASHINGTON, D. C.

PLATE No. 148. *Field No. 1, Issoudun. J. André Smith.*

Crayon and wash drawing. Undated. 8¼ x 13¼ inches.

ORIGINAL IN THE NATIONAL MUSEUM, SMITHSONIAN INSTITUTION, WASHINGTON, D. C.

The prominent artist, J. André Smith, who in 1915 had received the Panama-Pacific Exposition gold medal for his etching, was the first of the official artists commissioned in the Engineer Reserve Corps to be sent overseas. Mr. Smith in 1917 had gone to the Officers' Training Camp at Plattsburgh and had served for several months in Washington, helping with the organization of the first camouflage companies. At the beginning of 1918 he received his appointment as staff artist, and sailed for France in March. Of the 277 drawings sent in to the War Department by the middle of January 1919, 105 were by Captain Smith. He worked mainly in pencil on tinted

300

paper, accenting with touches of water color.

A volume of Captain Smith's war drawings, *In France with the American Expeditionary Forces,* was brought out in 1919 by Arthur H. Hahlo & Co., New York. The artist speaks in his foreword of the "orchestra seats in the theatre of war" enjoyed by many spectators besides the correspondents familiar in former wars—"novelists, poets, historians, propagandists, artists, sculptors, photographers, and moving-picture men (not to mention a liberal scattering of miscellaneous scientists)." Of his own contribution to the voluminous records produced by these auxiliaries, he says:

"War posed for me in the attitude of a very deliberate worker who goes about his task of fighting in a methodical and thorough manner. If the picture of war which the sum total of my drawings shows has any virtue of truth or novelty it is in this respect: It shows War, the business man, instead of War, the warrior. It is an unsensational record of things actually seen, and in almost every instance drawn, as the saying is, 'on the spot.' The drawings cover a wide area of the work of our Expeditionary Forces in France and picture our activities from our ports of debarkation along the line of our Services of Supplies, over many of our battlefields, and through Luxembourg into Germany and across the Rhine . . . The searcher after sensational pictures of conflict, the horrors of war, and the anecdotic record of soldier life and heroism will not find these subjects here. My drawings show merely the background of the A. E. F."

The first of the two drawings by Captain Smith here reproduced shows typical rest quarters of men back from the trenches, "behind the lines." Rebeuville is a tiny village in the Vosges.

Issoudun, a small town in the level plains of central France, southeastward less than a hundred miles from Tours on the Loire, the main headquarters of the American Army Air Service, was in 1918 the site of the splendid flying school to which most of our pilots came for their immediate pre-combat training. Mr. Smith's second drawing shows "Field No. One", with its row of hangars, and the small planes lined opposite, while other planes come and go in their proper element above. There were nine fields altogether at Issoudun, marking successive stages in the flyer's education; "Field No. Ten," visitors were informed, was the cemetery. Two other sketches from Issoudun, scenes outside and inside a repair shop, comprise drawings 25 and 26 in Mr. Smith's book.

PLATE No. 149. *First Lieutenant E. V. Rickenbacker, 94th Aero Squadron, standing in front of his Spad plane, near Rembercourt, Meurthe et Moselle, Oct. 18, 1918.*

Photograph by Sergeant Eikleberry, U. S. Signal Corps. Original glass negative. 6½ x 8½ inches.

ORIGINAL IN THE NATIONAL ARCHIVES, WASHINGTON, D. C.

Of individual names imprinted on American mass memory by the First World War, three stand preeminent—General Pershing, Sergeant York, and "Eddie" Rickenbacker. The President of Eastern Air Lines, leading authority on practical aviation in the United States, who in 1943 drifted for three weeks on a rubber boat in the Pacific while thousands of planes searched for him, was in 1918 our most glorious and glamorous "ace."

Rickenbacker, born in Columbus, Ohio, in 1890, was the son of a poor family and, losing his father at the age of 12, went to work to help his mother. He learned engineering through a correspondence course and got into an automobile company. At 20 he became an automobile racer, and for seven years was the daredevil of the race tracks, winning championships, national and international, right and left. A month after the war began he enlisted, with the idea of forming an air squadron entirely from automobile racing men, but June of 1917 found him in France as chauffeur for General Pershing. After two months he was transferred, at his insistent demand, to the Air Service, and went in late August to Tours for preliminary training as a flier. Then he was sent to Issoudun Field, to be chief engineer officer.

Lieutenant Rickenbacker was not pleased to be behind the lines, but authorities said he could not be spared to go and endanger himself at the front. He only won his way by getting himself hospitalized for two weeks, to show that the field still kept going without him. He was transferred to active duty with the 94th Aero Pursuit Squadron, first air unit of our army in action on the Western Front. His own "Hat-in-the-Ring Squadron"—the emblem is clearly visible on the side of the neat little plane in the photograph—was organized in September 1918, and brought down 69 German planes, the largest number to the credit of any American unit. Eddie himself accounted for 26. Major Rickenbacker, our top ace, came through without a scratch, wearing the Croix de Guerre, the Légion d'Honneur, the

D. S. C. with nine palms, and the Congressional Medal of Honor. When this picture was taken, on duty at Rembercourt in the last week of the war, he wore only his wings.

PLATE No. 150. *Sketch—The Machine Gunner.* ☆ *HD AEF.*

Charcoal and wash drawing by Harvey Dunn. Undated. 27 x 19½ inches.

ORIGINAL IN THE U. S. NATIONAL MUSEUM, SMITHSONIAN INSTITUTION, WASHINGTON, D. C.

HARVEY DUNN was born in Manchester, S. Dak., in 1884. Trained at the Art Institute of Chicago and, like George Harding, in Howard Pyle's school, he became a mural painter and portraitist, and illustrator for many magazines. Since the war he has lived at Tenafly, N. J., teaching at the Grand Central School of Art in New York. He published a book about the school, *Evening in the Classroom,* in 1934. In 1918 he was commissioned captain in the group of staff artists of the A. E. F. In France he went with the men over the top carrying a specially designed box with rollers to wind up the finished sketches and unreel a clean sheet of paper as he needed it. His rapid pictures are of exceptional vividness—witness the sketch of the machine gunner, a hard-boiled and completely self-reliant military figure, and one such as could be found only in an American army. The American type has changed in 80 years, and yet Dunn's machine gunner has something very definite in common with the young sergeant whom Edwin Forbes sketched in 1863 (Plate 99).

PLATE NO. 140. *Brig. Gen. John J. Pershing Crossing the Santa Maria River near El Valle, Mexico, 1916. Photograph by Underwood & Underwood.*

PLATE No. 141. *United States Troops Disembarking at Brest, July 22, 1918. Drawing by Walter J. Duncan.*

304

PLATE NO. 142. *In Belleau Woods. Drawing by Wallace Morgan, 1918.*

305

Plate No. 143. *Shadows. Etching by Kerr Eby.*

306

PLATE NO. 144. *Capturing St. Mihiel Salient:*
A Stuck Ammunition Wagon Holds Up a
Whole Column, September 13, 1918. Photo-
graph by Sgt. J. A. Marshall.

307

PLATE NO. 145. *Capturing St. Mihiel Salient:
Columns of German Prisoners Marching in the
Rain toward the Prison Pens, September 13,
1918. Photograph by Corp. R. H. Ingleston.*

308

VERDUN OFFENSIVE

PLATE No. 146. *Verdun Offensive. Montfaucon,*
September 1918. Drawing by George Harding,
1918.

309

PLATE No. 147. *In Rebenville. Drawing by J. André Smith, 1918.*

310

PLATE No. 148. *Field No. 1, Issoudun. Drawing by J. André Smith, 1918.*

PLATE No. 149. *First Lt. E. V. Rickenbacker standing in Front of his Spad Plane near Rembercourt, October 18, 1918. Photograph by Sergeant Eikleberry.*

312

PLATE No. 150. *The Machine Gunner. Drawing by Harvey Dunn, 1918.*

313

Graphic Index

*By the asterisk we have sought to distinguish lithographic artists or craftsmen, whose work is actually perceptible on the plates, from the proprietors of lithographic printing and publishing houses. There are evidently no terms which will make the distinction.

List of Library of Congress Negatives

All of the items reproduced in this book which are the property of the Library of Congress have been photographed, and the negatives kept on file. Prints (8 x 10 inches) from these negatives may be secured from the Library of Congress Photoduplication Serv-

ice, Washington, D. C. 20540. The negative numbers listed here should be used in ordering. A current price list is available from the Photoduplication Service upon request.

Plate Nos.	L.C. Negative No.	Plate Nos.	L.C. Negative No.	Plate Nos.	L.C. Negative No.	Plate Nos.	L.C. Negative No.
2	LC–USZ62–96	48	LC–USZ62–120	79	LC–USZ62–146	111	LC–USZ62–39
3	LC–USZ62–97	49	LC–USZ62–435	80	LC–USZ62–147	112	LC–B8171–7557
4	LC–USZ62–98	50	LC–USZ62–90	81	LC–USZ62–157	113	LC–USZ62–198
5	LC–USZ62–47	51	LC–USZ62–366	82	LC–USZ62–163	114	LC–USZ62–149
6	LC–USZ62–111	52	LC–USZ62–89	83	LC–USZ62–139	115	LC–USZ62–732
7	LC–USZ62–106	53	LC–USZ62–87	84	LC–USZ62–173	116	LC–USZ62–158
8	LC–USZ62–104	54	LC–USZ62–126	85	LC–USZ62–679	117	LC–USZ62–172
9	LC–USZ62–103	55	LC–USZ62–125	86	LC–USZ62–160	118	LC–USZ62–155
10	LC–USZ62–110	56	LC–USZ62–65	87–88	LC–USZ62–5769	119	LC–USZ62–176
16	LC–USZ62–108	57	LC–USZ62–131	89	LC–USZ62–533	120	LC–USZ62–169
17	LC–USZ62–42	58	LC–USZ62–64	90	LC–USZ62–142	121	LC–USZ62–144
18	LC–USZ62–113	59	LC–USZ62–127	91	LC–USZ62–143	122	LC–USZ62–161
19–20	LC–USZ62–94	60	LC–USZ62–192	92	LC–USZ62–30	123	LC–USZ62–171
21	LC–USZ62–472	61	LC–USZ62–130	93	LC–USZ62–178	124	LC–B8171–7748
22	LC–USZ62–191	62	LC–USZ62–190	94	LC–USZ62–153	125	LC–USZ62–140
25	LC–USZ62–107	63	LC–USZ62–132	95	LC–USZ62–151	126	LC–USZ62–152
26	LC–USZ62–44	64	LC–USZ62–128	96	LC–USZ62–137	127	LC–USZ62–88
28	LC–USZ62–52	65	LC–USZ62–752	97	LC–USZ62–138	128	LC–USZ62–532
29	LC–USZ62–45	66	LC–USZ62–66	98	LC–USZ62–148	129	LC–USZ62–193
30	LC–USZ62–109	67	LC–USZ62–129	99	LC–USZ62–46	130	LC–USZ62–40
34	LC–USZ62–121	68	LC–USZ62–133	100	LC–USZ62–73	131	LC–USZ62–196
35	LC–USZ62–118	69	LC–USZ62–124	101	LC–USZ62–35	132	LC–USZ62–80
36	LC–USZ62–433	70	LC–USZ62–32	102	LC–USZ62–75	133	LC–USZ62–194
37	LC–USZ62–434	71	LC–USZ62–33	103	LC–USZ62–159	134	LC–USZ62–432
39	LC–USZ62–116	72	LC–USZ62–156	104	LC–USZ62–164	135	LC–USZ62–134
40	LC–USZ62–122	73	LC–USZ62–36	105	LC–USZ62–37	136	LC–USZ62–135
41	LC–USZ62–8	74	LC–USZ62–154	106	LC–USZ62–175	137	LC–USZ62–534
42	LC–USZ62–31	75	LC–USZ62–775	107	LC–USZ62–197	143	LC–USZ62–436
43	LC–USZ62–93	76	LC–USZ62–174	108	LC–USZ62–34		
44	LC–USZ62–63	77	LC–USZ62–41	109	LC–USZ62–141		
47	LC–USZ62–115	78	LC–USZ62–150	110	LC–USZ62–38		

A print of Plate No. 38 may be obtained through the Geography and Map Division, Library of Congress. It should be ordered by title. Current Photoduplication Service rates apply.